The Age of Culpability

Why be lenient towards children who commit crimes? Reflection on the grounds for such leniency is the entry point into the development, in this book, of a theory of the nature of criminal responsibility and desert of punishment for crime. Gideon Yaffe argues that child criminals are owed lesser punishments than adults thanks not to their psychological, behavioural, or neural immaturity but, instead, because they are denied the vote. This conclusion is reached through accounts of the nature of criminal culpability, desert for wrongdoing, strength of legal reasons, and what it is to have a say over the law. The centrepiece of this discussion is the theory of criminal culpability. To be criminally culpable is for one's criminal act to manifest a failure to grant sufficient weight to the legal reasons to refrain. The stronger the legal reasons, then, the greater the criminal culpability. Those who lack a say over the law, it is argued, have weaker legal reasons to refrain from crime than those who have a say. They are therefore reduced in criminal culpability and deserve lesser punishment for their crimes. Children are owed leniency, then, because of the political meaning of age rather than because of its psychological meaning. This position has implications for criminal justice policy, with respect to, among other things, the interrogation of children suspected of crimes and the enfranchisement of adult felons.

Gideon Yaffe is the Wesley Newcomb Hohfeld Professor of Jurisprudence and Professor of Philosophy and Psychology at Yale. He is the author of *Attempts: In the Philosophy of Action and the Criminal Law* (OUP, 2010), as well as books about John Locke and Thomas Reid. He also collaborates with neuroscientists on experiments intended to be of relevance to criminal responsibility assessments.

The Age of Culpability

Children and the Nature of Criminal Responsibility

Gideon Yaffe

OXFORD
UNIVERSITY PRESS

Great Clarendon Street, Oxford, OX2 6DP,
United Kingdom

Oxford University Press is a department of the University of Oxford.
It furthers the University's objective of excellence in research, scholarship,
and education by publishing worldwide. Oxford is a registered trade mark of
Oxford University Press in the UK and in certain other countries

© Gideon Yaffe 2018

The moral rights of the author have been asserted

First Edition published in 2018
First published in paperback 2020

All rights reserved. No part of this publication may be reproduced, stored in
a retrieval system, or transmitted, in any form or by any means, without the
prior permission in writing of Oxford University Press, or as expressly permitted
by law, by licence or under terms agreed with the appropriate reprographics
rights organization. Enquiries concerning reproduction outside the scope of the
above should be sent to the Rights Department, Oxford University Press, at the
address above

You must not circulate this work in any other form
and you must impose this same condition on any acquirer

Published in the United States of America by Oxford University Press
198 Madison Avenue, New York, NY 10016, United States of America

British Library Cataloguing in Publication Data
Data available

Library of Congress Cataloging in Publication Data
Data available

ISBN 978-0-19-880332-4 (Hbk.)
ISBN 978-0-19-886002-0 (Pbk.)

Links to third party websites are provided by Oxford in good faith and
for information only. Oxford disclaims any responsibility for the materials
contained in any third party website referenced in this work.

For Oona, with my love, especially, but also with my respect.

Contents

Acknowledgments   xi

Introduction   1

1. Immaturity and Reduced Culpability   18
   - 1.0 Introduction   18
   - 1.1 Rationalizing Our Practice   19
   - 1.2 Arguments from the Premise that Kids Are Different   21
   - 1.3 The Proxy for Culpability Argument   22
     - 1.3.1 Initial observations about the argument   22
     - 1.3.2 The argument's empirical assumptions   26
   - 1.4 The Problem of Empirical Dependency   30
   - 1.5 A Ground for Ignoring the False Positive Rate?   40
   - 1.6 Conclusion   42

2. Kids Will Be Kids... Until They Grow Out of It   44
   - 2.0 Introduction   44
   - 2.1 Kids Will Be Kids   45
     - 2.1.1 Distinguishing from the Proxy for Culpability argument   47
     - 2.1.2 The problem with (KW3)   51
     - 2.1.3 Taking stock   54
   - 2.2 They'll Grow Out of It   55
     - 2.2.1 Learning to walk the line   55
     - 2.2.2 The very idea of special deterrence   58
     - 2.2.3 Life without parole   60
   - 2.3 Conclusion   64

3. Criminal Culpability   66
   - 3.0 Introduction   66
   - 3.1 Culpability and Wrongdoing   66
   - 3.2 Causal Responsibility   68
   - 3.3 Modes of Transaction with Reasons   70
   - 3.4 Culpability as Manifestation of Modes of Transaction with Reasons   71
   - 3.5 Faulty Modes of Transaction with Reasons   73
   - 3.6 Objection: Culpability for *Mala in Se* Crimes   75
   - 3.7 Reasons-responsiveness vs. Quality of Will   77
   - 3.8 A Character Theory? No   79
   - 3.9 Two Kinds of Excuse   80
   - 3.10 An Evidentialist Theory of Manifestation   84
     - 3.10.1 Evidencing   85

3.10.2 Norms structuring the background	86
3.10.3 Replying to objections to the evidentialist theory of manifestation	90
3.10.4 Manifestation of psychological state, rather than modes of transaction with reasons?	95
3.11 Conclusion	96
4. Desert for Wrongdoing	**98**
4.0 Introduction	98
4.1 Moving an Act's Place in the Space of Reasons	102
4.1.1 Rational support relative to an agent	104
4.1.2 The ideal agent	107
4.1.3 Similarity in forms of rational support	109
4.1.4 The currency of punishment	114
4.2 Criminal Punishment and Culpability	117
4.2.1 Culpability	117
4.2.2 Justified criminal punishment	119
4.3 Conclusion	123
5. The Weight of a Legal Reason	**125**
5.0 Introduction	125
5.1 Legal Positivism and the Incorporation of the Moral into the Legal	126
5.1.1 Positivism	127
5.1.2 Moral incorporation	130
5.1.3 Moral reasons, legal reasons	132
5.2 The Weight of a Legal Reason	135
5.2.1 The strength of a legal reason: three types	136
5.2.2 The weight of D's legal reason	143
5.2.3 The legal reasons to abide by criminal prohibitions	151
5.2.4 Returning to culpability and desert	153
5.3 Conclusion	156
6. Giving Kids a Break	**158**
6.0 Introduction	158
6.1 Having a Say	160
6.2 How Much Say Do Kids Have?	165
6.3 *Should* Kids Have Less Say Than Adults?	172
6.4 Conclusion	182
7. Who Else Is Owed a Break?	**185**
7.0 Introduction	185
7.1 Visitors and Immigrants, Legal and Illegal	189
7.2 Prisoners and Felons	196
7.3 The Poor	198
7.4 Conclusion	201
8. What Breaks Are Owed?	**203**
8.0 Introduction	203

8.1	Forms of Lenience	203
8.2	Interrogating Kids	208
8.3	Conclusion	216

Conclusion 217

Bibliography 223
Index 231

Acknowledgments

While it is traditional to begin an acknowledgments section by identifying when you began work on a book, in this case that moment is very difficult to date. From one point of view, I began when I was in graduate school at Stanford in the late 1990s working on my Ph.D. in philosophy. There I encountered for the first time P. F. Strawson's paper "Freedom and Resentment" and Gary Watson's paper "Responsibility and the Limits of Evil: Variations on a Strawsonian Theme." Reading those two brilliant papers launched literally years of somewhat unfocused thought about the question of why a quality like being a child should mitigate responsibility for bad behavior. Conversations over the years with philosophers and non-philosophers about the question, especially conversations with Gary Watson, fueled the fires, focused my thinking, and helped me to recognize that my many false starts were just that. I'm very grateful to him, and to others who were willing to think about the question with me. I have spoken to so many other people about these and related issues over the years that it is not possible to list them all. To those who I leave out, I am very sorry. For what it's worth, I have particularly vivid memories of directly relevant conversations with Bruce Ackerman, Kristen Bell, Michael Bratman, Marshall Cohen, Greg Daniels, Haley Daniels, Steve Finlay, Joey Fishkin, Harry Frankfurt, Cary Franklin, Heather Gerken, Pamela Hieronymi, Doug Husak, Greg Keating, Matt King, Al Klevorick, Hedy Kober, Issa Kohler-Hausmann, George Letsas, Yair Listokin, Daniel Markovits, Tracey Meares, Michael Moore, Robert Post, Judith Resnik, Jennifer Richeson, Jacob Ross, Jed Rubenfeld, Alex Sarch, Alan Schwartz, Scott Shapiro, Dan Speak, Nomi Stolzenberg, Amy Wax, and Taisu Zhang. But my outlook was also molded, I am certain, by conversations with many other people.

Work on the book began in greater earnest thanks to the MacArthur Foundation's Law and Neuroscience Project, with which I was involved. A significant amount of work funded by the Foundation involved study of the brains of adolescents, and the bearing of discoveries about their brains on their criminal liability. While I was not directly involved in that work, I, like other members of the project, had the opportunity to query and comment on the work of those who were. This threw me into regular contact with Richard Bonnie, B. J. Casey, Buffie Scott, and Larry Steinberg, who were the driving forces behind the adolescent research the Foundation was funding. I hope that the four of them will take it, as it is intended, to be an expression of the greatest respect for their work when I say that it was thanks to my finding wanting the fundamental theory, driving their research, of the grounds for leniency towards kids that I developed both my negative argument against their views, and the positive position offered in this book. Intensive intellectual engagement with the four of them was essential to the development of this book. Larry Steinberg's great generosity in discussing and reading the manuscript was of further help. Buffie Scott also read large sections and helped me to deepen my ideas. Also essential was my interaction with those in the project more sympathetic to my skeptical stance, especially Morris Hoffman, Read Montague, and Stephen Morse. The reactions of the members of the group to a presentation that I gave in November 2016 of the central ideas of the book were also a great help. Deep thanks are owed to the MacArthur Foundation for creating the conditions under which we were all able to knock heads, and to Owen Jones whose deft leadership made it possible.

My thinking developed further after spending many months visiting Commissioner Robert Totten's courtroom in Los Angeles. There I observed a wide variety of hearings and proceedings involving kids who had, or had allegedly, committed crimes. I am very grateful to Commissioner Totten for generously providing me with access. He and his staff are doing important and selfless work on behalf of children. Judge Michael Nash is also owed thanks for his dedication to transparency in Los Angeles's juvenile delinquency system. Without that commitment on his part, an outsider philosopher would never have been able to take a glimpse at how things really work. Thanks also to Yale Law School for paying my salary while I spent this time as an observer.

Still, I did not actually sit down to write anything that made it into this book until the Guggenheim Foundation gave me the one thing that is most essential to research in philosophy: time. Thanks to a Guggenheim Fellowship, and matching support from Yale, I was able to spend the entirety of the 2015–16 school year working on this book. Without that, there is no way this project would have been completed.

Parts of the book were presented at various universities and audiences in all of these cases were very helpful. Three very thoughtful, careful, and constructive referee reports from Oxford University Press helped me immensely in the final revision of the manuscript. I owe all three referees sincere thanks. And thanks are owed to Peter Momtchiloff for all the help that he gave in bringing this project to fruition. Walter Sinnott-Armstrong, who identified himself as a referee, offered exceptionally generous and detailed comments on the entire manuscript. His comments became my checklist for revision—I tried to do exactly what he suggested far often than not—and the book is much better thanks to them.

And, of course, as anyone who does hard intellectual work will tell you, the quality of the work is a product not just of what you do when engaged in it, but also what you do when you're not. Thanks to my wife, Sue Chan, and our daughter, Oona Yaffe, for making those hours the ones I look forward to most.

Introduction

The case of *Roper v. Simmons* (543 U.S. 551) presents a set of facts that test almost anyone's intuitions favoring the idea that kids should be shielded from the worst punishments, punishments that are justifiably heaped on adults. More for the thrill of it than anything else, Christopher Simmons, together with two friends, broke into a randomly chosen home in the middle of the night, abducted Shirley Crook from her bedroom, bound her hands, legs, and head tightly with duct tape, and threw her off a bridge. She drowned in the waters below. Simmons later bragged about the murder, saying that he did it "because the bitch seen my face." This repulsive remark was an evident lie, not that it matters, since there was ample evidence that Simmons had planned to kill Crook well before he and his friends even entered her home. Shirley Crook left behind a grief-stricken husband and daughter, both of whom testified at the sentencing phase of the trial to the havoc that the murder had wreaked on their lives. One and only one thing can be said on Simmons' behalf, and it was duly noted by the attorneys in the case when addressing the jury that sentenced him to die: Christopher Simmons was 17 years old at the time of the crime. Eventually the Supreme Court of the United States reached the conclusion that this one fact was significant enough to warrant withholding from Simmons the worst that the state can do to a person: the court saved Simmons' life, ruling that no one under 18 at the time of a crime could be executed for it, no matter how heinous the conduct.

This result can seem quite arbitrary. After all, had Christopher Simmons been born prematurely, and so had turned 18 the day of the murder, instead of a bit later, there would not have been the same objection to putting him to death. Still, the Supreme Court was right. Children should be given a break when they do wrong; they ought to be treated more leniently than adults. But why? Why should the age of the offender matter to criminal liability? The answer to be offered in this book is deceptively simple: kids should be given a break because they are disenfranchised, denied as much say over the law as adults, and so denied an equal role in authoring the law's demands. The book's goal is to make the case for this position.

Let me define a few terms. I am going to use the term "a break" to refer to a large class of treatments by the state, under the criminal law, of citizens that are diminished in severity in comparison to others. In the paradigm case, someone gets a break thanks to some fact about him if he is given a lesser sentence thanks to that fact. But there are many cases of breaks outside of the paradigm case. A person also gets a break if he is excused entirely from punishment. And he gets a break if his case is treated under procedures that tend to issue in lesser punishments, or are in some other way easier on defendants, even if they do not in fact result in lesser punishment in his case. To say that someone "gets a break" is merely to say that there is some respect in which he is treated more leniently by the state than others who are like him in many, but not all, crucial respects. So, the concept of "a break," in the sense in which I am using the term, is very broad. A person can get a break that another does not, even if, in the end, they serve the same amount of time in prison, or even if the former serves a longer sentence than the latter. Leniency is about more than outcome. To get a break while receiving the same punishment as those otherwise equivalent people who did not is not to get much of a break, of course; likely, being a kid warrants more of a break than that. But, still, at this early stage the term "a break" will be used in the broad sense to include what someone who is given a chance of lesser punishment enjoys, even if that chance does not materialize.

I'm going to use the term "kids" to refer to anyone under 18 years old. The terms "infant," "toddler," "child," and "adolescent" bring with them connotations of developmental stage that I want to avoid. In saying that someone is a kid, I intend that there should be no intrinsic implication at all about that person's development, whether physical or psychological. To say that someone is a kid is to say something only about the distance in time between that person's birth and the present moment: that distance is less than 18 years. I recognize that this is a very diverse group of people. Infants have less in common with 10-year-olds than 10-year-olds have with 50-year-olds. And of course even infants, not to mention 12-year-olds or 16-year-olds, differ mightily from one another. But I choose to lump this diverse group for an obvious reason: roughly speaking, they are lumped together by the criminal law. Kids who commit crimes are treated differently from adults who commit crimes.

That kids are given a break under the criminal law in the United States is obviously true of kids whose crimes are adjudicated in the juvenile system. Different procedures apply in the juvenile system, and different punishments are issued. But this is true even of kids who are transferred to the adult system and tried and punished as adults. They are treated differently from adults in at least the following small way: it takes an act of prosecutorial discretion to treat them in other ways as adults. By contrast, no act of prosecutorial discretion will result in an adult being treated in the way that most kids are treated. Prosecutors cannot decide to try a 25-year-old as a child. But also some kids whose cases are transferred to the adult system are also treated differently from adults in sentencing, given the recent Supreme Court decisions barring the death penalty for juveniles, barring life without parole for non-homicide offenses, and barring mandatory life without parole even in homicide offenses.[1] And even kids tried as adults, who get the same sentences as otherwise similar adults, do not serve their

---

[1] *Roper v. Simmons* (125 S.Ct. 1183 (2005)), *Graham v. Florida* (130 S.Ct. 2011 (2010)), *Miller v. Alabama* (132 S.Ct. 2455 (2012)), *Montgomery v. Louisiana* (577 U.S.___(2016)).

time in adult prison until they are old enough to be housed with adults. Crimes by kids are a special legal category.

It must be said loudly and unequivocally that I believe our social policy of giving kids a break is fully justified. In fact, I believe that, in the United States at least, it does not go *even close* to far enough in many ways. Kids generally ought to be given bigger breaks than they are given; and some categories of kids who are given at most very small breaks ought to be given far, far bigger breaks than they receive. Consider a kid who is transferred to the adult system after committing a crime of sufficiently low severity that not even an adult could be given life without parole for its commission. Such a kid receives only the break of being given *a chance* of being tried in the juvenile system, a chance that does not materialize. That is not even close to enough of a break. And even kids who are tried in the juvenile system are given smaller breaks than they ought to be given, I think, since they receive many fewer procedural protections than they ought to have.[2] They do not have jury trials, for instance, and perhaps they ought to.[3] And even in the juvenile system, many kids are given far harsher punishments, for not particularly objectionable behavior, than they ought to be given. A kid, for instance, who is arrested for painting graffiti on a building can find himself facing months of intrusive state supervision, during which time peccadillos such as mouthing off at teachers can trigger even greater limitations on his freedom. There is a substantial gap between the kinds of breaks kids ought to get and the kind they do get. We need to do much more; we need to be more lenient than we are. Although we are past the point in our history when we flattered ourselves into thinking that the things we did to child criminals, in the juvenile system, were not punishments but somehow gifts, given for their own good, we are not yet considering as carefully as we need to how much we punish kids. Assuming there is good reason to punish criminals, there are good reasons to punish kids who are criminals; but we should punish them less harshly than we do.

But, this point is entirely consistent with the fact that will be of primary concern to us here, namely that kids do indeed get a break, and ought to. Our question is *why*. What is the underlying philosophy of the nature of childhood, the nature of responsibility, the nature of crime, the justification of punishment, and the justification of the disenfranchisement of kids that supports and justifies us in giving kids a break? I am seeking, and will provide, an articulation of a *rationale* for a practice that *I am certain has a good rationale*.

---

[2] The landmark decision in *In Re Gault* (87 S.Ct. 1428 (1967)) granted juveniles many important procedural protections that they previously lacked, including conviction only on a finding of guilt beyond a reasonable doubt. But, still, the juvenile court system does not grant the same, or as many, procedural protections to defendants as the adult system does.

[3] For discussion, see Martin Guggenheim and Randy Hertz (1998) "Juvenile Justice Reform: Reflections on Judges, Juries, and Justice: Ensuring the Fairness of Juvenile Delinquency Trials" in *Wake Forest Law Review*, 33: 553–93.

The articulation of a philosophical rationale for a practice of giving kids a break is of interest in itself, of course; but it should matter, also, to those who are particularly interested in improving the justice of our policies and practices for responding to child criminals. In the last decades of the twentieth century, there was a move towards increasingly punitive policies towards child criminals in the United States—more transfer of juveniles to the adult system, longer sentences, fewer breaks for kids.[4] This trend was exacerbated by the label "super-predator," used to refer to a subset of adolescent offenders who were thought to be just like, or worse, than the very worst of adult criminals in their psychology and their behavior. John DiIulio, who coined the term, predicted in 1995 that there would be an enormous increase in violent juvenile crime if drastic steps were not taken to stop the "super-predators."[5] The resulting changes in criminal justice policy, changes that resulted in kids in many cases being given no breaks, and virtually always being given smaller breaks than before, were disastrous. It has been described, with good reason, as a case of "moral panic."[6] There is little doubt that Black boys were far more likely to be classified as "super-predators" than anyone else. Far more likely than White boys or boys of any other race; far more likely than Black girls, or girls of any race. So the harm done by the super-predator theory was borne almost entirely by Black boys and their families. Still, the central criticism that has been offered is that there really were no super-predators, or at least very few, and there was no good reason to expect the enormous increase in crime that DiIulio predicted.[7] In fact, DiIulio himself has repudiated his past position on these grounds.[8] To be sure, the late twentieth-century trend towards giving no or fewer breaks to kids when it came to criminal liability can be correctly criticized on these grounds. But it is important to see that it would have been a morally terrible trend *even if there were super-predators, and even if there was going to be a radical increase in juvenile crime*. This fact is easy to overlook if one is wedded to a view according to which kids are owed a break only in virtue of their psychological and behavioral differences from adults. If that were true, then the late twentieth-century trend in juvenile criminal justice in the United States *would have been appropriate had the empirical claims by which it was guided been true*. It was philosophical error, I will argue in this book, that made those empirical claims seem salient. It was only because people thought that kids were owed a break because they were different from adults in their psychology and behavior that it seemed to make sense to deny a break to the "super-predators," who were thought to be the exception. Until we correct that philosophical

---

[4] Franklin Zimring (1998a) *American Youth Violence*, New York: Oxford University Press.
[5] John DiIulio (1995) "The Coming of the Super-Predators" in *The Weekly Standard*, November 27.
[6] Elizabeth S. Scott and Laurence Steinberg (2008) *Rethinking Juvenile Justice*, Cambridge: Harvard University Press.
[7] Franklin E. Zimring (1998b) "Juvenile Justice Reform: The Youth Violence Epidemic: Myth or Reality?" in *Wake Forest Law Review*, 33: 727–44.
[8] Elizabeth Becker (2001) "As Ex-Theorist on Young 'Superpredators,' Bush Aide Has Regrets" in *The New York Times*, Feb 9, p. A19.

error, we are at the mercy of the possibility of future empirical error about the psychology of kids who commit crimes.[9]

A defensible rationale for giving kids a break under the law is not easy to produce. Facile slogans in this domain are so common as to obscure the fact that there is an enormous mystery here. The undeniable fact that kids who commit crimes are, almost invariably, victims of some of the most egregious forms of abuse and deprivation that one encounters in a developed nation obscures the mystery further. It makes one feel that to point out the gaps in a proposed rationale is to side with those abusers and neglecters who have turned some of our children into criminals. But, still, there are frequently large gaps. Consider, for instance, the position that kids who do wrong should be *taught* rather than punished. One might advocate such a position because one holds that punishment is never appropriately applied to those who can be taught to behave better without its aid. But many adults are teachable and many kids are not. So the goal, if it is a worthy one, of refraining from punishing when we can teach is at best imperfectly pursued through a policy of leniency towards kids. Besides, even the unteachable kids should get a break, and many a teachable adult should not. Rather, the idea that kids should be taught rather than punished merely *expresses* the view that kids who commit crimes ought to be treated leniently; it does not provide an independent ground for that view. And so the idea serves to paper over the mystery rather than to solve it. In fact, this is common. Much of what is said in defense of belief that kids should be treated leniently is, in the end, nothing more than fervent expression of that belief and involves not one step towards justifying it.

One might think that our policy of giving kids a break when it comes to criminal liability is defensible to the extent that it mirrors the moral fact that kids who engage in moral wrongdoing ought to be blamed less harshly than adults who do the same wrongful things.[10] Making good on this idea would require establishing several claims. It would require showing, for instance, that a policy of leniency towards a particular

---

[9] Consider Craig S. Lerner (2011) "Juvenile Criminal Responsibility: Can Malice Supply the Want of Years?" in *Tulane Law Review*, 86: 309–87. Lerner claims that there is an identifiable class of kids who commit terrible crimes who are, essentially, precocious enough to be held fully responsible. On these grounds, he advocates against leniency towards them. As I see it, Lerner is making the same philosophical error as those who he opposes. Both camps are committed to the view that if things are, empirically, as Lerner asserts, then there are a class of kids who are owed no breaks. This, as we will see, is a mistake, and a dangerous one.

[10] I believe that the question of why, exactly, children are diminished in moral blameworthiness remains under-theorized by moral philosophers. The most notable exception is Tamar Schapiro, whose work on this topic is filled with important insights. See Tamar Schapiro (1999) "What Is a Child?" in *Ethics*, 109(4): 715–38; Tamar Schapiro (2003) "Childhood and Personhood" in *Arizona Law Review*, 45: 575–94. However, Schapiro's position is also subject to some well-placed criticisms. See Michael Tiboris (2014) "Blaming the Kids: Children's Agency and Diminished Responsibility" in *Journal of Applied Philosophy*, 31(1): 77–90. Both Schapiro and Tiboris advocate positions under which there is no reason to take a precocious child, who is more like an adult than a typical child in the respects that they take to be crucial for blameworthiness, to be diminished in moral blameworthiness. This fact, for reasons explained in the main text, makes their positions ill-suited to justifying a legal policy of leniency towards even precocious child criminals.

group when it comes to criminal liability is justified when that group ought, also, to be subject to lesser blame when it comes to moral wrongdoing. Such a view requires controversial views about the point of criminal liability assignments. It requires, in particular, the view that a person's degree of criminal liability should mirror her degree of moral blameworthiness.[11] But if we grant such a position, and I think we should, we then need to see what the relationship is between the group of people singled out for leniency by our legal policy, namely kids, and the group of people who are reduced in moral blameworthiness for wrongful behavior.

The salient group reduced in moral blameworthiness, however, are not kids per se, at all. Rather, the group is bound together by the fact that they have one or another excuse for their behavior, or one or another mitigating factor is present, and where the relevant excuses and mitigating factors can be identified without mention of age, or even maturity. Say that A and B do exactly the same morally wrongful, harmful thing, but A acted while only dimly aware of the risks of harm, while B was vividly aware of them. Then, *ceteris paribus*, A is deserving of less blame than B. Or, say that A acted impulsively while B acted after sober reflection on the pros and cons of the behavior. Then, arguably, A is deserving of less blame than B. Or, say that A acted in a state of arousal brought on by the presence of peers thanks to which refraining from wrongful behavior was much harder for him, where B, by contrast, was not comparably aroused. Then again, arguably anyway, A is owed a break that B is not. Of course, kids are more likely than adults to be like A is, in all three of the scenarios just described.[12] And so we accept a moral rule of thumb which places the brakes on blaming when the wrongdoer is a kid. But this can be overridden by the recognition that the kid before us was vividly aware of the risks, did not act impulsively, and was not in any special state of arousal that interfered with his capacity to behave better. Christopher Simmons, probably, deserves no lesser degree of *moral* blame than he would have if he had been a bit older when he brutally murdered Shirley Crook.

That there is nothing *morally* salient about being young, in and of itself, considered independently of the features that are ordinarily found in the young, features that we gesture towards, without specifying, with talk of "immaturity," can be seen by reflecting on the extraordinarily wide range of parental responses to child wrongdoing that are perfectly appropriate. Neighbors whose kids together inflict a small unjustified harm—perhaps they together hurt or are rude to a visitor—might respond very differently towards their kids; one might get grounded, another be required only to

---

[11] This claim can be denied. For a recent paper in which it is denied, see David Shoemaker (2012) "Blame and Punishment" in *Blame: Its Nature and Norms*, D. Justin Coates and Neal A. Tognazzini (eds.), New York: Oxford University Press, pp. 100–18.

[12] For discussion of the evidence for this, see, for instance, Catherine A. Hartley and Leah H. Somerville (2015) "The Neuroscience of Adolescent Decision-Making" in *Current Opinion in Behavioral Science*, 5: 108–15; B. J. Casey and Kristina Caudle (2013) "The Teenage Brain: Self Control" in *Current Directions in Psychological Science*, 22(2): 82–7; Anna C. K. Van Duijvenvoorde and Eveline A. Crone (2013) "A Neuroeconomic Approach to Adolescent Decision Making" in *Current Directions in Psychological Science*, 22(2): 108–13.

promise not to do it again or to apologize. These two different responses might both be completely fitting, despite the fact that the kids are of exactly the same age. The reason is that the kids might differ in maturity and so might differ in their culpability for their wrongful act. Perhaps one knew better, as it were, and the other did not. *Age* just isn't what matters in itself when it comes to moral blameworthiness. Age matters only as evidence of something else that matters, something about the psychology of the wrongdoer.

But this is exactly why it is hard to justify a social policy of giving *kids* a break through appeal to the way in which being a kid bears on moral blameworthiness. The moral category of interest is disjunctive, and age is at most indirectly relevant to its boundaries.[13] The relevant moral category of people have one or another of a familiar list of blame-reducing features. But we do not need to add a policy of leniency towards kids to the law in order to give a break to *this* group of people; *they are already given a break under the criminal law*. A person who was not vividly aware of the risks of harm that his act caused will often be characterized as negligent, rather than reckless, and subject to lesser penalties. A person who acted impulsively, or without sober reflection on the pros and cons of conduct, will sometimes have a less objectionable grade of *mens rea*, or, if not, will at least be able to hope for sentencing mitigation in light of this fact. The law already recognizes a wide range of excuses, tailored to approximate, to the extent law can, moral differences in blameworthiness. Of course, the law of excuses and mitigation is far from perfect. We should improve it. But if the law gets the excuses morally wrong, then it gets them morally wrong whether the offender is a kid or an adult. Giving *kids* a break does not solve the problem.

In addition, the facts about the reduced moral blameworthiness of (many) kids cannot serve to justify a policy of lenience since that policy applies even when it comes to the assignment of criminal liability in the absence of any moral blameworthiness. Say that a state criminalizes a form of morally permissible behavior. The state should not do this—criminal sanctions should be reserved for morally wrongful conduct—but it does. The state perpetrates an *additional* injustice if it also punishes kids who violate the law banning morally permissible behavior just as harshly as it punishes adults who do so. Kids are owed leniency in comparison to adults, that is, even when adults are morally deserving of far less punishment than they are given under the criminal law. This fact cannot be explained by a view that appeals to the reduced moral blameworthiness of kids since, when the law prohibits morally permissible behavior, *kids are no less morally blameworthy than adults since neither are morally blameworthy for their crimes at all*. No, we cannot justify our policy of giving kids a break when it comes to criminal liability by appeal to the reduced moral blameworthiness of kids. And yet that policy is justified. How so?

---

[13] The point that I am making in these paragraphs is made very clearly and forcefully in Stephen J. Morse (1997) "Immaturity and Irresponsibility" in *Journal of Criminal Law and Criminology*, 88: 15–65.

The relationship just outlined between the policy this book is concerned to justify—the policy of giving kids a break—and the policy of, on the other hand, apportioning criminal penalties in a way that is constrained by the appropriate degree of moral blame, makes evident what is wrong with a facile objection to the positive view to be defended in this book. As indicated, this book argues for the claim that kids are to be given a break because they are diminished in their say over the law. Since the primary mechanism (although not, as we will see, the only mechanism) through which anyone in a democracy has a say over the law is the vote, the thesis of this book is that kids in a democracy are owed a break in large part because they are denied the vote. The facile objection derives from the observation that this implies that were we to lower the voting age to, say, 14, then we would have no reason to give a break to the 14-year-olds, or any other kids between the ages of 14 and 17 to whom we give a break in our current system. To many this will seem manifestly objectionable. To many, that is, unmitigated criminal liability for a 14-year-old appears *just wrong*, no matter what the voting age. (This objection will be discussed again in chapter 5.) However, the objection is mistaken; in fact, that it is mistaken is a simple corollary of what has already been said about the relationship between the moral rule of thumb that kids are reduced in moral blameworthiness and the policy of giving kids a break under the criminal law. What is true is the following: *14-year-olds tend to differ from, for instance, 20-year-olds in ways that matter to their moral blameworthiness and so should be reflected in the laws of excuse and mitigation, no matter what the voting age.* What is false, however, is what is essential to the objection: *Our policy of giving kids a break is a way of bringing our institutional behavior in line with this truth.* This is precisely what I deny. The policy of giving kids a break has another purpose, to be described in detail. This is entirely consistent with the further point that age is highly probative of moral blameworthiness and so it is probative of the likelihood that a person has an excuse, or is owed mitigation, under some legal doctrine that is aimed at apportioning punishment in accordance with moral blameworthiness. Five-year-olds and 16-year-olds are equally denied the vote. But I do not assert that they therefore ought always to be treated the same under the criminal law; that would be absurd. A given 5-year-old and a given 16-year-old almost always differ in their psychology and their behavior in a way that makes appropriate differential treatment under laws of excuse and mitigation aimed at apportioning punishment in accordance with moral blameworthiness. Put in intuitive terms, 16-year-olds often know better, and 5-year-olds do only exceedingly rarely; when we find this difference, as we almost always do, they ought not be treated the same. The fervent assertion that we ought to treat 14-year-old criminals differently from 20-year-old criminals, no matter what the voting age, amounts to the fervent expression of the thought that they almost always differ psychologically or behaviorally in ways that support greater moral blame for the 20-year-old than the 14-year-old. True enough; who would deny it? But it does not in any way undermine the rationale for giving kids a break offered here.

Writing about the question this book aims to address, the important philosopher of law R. A. Duff suggests that the issue is not whether kids should be treated more leniently than adults *are actually treated*, but, instead, whether they should be treated more leniently than adults *ought to be treated*.[14] After all, if no one should be treated as harshly as we actually treat adult criminals, then child criminals should not be treated that harshly either. The hard question is why an offender's youth counts in his favor when it comes to the question of how harshly to treat him. Duff's point is important, I think. Overlooking it tends to obscure the fact that some of the reasons one might have for wanting to see a particular child treated leniently derive from the belief that it would be wrong to deny even an adult such leniency. Those, for instance, whose opposition to the death penalty is what motivated their support for shielding Christopher Simmons from execution were not moved by considerations that favor the policy of leniency towards kids that this book is concerned to justify. Leniency towards a child was merely a symptom of what they really favored, namely leniency towards anyone sentenced to die, whether child or adult.

However, it is also important to recognize that we do not need to know how, exactly, adult criminals ought to be treated in order to address the question of why child criminals ought to be treated more leniently. Rather, what we need to identify is an argument for treating children more leniently that does not use as a premise the claim that otherwise identical adults are treated too harshly. What we need, that is, is an argument that supports the claim, for instance, that Christopher Simmons should not be executed *even if an otherwise identical adult should be*. That is, we need an argument for leniency towards kids that assumes, *for the sake of argument*, that what the law authorizes to be done to otherwise identical adults is appropriate. Since this is what we need, this book will not provide an account of how we ought to respond to crime by adults. But this is not to say that I remain neutral about all debates that rage about this question. In particular, I am not neutral on the question of whether criminal punishment is an appropriate response to crime: I hold that it is, and assume as much throughout this book. You have to start somewhere. But to assume that punishment by the state is the right response to crime is to leave open the questions of what should be criminalized, how much punishment should be issued to fully responsible adults who commit this crime or that, what form punishment should take, how we should measure which punishments are harsher than others, and many other questions of this nature. While some things need to be said about some of these issues along the way, I do my best to remain neutral here, to the extent that I can, on many of the central questions in the philosophy of criminal law.

However, despite my neutrality on many issues about the philosophy of criminal punishment, my central goal in this book, despite appearances, is not to justify leniency towards child criminals. That, rather, is an entry point—of intrinsic interest, but, still

---

[14] Antony Duff (2002) "Punishing the Young" in *Punishing Juveniles: Principle and Critique*, Ido Weijers and Antony Duff (eds.), Oxford: Hart Publishing, pp. 115–34.

merely an entry point. *My central goal is to forward theories of the nature of criminal culpability, of desert for wrongdoing, and of the kind of participation in the law that is required to support unmitigated liability for crime.* This book offers a simple argument for a collection of philosophical theories about these topics: when we accept my views with respect to these issues we are able to explain a fixed point in theorizing about criminal law, namely that we ought to be lenient towards child criminals. The capacity of my general theories of the nature of crime, desert, and culpability to explain this undeniable normative fact, that is, provides a powerful argument for those general theories.

Still, despite my positive ambitions, this book's first task is to argue for a purely negative claim. It makes the case for the claim that the policy of giving kids a break for their criminal behavior is not justified by any intrinsic difference between children and adults. We are not, contrary to popular opinion, justified in giving kids a break because of something about their brains, or something about their psychological frame of mind, or something about the developmental normality of their bad behavior, or something about the impermanence of their condition. *The justification of our leniency outstrips the leniency that is warranted by the intrinsic features of children.* This sets the stage for the book's second part, in which a positive argument, a justification, of our practice of giving kids a break is offered. The concluding chapters of the book examine the extent to which the argument for giving kids a break extends to other groups, and takes small steps towards articulating the argument's implications for the crafting of specific policies for the treatment of child criminals.

It might seem surprising, given what has just been said, but under the positive position presented here, children ought to be given a break because they are diminished in their culpability for criminal wrongdoing, and deserving of lesser sanction. However, they are not diminished in their culpability *because of anything intrinsic about their psychology or their behavior*. In that way, the excuses they have are entirely different from the excuses that we ordinarily find in the law, such as excuses of mistake, insanity, or duress. Rather, children are diminished in culpability thanks to the fact that we have constructed our institutions in such a way as to weaken the legal reasons that they have to refrain from crime. The primary way we have done so is through denying them equal authorship over the law's demands. By denying the vote to children, we cause it to be the case that they are less complicit in the government's actions against criminals, including themselves, than are adults. But the strength of a person's legal reason to refrain from a crime is a function of the degree to which he would be complicit in government action guided by his disregard of that reason, namely his punishment for that crime. The result is that when kids do commit crimes, they disregard less pressing legal reasons to refrain than do adults who engage in exactly the same objectionable behavior. Add the view, also to be presented here, that culpability consists in disregard of legal reasons to act otherwise, and we have the result that children are diminished in criminal culpability, even when they are psychological and behavioral duplicates of adult offenders. There was less strong legal reason for

Christopher Simmons to refrain from wrapping someone in duct tape and throwing her from a bridge than there was for any adult to refrain from such behavior. And so, in disregarding his legal reasons to refrain from such behavior, Simmons' frame of mind was less objectionable than that of any adult who did exactly the same thing, in exactly the same frame of mind. But where there is reduced culpability, there ought to be more lenient treatment. In fact, those who are reduced in culpability are *deserving* of more lenient treatment. And so children are diminished in culpability, and owed more lenient treatment in light of that, merely because they are denied the vote. Age matters because it has a *political meaning*. That is the positive position to be argued for here.

The position I offer is easily confused with a different and irremediably flawed position according to which children are owed a break because they do not, or cannot be expected to know as much about what the law demands of them as adults. If two people differ in their knowledge of what the law demands of them, then they differ in their psychology. Whether that difference implies a difference in criminal culpability is controversial.[15] But to appeal to such a psychological difference between children and adults to justify leniency towards children is to pursue the very same strategy as those who appeal to other psychological differences, such as impulsivity, myopic discounting of future goods and evils, or susceptibility to peer influence in justifying leniency. The psychological features thought to be of importance are different, but the strategy is otherwise the same and no more defensible. Instead, under the position offered in this book, there would be good reason to be lenient towards a child, in comparison to an adult, *even if the two had precisely the same appreciation of the respective legal demands on their conduct*. It is not that children are less equipped than adults to meet a fixed standard. It is, rather, that *they are to be held to lower standards*.

To see the point, consider the following riddle: Twin high-jumpers, identical in every respect, run on identical tracks towards respective high-jump bars. They run just as hard, jump just as hard, and jump in precisely the same way, with precisely the same muscle contractions and body motions, aiming to overcome precisely the same gravitational forces, and yet one sails over his bar while the other crashes into his. How can this be? Surely there was some difference between them! The answer to the riddle is simple: the bar was set lower for the one than the other. Perhaps the successful and failed jumpers know the height of their respective bars; perhaps their psychological states are different in this respect. But that is not what explains why the one succeeds and the other fails. What explains that is that the bar was lower for the one than the other, period. Similarly, I suggest, while children and adults very often do differ in their psychology in ways that matter to culpability, including in their appreciation of the law's demands on them, *that is not what justifies giving a break to kids*. What justifies

---

[15] There is no shortage of material to be found about the question of whether or not, or in what sense, ignorance of the law excuses. A recent treatment of the issue can be found in Douglas Husak (2016) *Ignorance of Law: A Philosophical Analysis*, Oxford: Oxford University Press. My take on the issue, criticized by Husak, is Gideon Yaffe (2009) "Excusing Mistakes of Law" in *Philosopher's Imprint*, 9(2): 1–22.

that is that when it comes to criminal culpability the bar is lower for them than for adults. The reason that the bar is set lower is that kids have less say over the law than adults do; in particular, they don't have the vote.

So, as we will see before all is said and done, the rationale presented here for leniency towards child criminals has the implication that there is a very good reason to link two things: the voting age, and the age at which people who commit crimes are to be treated as adults. The reason that these two ages should be linked is that the strength of a legal reason for a particular person to refrain from action is in part a matter of the degree to which the person is a source of the legal authority of the prohibition against the relevant kind of action. Exactly what this means will be explained in the course of this book. But the result is that a person has available to him the distinctive ground for lenient treatment that, it is argued here, is available to kids, only if, in fact, the legal reasons to refrain from the kind of behavior in which he or she engaged are weaker than they are for those who are fully culpable for such bad behavior. People who are given full and complete representation in the government do not, ordinarily, have weakened reasons to refrain from crime. The result: If we are to raise the age of maturity, and so, for instance, treat 18- and 19-year-olds more leniently than those above those ages, we would also need to raise the voting age. This implies that reform efforts currently underway in some jurisdictions in the United States to raise the age of maturity for purposes of criminal liability, efforts which do not include an effort to raise the voting age, are subject to principled critique: they will result in mismatches between punishment and culpability.[16] This is one of the more important practical implications of the view to be argued for at length in this book.

It might seem impossible that there should be a moral justification for treating everyone under any given age, much less 18, leniently. There is cross-cultural and cross-historical variation in the age of maturity for purposes of treatment under the criminal law. To suggest that everyone under 18 should be given a break would seem to imply that a society that sets the age threshold at 21 or 16 is making a moral error. But that is actually not an implication of the view to be presented here. The moral principle that is constant across cultures and historical periods is to treat people who are reduced in culpability more leniently. But, for reasons to be explained here, a social decision to set the age of maturity at a particular number, for the purposes of full participation in government, causes it to be the case that those below the threshold are reduced in culpability in comparison to those above it. Under the view to be presented here, defense of our policy of giving kids a break does not necessarily serve to support the policy of giving those under 18 a break in, for instance, a country that sets the age of maturity at 21. Such a society might very well be perpetrating injustice were they to punish their 19-year-olds as harshly as we punish ours *even if their and our 19-year-olds are exactly alike in their intrinsic psychological and behavioral properties.*

---

[16] Jacqueline Rabe Thomas and Mark Pazniokas (2015) "Malloy: Raise the Age for Juvenile Justice System to 20" in *The Connecticut Mirror*, November 6.

Whether to be lenient towards a criminal is a matter, in part, of the strength of the legal reasons the criminal had to refrain. That, in turn, is a function, in part, of the age of the offender. But it is not solely a function of that. Change other things about the legal system, like, for instance, the voting age, and one can change the strength of the legal reasons to refrain from crime for age-mates differing only in the legal systems under which they live.

What has just been very briefly described is a repeating theme in this book: the dependency of the facts about criminal culpability on the social facts about law. In settling on certain legal standards we thereby constitute legal reasons with certain strengths. Since criminal culpability consists in a failure to insufficiently regard legal reasons, by setting the legal standards as we do, we set the bar for criminal culpability. And since we are morally required to treat the less culpable less harshly, it follows that by setting the legal standards as we do we constitute *moral* reasons to treat some people more leniently than others. One implication of this line of thought, which will be emphasized throughout, is that *age*, and not just maturity in some respect, which often goes along with age, matters *morally* to criminal liability. There is a moral reason to treat kids more leniently precisely because we have, perhaps arbitrarily, set 18 as the legal standard for having a full say over the law.

How does this last point connect to the point made earlier in this introduction that the policy of giving kids a break is not justified by their reduced moral blameworthiness? The answer is this: our moral reason not to treat people more harshly than is justified by their *criminal culpability* is distinct from our moral reason not to treat people more harshly than is justified by their *moral blameworthiness*. The distinction between criminal culpability and moral blameworthiness is demonstrated by the fact that there can be criminal culpability for morally permissible action, as when the law prohibits morally permissible action, but there cannot be moral blameworthiness for such action. My claim is that criminal culpability has independent and distinct moral significance for what the state is justified in doing to someone that does not reduce to the moral significance of moral blameworthiness. The case for this claim develops over the course of this book.

The chapters of the book proceed as follows. Chapter 1 argues against the view that we are justified in giving kids a break thanks to the fact that kids lack certain psychological states or capacities that are essential for full responsibility. Psychological states and capacities matter to culpability. Where we find differences of that sort, we find differences in culpability. And there is empirical research that confirms "what every parent knows" about the psychological states and capacities of kids: they lack a lot that is necessary for full responsibility. *But that is not why we are justified in treating them leniently.* At least, so chapter 1 argues. Chapter 2 continues the negative side of the argument by showing that we are not justified in our leniency towards kids by either the developmental normality of the facts about them that give rise to wrongful behavior, or the impermanence of their criminogenic condition. If this negative argument succeeds, then, combined with argument of chapter 1, the conclusion is inevitable that the moral justification of our social policy of giving kids a break does not derive from some special merit in children in contrast to adults to whom leniency is denied.

Chapter 3 begins the presentation of the positive side of the book, the account of why we are morally justified in giving kids a break. Chapter 3 offers a general account of the nature of criminal culpability. The view presented fits snugly with philosophical work on the nature of responsibility, and work in jurisprudence, by myself and others, on the import of *mens rea* to criminal culpability. Roughly speaking, the position to be argued for in chapter 3 is this: to be criminally culpable for wrongful conduct is for that conduct to manifest a failure to properly recognize, weigh, or respond to the legal-reason-giving force of the features of one's conduct. To be criminally culpable, for instance, for theft is to fail to treat the fact of the absence of the owner's consent as reason-giving in a way that conforms to the legal reason to refrain from taking property that that fact actually provides. The result of this theory of culpability is that every criminal statute prohibiting behavior establishes two legal norms: one with respect to which a person's conduct is to be measured—it identifies a form of conduct as not-to-be-done—and another with respect to which the person's modes of transactions with reasons, manifested in behavior, are to be measured. Thanks to statutes barring theft, there is a legal demand not to take things that do not belong to you, and a legal demand not to manifest in one's behavior a lack of regard for the legal reason-giving force of the fact (among others) that an object belongs to someone else.

One of the most important conceptual innovations offered in this book starts to emerge in chapter 3. The chapter identifies a distinctive form of excuse, overlooked, I believe, in prior efforts to categorize the excuses. Aristotle famously noted the difference between excuses of ignorance and excuses of compulsion.[17] But there are some facts about an agent that seem to shield from blame for wrongful, unjustified action which do not fall naturally into either category. Conditions, for instance, that disable an agent from engaging in the basic human interactions involved in being held and holding another responsible for bad behavior—conditions such as some serious forms of mental disability or mental disorder—are not naturally characterized as excuses of either ignorance or compulsion. Moved by this point, theorists who recognize Aristotle's two categories of excuse have sometimes added a third, to which a variety of names have been given. Gary Watson calls them "exemptions" because when an agent is disabled in these ways she is exempt from being held to the same standards of behavior appropriate for the rest of us, even when her acts are performed neither from compulsion, nor ignorance.[18] Michael Moore has named them "status excuses" because, the thought is, there is a certain status, aptly labeled as "personhood," that the agent falls short of possessing fully and the possession of which is necessary for

---

[17] Aristotle (2012) *Nicomachean Ethics*, Robert C. Bartlett and Susan D. Collins, trans. Chicago: University of Chicago Press, book 3, ch. 1, 1110a, p. 42.

[18] Gary Watson (2004) "Responsibility and the Limits of Evil: Variations on a Strawsonian Theme" in *Agency and Answerablity: Selected Essays*, Oxford: Oxford University Press, pp. 219–59.

unmitigated blame for bad acts performed neither from compulsion nor ignorance.[19] But why should we think that the only status of relevance to responsibility is personhood? Personhood is, of course, central to *moral* evaluation, but of equal import to *legal* evaluation under the criminal law is the status of *citizen*. Although the full argument for the claim emerges not solely in chapter 3, but also in chapter 5, those, I contend, who are diminished in this status, the status of citizenship, are also diminished in criminal culpability. The more diminished their status as citizens, the more diminished their culpability. If they are not citizens at all, they have a citizen-based status excuse from criminal responsibility. This is another way of putting the central idea of the book, developed over the succeeding chapters: kids are not full citizens, and that is why they are reduced in criminal culpability; the status of citizenship is a necessary condition for holding someone to the standards of culpability applied in cases of unmitigated criminal responsibility. We have constructed our laws in such a way as to disable kids from full participation in the roles central to citizenship, and thereby imposed on them a disability analogous to that suffered by the mentally disabled, who are incapable of full participation in the roles central to personhood.

Chapter 4 extends the general theory of criminal culpability offered in chapter 3 through the presentation of an account of desert for wrongdoing. The question addressed is what a person deserves for having engaged in wrongful, criminal behavior. The answer offered and defended in chapter 4 is this: he deserves that thanks to which the wrongful act is, by his prospective standards, opposed by reasons to the same degree and in the same way as that act is, for ideal citizens, opposed by reasons. To get what one deserves for doing wrong, that is, is for something to be attached to one's wrongful act thanks to which the act occupies the position in the space of reasons that the act in itself occupies for law-abiding citizens. This position explains why a person deserves a lesser punishment when her conduct is diminished in culpability, under the theory of culpability offered in chapter 3. The position also implies that what a person deserves for her wrongful conduct is in part a matter of the strength of the reasons she had to refrain from that conduct. The stronger the reasons to refrain, the greater the harm to her that must be attached to the act if the act is to occupy the place in the space of reasons for her that it ought to have occupied.

Under the views of criminal culpability and deserved legal sanction developed in chapters 3 and 4, both are in part a matter of the strength of the legal reasons the agent had to refrain from prohibited conduct. But what, exactly, is it for one legal reason to be stronger than another? Chapter 5 offers a theory of the strength of a legal reason and explains why, given the accounts of culpability and desert offered in chapters 3 and 4, how the law is constructed can make a difference to the degree to which wrongdoers are culpable, and, in turn, make a difference to what they deserve. By constructing the law as we do, we change the landscape of legal reasons. And that landscape is in part

---

[19] Michael Moore (2015) "The Quest for a Responsible Responsibility Test: Norwegian Insanity Law After Breivik" in *Criminal Law and Philosophy*, v. 9, pp. 645–93.

constitutive of the standards for criminal culpability, and for what is deserved for wrongdoing. The claim argued for in chapter 5, which is of greatest importance to the central argument of the book, is the claim that the strength of a person's legal reason to refrain from behavior prohibited by a statute is often a function, in part, of how much say the person has over the legal authority of the statute.

Chapter 6 applies the philosophical machinery developed in chapters 3, 4, and 5 to the question of why we are justified in giving kids a break under the criminal law. Doing so requires, first, developing an account of what it is *to have a say over the law*. Chapter 6 suggests that to have a say over the law is to satisfy three conditions. It is to be entitled to exert influence over the law, to be entitled to be free of reasonable obstacles to the exercise of that entitlement, and to be actually free of the obstacles one is entitled to be free of. I claim, in the chapter, that when a person has a say over the law in this sense, he is complicit in government action authorized by the law, including actions taken against himself. The greater the say, the greater the complicity. The result is completion of an argument in support of the central claim of chapter 5: how strong one's legal reasons are to refrain from crime is, in part, a function of how much say one has over the law.

Chapter 6 also explains the sense in which kids do have a say over the law—primarily, I suggest, through free speech protections—and the sense in which they do not, in comparison to adults. Kids' say over the law is limited both by parental-gating on speech protections—kids, roughly, are not given the right to a real and meaningful opportunity to say things their parents do not want them to say—and, most importantly, by denying them the vote.

Finally, chapter 6 argues that the policy of denying kids the vote is justified not, as one might have thought, by the fact that kids aren't equipped, psychologically, to vote, but, instead, by the need for any self-governing state to provide mechanisms through which we, who are the authors of today's law, can have a say over future law, including the law in place after our deaths. Given that we are entitled to try to exert influence over our kids' values, by denying them the vote, and granting it to them after we have the opportunity to influence their values, we create a mechanism through which we now can have a say over tomorrow's law. All of this in turn implies, given the theories of culpability and desert offered in chapters 3 and 4, that kids are diminished in culpability for their wrongful behavior, and are deserving of leniency.

What the proposed rationale for denying the vote to kids provides is a way of understanding how facts about child psychology do matter, after all, to our policy of giving kids a break. What matters are not facts that bear on culpability. What matters, instead, are facts about the plasticity of kids' values, in comparison to adults. If we are to give today's adults a way of influencing tomorrow's law, we need to give them reasonable opportunity to mold their children's values. This requires setting an age threshold before which children lack the vote and after which they have it. What age threshold is reasonable in this respect will be a function, in part, of how plastic kids' values generally are and to what age. This is a tractable empirical question. If we were to find that, in fact, children generally are no longer moldable at the age of 14, or that they are moldable by their parents well into their twenties, then such discoveries would provide us with reason to alter the voting age, and with it the facts about criminal culpability.

Chapter 7 turns to the question of who else might be owed lenient treatment under the criminal law, given the argument offered for our leniency towards kids. Central to the lines of thought developed in chapters 5 and 6 is the idea that much state power, used against criminals, is authorized by the fact that those against whom it is used had a say over the law they violated. But in this chapter it is argued that there are other facts about people that can contribute to the state's authorization to use force against them. So, in many cases, other disenfranchised groups—such as visitors, both legal and illegal—are not owed leniency. However, the chapter argues that the situation is substantially more complicated when it comes to groups such as members of traditionally oppressed minorities, and the very poor, who have a claim to some sense of disenfranchisement. Some of them may have a claim to leniency for reasons related to the reasons that kids do. The chapter also considers the culpability and desert of those who are disenfranchised during the course of prison terms, and argues against the current policy, in place in many jurisdictions, of disenfranchising felons, even after they have served their sentences, and yet holding them to the same standards as enfranchised adults when it comes to criminal liability.

Chapter 8 turns to the question of what form the leniency we are required to give to kids should take, given the principled argument for leniency developed over the course of the preceding chapters. I argue that the primary and most important way we ought to give kids a break is through laws that produce mitigation of sentence, either by granting sentencing judges the power to mitigate the sentence of a kid *because he is a kid*, or by barring them from issuing harsh sentences that they have the power to give to adults. However, the chapter also suggests that the rationale for giving kids a break has implications for police practices, as hinted in a recent Supreme Court case. The chapter aims to demonstrate this by arguing that there will be deceptive interrogations of kids who are suspects that are impermissible even when the very same interrogations of psychologically and behaviorally identical adults are permissible.

The aspiration of the book, overall, is to provide a moral and conceptual framework that can guide our criminal justice policy with respect to children. The philosophical issues are interesting and important in their own right. And the book aims to make substantial progress on those issues. But the issue matters to policy too. We need more than just to know, in our guts, that kids should be given a break. We need to know, and to articulate *why that is true* so that we can figure out which kids ought to be given what breaks for what kinds of wrongful behavior. The book's aim is to provide a foundation on which thoughtful and just public policy in this domain can be built.

1
Immaturity and Reduced Culpability

1.0 Introduction

These days it is rare to find something written about kids and crime that does not mention current research on the brains of children. We are entranced by the idea that kids commit crimes because of something about their brains. And that is absolutely true. Gripped by this thought it is easy to forget that it is also true that *adults* commit crimes because of something about their brains. Where there is behavioral smoke, there is neural fire. Where there is crime, there is a neural source, whether the crime is committed by a kid or an adult. But when we are careful, we are attracted to the bearing of recent neuroscientific discoveries about kids' brains on their criminal liability not simply because such studies support the thought that there is a neural source of bad behavior—we already knew *that*—but, instead, because we think that such studies show that kid criminals are different from adult criminals in some important way that warrants giving them a break. We care about kid brains because we think that what is being learned about them shows us that kids are different in some way that matters to their culpability for crime. My aim here is to diffuse the power of this thought.

The central goal of this chapter is negative. The goal is to show that the justification for our practice of giving kids a break cannot be that kids are different from adults in some way that shows them to be reduced in culpability. We have to seek the justification for our practice elsewhere. But although I believe this is true, and will establish it in what follows, it is also important not to throw the baby out with the bathwater. Neuroscience, developmental, and cognitive psychology help us to appreciate features of people that bear on the assessment of their culpability for crime. Those tasked with deciding whether a person should be given a break—such as legal actors, like judges and prosecutors—should, of course, be as informed as possible about the features of the person that matter to the question. This is just as true when the person being assessed is an adult as when he or she is a child. And so I have no quarrel with the claim that justice can be furthered by informing discretionary actors in the criminal justice system about recent developments in brain science and psychology; this is surely true.[1] But I believe that there is something deeply

---

[1] See, for instance, Laurence Steinberg and Robert G. Schwartz (2000) "Developmental Psychology Goes to Court" in Thomas Grisso and Robert G. Schwartz (eds.), *Youth on Trial: A Developmental Perspective*

wrong with a system that allows for the possibility that some kids will be given no breaks, even if the decision to deny it to them is made by a discretionary actor informed by the most recent developments in neuroscience and psychology. As we will see here, we cannot justify a system that, instead, gives breaks to kids, all kids, by appealing to the growing and important empirical work mapping and quantifying the neural and psychological differences between kids and adults. But such a system is what justice requires.[2]

1.1 Rationalizing Our Practice

I think it is helpful to think of a rationale for a particular practice as *an argument* the conclusion of which is that we ought to engage in the practice. A rationale for the practice of allowing same-sex marriages is an argument with premises concerning the universality of certain kinds of rights, and the impermissibility of government behavior that curtails such rights, leading to the conclusion that we ought not to bar same-sex couples from marrying. The more of the premises we articulate, the better we understand the proffered rationale. And the better we defend those premises, the better grounded is the practice. If the argument is valid and can repel the usual sorts of objections that can be given to any argument—if its premises do not presuppose its conclusion, if its conclusion does not have absurd implications, etc.—then it provides a successful rationale for the practice of allowing same-sex couples to marry. Similarly, a rationale for the practice of giving kids a break will be an argument ending in the conclusion that we ought to give kids a break.

Everybody thinks that kids ought to be given a break, although there are significant differences about *which* kids, who do *what*, should be given *what kinds* of breaks. Even the *dissenting* opinions in cases like *Roper v. Simmons*, described in the introduction to this book, betray that sympathy. When the dissenting judges say that a policy of individual culpability assessment would be preferable to a blanket policy under which all kids are given a break, the issue is not whether kids should be given a break but, instead,

---

on *Juvenile Justice*, Chicago: University of Chicago Press, pp. 7–31. Related points are explored helpfully in Kim Taylor-Thompson (2003) "States of Mind/States of Development" in *Stanford Law and Policy Review*, 14: 143–73.

For discussion of the bearing of recent neuroscientific studies of kids on *mens rea*, in particular, see Jenny E. Carroll (2015) "Brain Science and the Theory of Juvenile Mens Rea" in *North Carolina Law Review*, 94: 539–99. See also Cindy Lederman (2011) "From Lab Bench to Court Bench: Using Science to Inform Decisions in Juvenile Court" in *Cerebrum*, The Dana Foundation: http://dana.org/Cerebrum/Default.aspx?id=39466 (accessed April 16, 2016).

[2] The negative position developed in this chapter is in agreement with the negative side of the view offered in Cynthia Ward (2006) "Punishing Children in the Criminal Law" in *Notre Dame Law Review*, 82(1): 429–79. Ward writes, for instance, "Whatever differences in ability, temperament, or proclivities separate children from adults, it is almost certainly true that some children, even pre-adolescent children, do possess the capacity to form intent, do have a threshold understanding of the harm they intend to inflict, and do possess the ability to assemble the means and execute on a plan to commit that harm. Holding such children criminally responsible is not unjust because of any innate internal differences between children and adults—but because of the different treatment of children by the law." (p. 479) Where Ward and I differ is in our accounts of what forms of treatment of children by the law matter and why.

how best to implement that. The dissenting justices assume, that is, that fact-finders would end up concluding that almost every kid defendant before them ought to be given a break. The justices just do not want to take that decision out of the hands of fact-finders. And so everybody implicitly accepts *some* argument ending in the conclusion that kids ought to be given a break—although we might not all accept the same argument. We can think of our task, then, as uncovering a secret—a secret argument that we implicitly accept, an argument so secret that even those who accept it do not know how it goes.

When people are asked why they think kids ought to be given breaks, when they are asked to articulate the content of the argument to which they subscribe, they typically cite an amalgam of things as though it were obvious how the things they cite support the claim. Consider, for instance, these remarks from the important recent Supreme Court opinion barring mandatory life without parole for juvenile offenders:

[C]hildren have a lack of maturity and an underdeveloped sense of responsibility, leading to recklessness, impulsivity, and heedless risk-taking…[C]hildren are more vulnerable…to negative influences and outside pressures, including from their family and peers; they have limited control over their own environment and lack the ability to extricate themselves from horrific, crime-producing settings. And…a child's character is not as well formed as an adult's; his traits are less fixed and his actions less likely to be evidence of irretrievable depravity.

[Studies show] that only a relatively small proportion of adolescents who engage in illegal activity develop entrenched patterns of problem behavior…And…developments in psychology and brain science continue to show fundamental differences between juvenile and adult minds—for example, in parts of the brain involved in behavior control.…[T]hose findings—of transient rashness, proclivity for risk, and inability to assess consequences—both [lessen] a child's moral culpability and enhance the prospect that, as the years go by and neurological development occurs, his deficiencies will be reformed.

(*Miller v. Alabama* 132 S.Ct. 2455, 183 L. Ed. 2d 407 (2012) at 2464, citations omitted)

It is hard to count all of the various features ascribed to children in these paragraphs, since some (e.g. "impulsivity" and "transient rashness") appear to overlap. Not to mention that it would be over-counting to take both kids' problems with self-control to count in their favor *and* to take the fact that there is a neural basis for such problems to count. The neural facts matter, if they do, only because they underlie a psychological state or capacity that matters. But suffice it to say that there are at least ten features mentioned here. And it is beyond question that the court takes them, somehow, to support giving kids a break (and not just any break, but the very particular break involved in removing the possibility of a mandatory life without parole sentence when tried as an adult). But this amounts to asserting as a premise that kids have the distinctive features mentioned here, and asserting the conclusion that kids ought to be given a break, without articulating the missing premises, premises which presumably provide a link between these two things. And without knowing what, exactly, the missing premises are, there is no way to assess whether the court has offered a legitimate rationale for what we all know to be true, namely that kids ought to be given a break.

So, it is worth considering various possible arguments that might be brought to bear in support of the claim that kids ought to be given a break, various possible ways of filling in the missing premises. As we will see between this chapter and the next, none of the arguments that immediately spring to mind are successful. If it weren't so obvious to all of us that kids ought to be given a break, and if we weren't so committed to advocating for that claim (in words at least, and maybe in deeds) these arguments would be recognized as failed efforts to articulate the underlying philosophical theory that supports our conviction that kids ought to be given a break. We need a better account of the foundation on which our conviction rests.

1.2 Arguments from the Premise that Kids Are Different

Roughly speaking, there are three distinct and separable kinds of arguments that begin with the distinctive features of kids of the sort cited by the Supreme Court and end with the claim that kids ought to be given a break:

Proxy for Culpability: Thanks to the way kids are, they lack a feature, or set of features, that are necessary for full responsibility for wrongful behavior. Any category of people who lack that feature, or set of features, is owed a break. So: kids should be given a break.

Kids Will Be Kids: Wrongful, criminal behavior by kids is a product of the way they are. But being that way is developmentally normal for kids. If wrongful, criminal behavior is developmentally normal for people in a certain category, then anyone in that category is owed a break. So: kids should be given a break.

They'll Grow Out of It: Wrongful, criminal behavior by kids is a product of features of kids that they typically grow out of. Any category of people who perpetrate wrongful, criminal conduct thanks to qualities that they will lose through the passage of time, and without special intervention, are owed a break. So: kids should be given a break.

Conversations about why kids deserve a break often float among these arguments in ways that make them difficult to adequately assess. Say that you challenge someone who cites the fact that kids are drawn to risk as a premise in the Proxy for Culpability argument. You ask *why* being drawn to risk is incompatible with full responsibility—some, in fact, might take it to be inculpating rather than exculpating. The question is likely to be evaded with the answer, "Well, it's normal for kids to be that way." This is to shift from the Proxy for Culpability argument to the Kids Will Be Kids argument. And when it is then objected that it's not actually normal at all to be so drawn to risk that you bind someone with duct tape and throw her off a bridge, this objection might be met with the rejoinder that, "But that perversity is something that people like Christopher Simmons grow out of, if they succumb to it at such an early age." This is to shift the ground to the They'll Grow Out of It argument. But these shifting sands amount to evasions. If none of these argument succeeds on its own terms, then shifting from one to another in response to objections is not progress.

Of course, it is possible that the arguments somehow combine to support giving kids a break. It is possible, that is, that no one of them can support that conclusion on its own, but together they do. One way in which that might happen is that one argument establishes that we should be lenient towards kids of one sort, and another of another sort, and all children fall into one category or the other. (Analogously: We should travel to New York because I have to be uptown and you have to be downtown.) Or, alternatively, one argument provides an insufficient reason for lenience, another another, but together the two reasons are sufficient. (Analogously: We should drive to New York, rather than take the train, because two train tickets cost more than driving, although one costs less.) There are so many different potential ways to combine arguments into new arguments, that it is difficult to rebut *all* such efforts without disclosure of the details. But suffice it to say that if there are decisive objections to one argument, and decisive objections to another, the best strategy of response is to seek a third, new argument rather than to seek a way to combine them. What we need is to slow down and examine each argument for leniency towards kids in turn. If we find, as I claim we do, that they are individually deeply flawed, then that is reason enough to develop an alternative. My target in this chapter is the Proxy for Culpability argument; the Kids Will Be Kids and They'll Grow Out of It arguments are discussed in chapter 2.

1.3 The Proxy for Culpability Argument

1.3.1 Initial observations about the argument

Advocates of the Proxy for Culpability argument can vary in their identification of the relevant feature taken to be necessary for fully responsible action; some might point to multiple features that are thought to be either individually or collectively necessary. They can start in different places and with different theories both of the nature of fully responsible action and of the features of kids that interfere with it. In perhaps its most plausible form, the Proxy for Culpability argument involves noting the ways in which kids, in contrast to adults, are often incapable of appreciating the wrongfulness of their wrongful conduct.[3] They are not merely oblivious to the fact that what they are doing is wrong, but are diminished also in their capacity to remedy this deficiency. They need more experience to develop such appreciation. But this is not the only form that the Proxy for Culpability argument can take. Those, for instance, who cite the fact that kids are highly

---

[3] The term "normative competence" is sometimes used to capture the collection of features that are taken to be necessary for culpability and are often absent in kids. For an extremely enlightening presentation of the Proxy for Culpability argument employing that term, see David Brink (2004) "Immaturity, Normative Competence, and Juvenile Transfer: How (Not) to Punish Minors for Major Crimes" in *Texas Law Review* 82: 1555–85.

susceptible to peer influence, in explanation for their belief that kids deserve a break, are often also implicitly offering the Proxy for Culpability argument. They hold that people who are fully responsible for wrongful behavior do not do bad things because they happen to be around others whom they want to impress, or whose presence arouses them somehow; fully responsible wrongdoers, the thought is, have a kind of autonomous ownership over the mechanisms that generate their conduct, a kind missing in those who are highly susceptible to peer influence. And so kids are diminished in responsibility because they are unlike the fully responsible in this respect. If susceptibility to peer influence is replaced with some other quality of kids, or some other qualities are added to the list, the argument remains fundamentally the same: that quality, or collection of qualities, can be inferred to be absent from the fact that the wrongdoer is nothing but a kid.

As the peer influence example illustrates, it is often far from obvious whether noting a distinctive fact about kids is intended to be a way of offering the Proxy for Culpability argument or one of the other arguments instead. Consider, for instance, appeal to kids' sensitivity to criminogenic circumstances. Someone who holds that crimes by kids are reflective of their circumstances rather than their essential natures (in contrast, presumably to crimes by adults), and who on that basis reaches the conclusion that kids should be given a break, could, in theory, be offering any of the three arguments. Such a person might take heightened sensitivity to criminogenic circumstances to be normal for kids, or temporary—something they will escape over time—and so might be offering either the Kids Will Be Kids or They'll Grow Out of It arguments. But others who are moved by the ways in which kids are sensitive to criminogenic circumstances might instead take that fact about a person to diminish his criminal culpability. The thought is that we are only fully responsible for wrongful behaviors that can be attributed *to us* rather than to our environments, and kids, because they, for instance, "lack the ability to extricate themselves from horrific, crime-producing settings,"[4] engage in wrongful behavior that is ordinarily attributable to circumstances.[5,6]

---

[4] *Miller v. Alabama* 132 S.Ct. 2455, 183 L. Ed. 2d 407 (2012) at 2464, citations omitted.

[5] A sensitive discussion of the bearing of kids' susceptibility to criminogenic circumstances on their culpability can be found in Jeffrey Fagan (2000) "Contexts of Choice by Adolescents in Criminal Events" in Thomas Grisso and Robert G. Schwartz (eds.), *Youth on Trial: A Developmental Perspective on Juvenile Justice*, Chicago: University of Chicago Press, pp. 371–401, esp. 389–91. As Fagan explicitly notes, the issue is not specific to kids. It is explored more generally in Tracey Meares (1998) "Place and Crime" in *Chicago-Kent Law Review*, 73: 669–705. A different kind of exploration of the idea can be found in Richard Delgado (1985) "Social Background: Should the Criminal Law Recognize a Defense of Severe Environmental Deprivation?" in *Law and Inequality*, 3: 9–45. For a critical discussion see, for instance, Stephen J. Morse (2011) "Severe Environmental Deprivation (AKA RSB): A Tragedy, Not a Defense" in *Alabama Civil Rights & Civil Liberties Law Review*, 2: 147–72.

[6] A novel account of the relevance of sensitivity to criminogenic circumstances to giving kids a break is offered in Cynthia Ward (2006) "Punishing Children in the Criminal Law" in *Notre Dame Law Review*, 82(1): 429–79. Ward seems to accept a kind of estoppel argument: Since the law makes it difficult for children to extricate themselves from criminogenic circumstances, the law should also take some responsibility for their bad behavior and so cannot represent children as fully responsible for their crimes. The question, however, is why there is not enough responsibility to go around. Why shouldn't the state (or "the law") blame itself while recognizing that some kids, even if not all, are also fully responsible for their behavior?

So, the Proxy for Culpability argument, in all its forms, runs like so:

(PC1)   Kids lack feature F.

(PC2)   Agents are fully responsible for their wrongful conduct only if they have feature F.

(Diminished Responsibility)   ∴ Kids are not fully responsible for their wrongful conduct.

(PC3)   Agents should be given a break for their wrongful conduct if they are not fully responsible for it.

(Conclusion)   ∴ Kids ought to be given a break for their wrongful conduct.

In the form in which I will here consider this argument, (PC1), if true, is a contingent truth. That is, F is not a logically or metaphysically essential feature of kids, nor is (PC1) analytic. F is not, for instance, the feature of "not being a kid" which is, of course, lacked by all kids. Further, (PC1) cannot be interpreted as the claim that each and every kid lacks feature F. For any choice of F that supports the truth of (PC2), (PC1) would turn out to be false if so interpreted. Some kids fully appreciate the wrongfulness of their wrongful conduct. Some kids are perfectly well equipped to extricate themselves from their criminogenic circumstances. Some kids are not particularly susceptible to peer influence. Rather "Kids are susceptible to peer influence" is true when interpreted as a generic statement, like "Sharks eat people"—true enough despite the fact that many do not. To put it another way, under the Proxy for Culpability argument, age has no moral significance in itself. It matters morally because it is a guide to the absence of feature F, which is morally significant because F is necessary for full responsibility. And so, similarly, (Diminished Responsibility) has to be understood as a contingent, true generic. Many will see this as a virtue of the Proxy for Culpability argument because they cannot see how the mere fact that a person has been on the earth for a short or a long period of time could possibly matter normatively in and of itself. Surely what matters is what has *happened* during the life before wrongful action, not the length of that life. And surely that matters because what has happened in one's life indicates a lot about the psychological states and capacities one has attained at the time of wrongful action. If the agent quickly acquired feature F where others take a few more years to get it, then, the thought goes, the agent is just as responsible as those who take longer to get there. Still, from the fact that a person is a kid we are able to infer that the person lacks feature F with a degree of reliability that supports the further conclusion that we ought to give kids a break.

It is important to see that narrowing our gaze to versions of the argument in which (PC1) is a rough generalization, like "Kids are short," and not a contingent, non-analytic truth, does exclude some initially appealing versions of the argument. But, I suggest, their appeal dissolves under scrutiny. Consider the idea that kids who do wrong are owed a break because they have not had a fair opportunity to become good people. They never had a chance, we might say. Under one natural interpretation, this idea involves the following pair of claims: (i) A person is fully responsible for his bad behavior only if he had a fair opportunity to be a better person; and (ii) A person had a fair opportunity to be a better person only if he is older than 18. The first of these claims is a specification of feature F; F is a fair opportunity to be better. If claim (ii) is true, and is understood as more than just the rough generalization that hardly any bad kids ever had a chance to be better, then (PC1) is analytic; bad kids, by definition, have not had a fair opportunity to be good.[7] But why think that (ii) is true? If it is, it is not because of some conceptual link between opportunity and age. People vary in their capacities to learn; some learn quickly, some need more time. This is just as true when what is at issue is moral learning. Of course, more than one's capacity to learn matters to opportunity. To have an opportunity to learn something in, say, one year requires both that one is a fast enough learner, and that one has available, or has the capacity to gain, the resources one needs to learn that thing in that period of time. Fast learners, awash in resources, then, are given opportunities when they are given short periods of time to learn. And so it is just false that there is any set amount of time that is necessarily required for a person to have an opportunity to learn anything, whether it is learning to be good or learning anything else.

But perhaps (ii) is true not because of a conceptual or metaphysical link between age and opportunity, but because of such a link between age and *fair* opportunity. A test-taker who is perfectly capable of finishing an hour-long test in thirty minutes is given an opportunity, but not a *fair* opportunity to complete the test when he is not given the full hour. If he fails to finish in thirty minutes, and the test is snatched from him, he has a complaint of fairness; he is owed the full hour, even though he does not need it. Perhaps being good is like that. Perhaps everyone is owed the full 18 years before they can be faulted for not being good, even if they are capable of getting there in less time. If this is right, then (ii) is a conceptual or analytic truth, and so is (PC1). Kids have not had fair opportunities to be good because *fair* opportunities require at least 18 years. So understood, (PC1) is a claim about our moral entitlements, about what we are *owed*. But even if it is true, it does not help the argument because under it (PC2) is false. Consider the test-taker who had the opportunity to finish the test in thirty minutes, but did not. He might explain himself by saying that he *expected* to have the full hour, and so cannot be faulted for dawdling with the intention of finishing in the time that, as it happened, he was denied. But this is not a complaint of fairness. Imagine that he knew, in advance, that he would have less than the amount of time owed him to complete the test; he would have only thirty minutes, enough for him to finish, but less than he is owed. The fact that he will not get the time he is owed does not provide him with a license not to complete the test. When he fails to finish the test, he is fully responsible for his failure. The reason he did not finish is because he failed to exercise his capacities in a situation in which he knew full well that he was required, albeit unfairly, to do so.

---

[7] If one understands (ii) as nothing other than a rough generalization, then the form of argument being proposed will fall to the objections offered in the rest of this chapter, which are directed against forms of the Proxy for Culpability argument in which (PC1) is not analytic.

This is not to say that there is no problem here. Perhaps he is owed an apology, or even another chance to take the test. But that there is a need for a remedy of some kind does not show what is needed to support this proposed version of the Proxy for Culpability argument for it does not show that what the person who is denied a fair opportunity to be good is owed is *a break*.

In fact, I believe that any effort to specify feature F in such a way as to make (PC1) a conceptual, analytic, or metaphysical truth, and so more than just a rough generalization, will fall to the form of argument offered in the last two paragraphs against the equation of F with the fair opportunity to be good. Under the proposed account, either (PC1) will, in the end, turn out not to be the conceptual truth it is claimed to be, or (PC2) will be false.

Note that if (PC2) is true under a given specification of F, then a finding that a particular defendant lacks feature F should not be ignored: it speaks against full responsibility, and so speaks in favor of giving that person a break. I believe that many of the distinctive features of kids are not such that (PC2) is true. There is an enormous gap, for instance, between the claim that a person is positively attracted to risk and the claim that he is less than fully responsible for his behavior. It is far from clear that a theory of the necessary and sufficient conditions for full responsibility that fills this gap would be defensible. The same is true of the theory of responsibility, very briefly sketched just above, that fills the gap between the claim that someone is susceptible to peer influence and the claim that he is diminished in responsibility. Why, exactly, is someone who commits rape or robbery to impress his friends diminished in responsibility in comparison to someone who does it for the thrill of it? This is not to say that *no* features of kids diminish the responsibility of those who possess them, only that many that are distinctive of kids do not. But for our purposes here, I am granting (PC2). The claim to be argued for in this chapter is that *even if F is necessary for full responsibility*, and *even if being under 18 is a good proxy for the absence of F*, the Proxy for Culpability argument fails to identify the fundamental rationale for giving kids a break.

1.3.2 *The argument's empirical assumptions*

Any advocate of the Proxy for Culpability argument must supplement it substantially in order to reach the further conclusion that we should *adopt a social policy* of giving kids a break. The reason is that the social policy attaches a break to the quality of being below a certain age, not to the absence of feature F, while acknowledging that some kids have feature F and some adults lack it. So, the social policy will be both over- and under-inclusive, by the standards presumed in the Proxy for Culpability argument. Some who do not deserve breaks will get them, and some who do will not. When a policy is neither over- nor under-inclusive, it is easy to see why we should adopt it; but when the policy catches too much or too little in its net, more needs to be said.

This, by itself, is just an observation; it is not an argument against the Proxy for Culpability argument. After all, very good, fully justified social policies often predicate government behavior on proxy properties, rather than on the morally significant properties that make such government behavior appropriate. Policies of this kind aim to predicate receipt of a benefit or a burden on the presence of a *target* property that is often difficult or expensive to observe, and so, in pursuit of that aim, assign the benefit or burden on the basis of the presence of an easily observed proxy property that is thought, for independent reasons, to correlate with the target property. In fact, age is a common example of such a proxy property. For instance, we aim to give licenses to drivers who can be trusted to drive reasonably safely, and so we institute a policy that allows people to seek licenses only when they are 16 or older. We know that there are some 14- and 15-year-olds, for instance, who can be trusted behind the wheel, and some who are over the age threshold for licenses who cannot. We know that this is true even if we limit ourselves to the pool of people who can pass driving tests and any other tests of that kind that we require for licenses. But, still, we predicate license eligibility in part on the proxy property of age, rather than the target property of trustworthiness, because age is easy to observe and verify and trustworthiness is not. This policy produces four familiar categories of cases (Table 1.1).

Table 1.1.

	Target Present (e.g. trustworthy driver)	Target Absent (e.g. not trustworthy driver)
Proxy Present (e.g. 16 or over)	True Positive	False Positive
Proxy Absent (e.g. under 16)	False Negative	True Negative

And, of course, if we knew the size of the population affected by this policy, and the distribution within that population of the target and proxy properties, that would help us to make an assessment of the overall value produced by the policy. How bad is a false positive or a false negative? How good is a true positive or a true negative? How many people fall into each of these four categories? If we were to answer these questions with respect not just to the policy on the table, but also with respect to competing alternative policies that are equally implementable—such as a policy of setting the age threshold at 14 or 19—then we could, potentially, produce a rational ground for acceptance of the policy of setting the age threshold at 16. If the overall value generated by such a policy—taking into consideration the value and disvalue of all four resulting classifications—is higher than that of equally implementable alternatives, then that is a strong reason to accept the policy. I do not mean to suggest that these are *the only* factors of relevance to an assessment of a social policy; there are often considerations of principle that are poorly modeled by appeal to value generated by classifications. But, still, this is one good way to assess a social policy in comparison to competitors.

In its most powerful form, the Proxy for Culpability argument involves offering this kind of reason for accepting the policy of giving kids a break.[8] The target property is the absence of feature F, necessary for full responsibility. The proxy property is being a kid, or being under 18. The policy of giving kids a break will generate true and false positives, and true and false negatives each at particular rates. It will give a break to some who lack feature F (true positives) and to some who do not (false positives), and it will deny a break to some who have F (true negatives), and also deny it to some who do not (false negatives). The claim of someone who offers the Proxy for Culpability argument is that the overall value generated by the policy of giving kids a break is greater than that of equally implementable policies, such as policies that set the age threshold for full criminal responsibility at 21 or at 16, given the values that attend each of these four classifications, and the numbers of people who fall into each, thanks to the policy.

Note that the court in *Miller*, as illustrated by the remark quoted above, seems to dwell primarily on the value of the true positives associated with the policy of giving kids a break. The court points to the features of kids that make them different, and presumably less culpable for their crimes, than adults. In doing so, the court draws our attention to what we achieve by giving a break to people who have these distinctive features. What we achieve, the court seems to think, is justice, a fit between what we do to an offender and what he deserves, in light of his distinctive psychological features. And, to be sure, this is an important point in favor of the policy of giving kids a break. Some of them really are different from typical adults with respect to psychological features that matter to culpability and so are deserving of breaks on those grounds. But the court seems to ignore the other three categories—the true negatives, the false positives, and false negatives. To know whether what we gain by giving a break to those kids who lack feature F is worth achieving overall, we need to also know what we lose by, for instance, giving a break to precocious kids whose psychological profiles are like the typical, responsible adult (the false positives), and what we lose by denying a break to those adults who are behind the developmental curve, and so have a psychological profile like that of the typical kid (the false negatives). If we set the threshold at 14, for instance, rather than 18, then we would have fewer true positives, which would be a loss of value, but we would also have fewer false positives, which would be a gain.

---

[8] I believe that this form of the Proxy for Culpability argument is very widely accepted, although rarely explicitly. However, explicit acceptance of it can be found in, for instance, Franklin E. Zimring (1998c) "Youth Violence: Toward a Jurisprudence of Youth Violence" in *Crime and Justice*, 24: 477–500; Franklin Zimring (2000) "Penal Proportionality for the Young Offender: Notes on Immaturity, Capacity and Diminished Responsibility" in Thomas Grisso and Robert G. Schwartz (eds.), *Youth on Trial: A Developmental Perspective on Juvenile Justice*, Chicago: University of Chicago Press, pp. 271–89; Richard J. Bonnie and Thomas Grisso (2000) "Adjudicative Competence and Youthful Offenders" in Thomas Grisso and Robert G. Schwartz (eds.), *Youth on Trial: A Developmental Perspective on Juvenile Justice*, Chicago: University of Chicago Press, pp. 73–103; Elizabeth Scott and Laurence Steinberg (2003) "Blaming Youth" in *Texas Law Review*, 81: 799–839; Elizabeth Scott (2000) "Criminal Responsibility in Adolescence: Lessons from Developmental Psychology" in Thomas Grisso and Robert G. Schwartz (eds.), *Youth on Trial: A Developmental Perspective on Juvenile Justice*, Chicago: University of Chicago Press, pp. 291–324.

Whether the overall value would be higher or lower will depend on the values associated with each of these classifications and the number of people who fall into different boxes under the one policy in comparison to the other.

The benefit of thinking about the Proxy for Culpability argument through this lens is that it forces us not to fall prey to the common tendency to overlook the loss in true positives of a policy that succeeds in avoiding some very awful false positives, or conversely, to overlook the loss of an increase in false positives of a policy that increases its true positives. Say we are contemplating a world in which kids are not given a break. We note that this would be awful since there would be a lot of people lacking feature F who are punished as though they are fully responsible. True. But there would also be a lot of people who have feature F who would be so punished, and who would not be so punished if we gave kids a break. The question of which policy is better, giving kids no break or giving them a break, then, depends on the overall value of the false positive and true positive rates associated with each of these two methods for detecting feature F, and the distributions of the relevant target and proxy properties in the population. Cite just one of these two to the neglect of the other, as we see the court do in *Miller*, and judgment can easily be clouded. After all, who would deny that it's better not to convict people who have all the various distinctive psychological states and capacities that so many kids have? No one would deny it. But the policy that involves giving them a break also gives one to kids who are different from the rest and fully responsible for their behavior.

So, there are empirical assumptions underlying any claim to the effect that we are justified in adopting a social policy that predicates government behavior on the presence of a proxy property rather than on the target property of interest thanks to which that behavior is appropriate. *Such a claim presupposes that the overall value of the classification of cases produced by the policy is superior to any other equally implementable policy.* The Proxy for Culpability argument assumes that by setting the threshold for a break at 18 years old—by giving a break to *kids*—we get a superior mix of true and false classifications than we get through any other policy that could be implemented. The Proxy for Culpability argument justifies giving a break to kids only if at the 16 threshold, for instance, the resulting decrease in true positives (cases of people who are given a break and also are owed it since they lack feature F) would not be outweighed in value by an appropriately large decrease in false positives (cases of people who are given a break despite possessing feature F). Anyone who thinks this is committed to empirical claims about the numbers of people between the ages of 16 and 18 who possess those features thanks to which they are fully responsible for their wrongful conduct. Maybe such claims are true; but the point of interest for us right now is that *they need to be* if the Proxy for Culpability argument is going to succeed.

Some people who have thought hard about policies involving age thresholds have embraced this empirical dependency in order to support different age thresholds in different domains. For instance, Laurence Steinberg has suggested that it makes sense to give kids who commit crimes a break while, at the same time, to entrust them to make decisions about abortion.⁹ His reason is that decisions to engage in crime (at least, of the sort that kids ordinarily commit) are typically made in a rush in circumstances of heightened emotion, while decisions about whether to abort a fetus are made more calmly and after greater deliberation. He thinks, and with good reason, that as an empirical matter kids have significant deficits when it comes to decision-making of the former kind, and not of the latter. And so he thinks that being between, for instance, 16 and 18 is a good proxy for diminished capacities to make decisions in the one domain, but not in the other. Ultimately, this is a claim about the comparative value of two policies that do not differ in proxy property (age), threshold (18), or in target property (decision-making deficits). Where the two methods differ is in the domain of particulars over which they range: one ranges over wrongful conduct typically chosen in circumstances of heightened emotion; the other ranges over decisions to abort, or not to, made in somewhat calmer, less time-pressured circumstances. The claim is that the overall value generated by the former policy is optimal relative to competitors, while the latter is not; a system that allows 16–18-year-olds to make up their own minds about abortion, he thinks, outperforms it. And this claim is ultimately defensible only given these empirical claims—claims with implications about the relative value of false and true positives and negatives—over these different domains. The point is that Steinberg tries to use the empirical assumptions of the Proxy for Culpability argument to his advantage in order to support different age thresholds for different domains of conduct.

1.4 The Problem of Empirical Dependency

At the very least, then, this much is clear: the Proxy for Culpability argument is empirically dependent. It provides support for the policy of giving kids a break only if competing, implementable policies do not offer better mixes of false and true positives and negatives. What this implies is that if it should turn out that another competing policy does, as a matter of empirical fact, offer a better overall score in this respect, then those who advocate the policy of giving kids a break should abandon it in order to accept the alternative position. *But would they be willing to do so?* Put in its baldest form, the central point of this section—the point which I will call "the problem of empirical dependency"—is that they would not and should not. What that shows, as we will see, is that the Proxy for Culpability Argument does not capture the rationale to which we are committed for giving kids a break.[10]

---

[9] Laurence Steinberg (2009) "Should the science of adolescent brain development inform public policy?" in *American Psychologist*, 64(8): 739–50.

[10] I take the point that I am making in this section to be closely allied to the critical position forcefully advocated by Emily Buss. See Emily Buss (2009a) "Rethinking the Connection Between Developmental Science and Juvenile Justice" in *The University of Chicago Law Review*, 76: 493–515; Emily Buss (2009b) "What the Law Should (And Should Not) Learn from Child Development Research" in *Hofstra Law Review*, 38: 13–65.

Consider the policy of giving males under the age of 18 a break, but giving females a break only if they are under 16. Unlike the policy of giving kids a break, regardless of gender, this policy is gender-sensitive. In fact, the state of Oklahoma at one time adopted just this policy, but with the genders reversed; 16–18-year-old males were treated as adults for purposes of criminal responsibility, while their female age-mates were treated as children. At the time, the state justified its approach through appeal to "the demonstrated facts of life." The 10th circuit struck down the policy on the grounds that the state had not specified what "facts of life" made the policy reasonable and in the absence of such specification the policy was in violation of constitutional requirements of equality.[11] But let's allow that although the facts of life do not support Oklahoma's former policy, they do support the gender-sensitive policy of giving breaks to girls under 16 and boys under 18. After all, girls do mature faster than boys, and so the probability that a girl between the ages of 16 and 18 has feature F is higher than the probability that a boy in that age group does.[12] Does the gender-sensitive policy employ a better proxy for culpability than the policy of giving a break to all those under 18, regardless of gender? Very possibly. Given differences in maturation rates, adding consideration of gender is an efficient way to gain an uptick in the true positive rate in contrast to the policy that gives a break to all kids. Is that uptick accompanied by an unfortunate and sufficiently large increase in the false positive rate, enough of an increase to outweigh the improvements? It is hard to say. Consider Blackstone's Ratio, according to which it is better that ten guilty people go free than that one innocent person be sent to the gallows. Or, anyway, since it is a bit unclear what, exactly, is meant by this, consider the accompanying idea that we should be exactly ten times as averse to a conviction of an innocent party as to an acquittal of a guilty one. The policy of denying a break to the 16–18-year-old females results in some convictions of innocents. But if for each one there are more than ten guilty people convicted who would have otherwise gone free, Blackstone's Ratio would counsel acceptance of the policy. I do not think anyone can confidently say that this is what such a policy provides. But I do not think anyone can confidently *deny it* either. It's an empirical question. It also might change over time. Age of puberty onset in girls has been declining.[13] Perhaps this change is accompanied also by a decline in the age at which girls, on average, acquire the features that are necessary for full responsibility. If so, then the Proxy for Culpability argument, considered on its face and without supplementation, would

---

[11] *Lamb v. Brown*, 456 F.2d 18, 19 (10th Cir. 1972).

[12] The traditional rule in Judaism is that girls are subject to the law at the age of 12 while boys achieve that status at 13. But this rule is supported by the logic of the religion by the further fact that girls and boys are subject to separate norms of conduct; things are required of girls that are not required of boys, and vice versa. So it is not the case that the rule is reflective of the idea that boys and girls have what it takes to be subject *to the same norms* at different times in development. It is, by contrast, that idea that fuels the Proxy for Culpability argument.

[13] Susan Y. Euling, Marcia E. Herman-Giddens, Peter A. Lee, Sherry G. Selevan, Anders Juul, Thorkild I.A. Sørensen, Leo Dunkel, John H. Himes, Grete Teilmann, and Shanna H. Swan (2008), "Examination of US Puberty-Timing Data from 1940 to 1994 for Secular Trends: Panel Findings" in *Pediatrics* v. 121, pp. S172–91.

support lowering the age under which girls are given a break. If you recoil at this idea *even if it should turn out to be empirically supported* then you ought also to recoil from the Proxy for Culpability argument. At the very least, you have to recognize that the argument requires significant supplementation if it is to support the policy of giving kids a break.

While I think that reflection on a policy that appeals to gender, and thereby improves classification, is instructive for a variety of reasons to be described below, it's also important to see that the central problem for the Proxy for Culpability argument can be expressed with less controversial examples. Consider, for instance, a height-sensitive policy: give a break to anyone under the age of 18, provided they are not over five foot four. This policy, like the gender-sensitive policy, might employ a superior proxy to age alone. Height, after all, is a marker of development: taller kids tend to be further along in their development than shorter kids. So, the height-sensitive policy will result in some improvements in the true positive rate: taller 16- and 17-year-olds possessing feature F, whatever it is, will be denied breaks. It will also result in an increase in the false positive rate: taller 16- and 17-year-olds lacking F will also be denied breaks. It's an empirical question whether the improvements outweigh the losses. But the advocate of the Proxy for Culpability argument ought to recognize a significant loss in persisting with a policy that gives breaks to all kids, regardless of height, should the height-sensitive policy offer a superior mix of hits and misses. Such a person ought to hold, that is, that to persist in giving all kids a break when we know that the combination of age and height are a superior proxy is a government failure. But it seems to me that our implicit rationale for giving kids a break does not have this implication. Government behaves better, as an intuitive matter, when kids are given a break regardless of height than when the government, instead, adopts the height-sensitive policy. If that is right, then our implicit rationale is not captured by the Proxy for Culpability argument.

Before considering some ways of resisting my objection to the Proxy for Culpability Argument, let's get a bit clearer on exactly how the objection proceeds. My claim is not that, in fact, an alternative to the policy of giving kids a break, such as the gender- or height-sensitive policies, offer a better mix of true and false positives and negatives. No one can assert that without also offering empirical evidence. My claim is, rather, that *if this is true* then advocates of the Proxy for Culpability argument would have to prefer the policy that is superior in this respect, or else offer some other reason for maintaining a preference for the policy that uses age alone as a proxy for culpability. In fact, an even weaker claim than this will serve my purposes. All that is essential to the argument is the observation that advocates of the Proxy for Culpability argument must take the policy of giving all kids a break to involve *a failure* on the government's part, relative to ideal government behavior, in light of the discovery that there is a better proxy for F than age. Even if the advocate of the Proxy for Culpability argument prefers, all things considered, to continue giving breaks to all kids, he would have to also acknowledge that this is in one important respect non-ideal behavior on the government's part, for in at least one respect, he is committed to thinking, the government would do better by using the alternative, superior proxy for F. But since our implicit, and unarticulated rationale for the policy of giving kids a break is not sensitive to this empirical fact—the policy of giving kids a break is not shown by such empirical discoveries to even involve a governmental failure, not even one that is outweighed—this shows that the Proxy for Culpability argument, without supplementation, fails to capture our implicit rationale. This is the problem of empirical dependency.

Notice that the problem of empirical dependency does not have bite against many public policies predicating government treatment on the presence of a proxy property which are justified on the grounds that they offer superior classification than any implementable competitors. Consider the case of driver's licenses. If it turns out that a better mix of true and false classifications can be achieved by either giving everyone the opportunity to get a license, regardless of age, or by replacing it with some other proxy property (such as a score on a timed decision-making test with high stakes) then that would be a strong reason against the policy of denying licenses to those under 16. Age isn't intuitively ethically sticky when what we are talking about are driver's licenses. If it is appealing to use age thresholds for licenses, that appeal disappears given a different set of empirical facts under which age is not the best proxy for the qualities that really matter morally. But age is sticky in this way when it comes to criminal responsibility. There is appeal to predicating government treatment on it in that domain that outstrips the empirical presumptions of the Proxy for Culpability argument.

From one point of view, the objection is made out much more powerfully by appeal solely to the example of the height-sensitive policy than by appeal to the gender-sensitive policy. After all, the very idea of predicating differential treatment on gender introduces noise. However, wherever we find intuitive resistance to a policy that employs a given proxy property, such as height, when contrasted with a simple age proxy, there is the possibility that our intuitive resistance is informed by the recognition that the relevant property is a superior proxy *simply because it is, itself, a proxy for a property like gender or race*. In fact, this is probably true of the property appealed to in the height-sensitive policy. Almost all of the true positives under such a policy who would have been false negatives under the policy of giving a break to all the 16- and 17-year-olds regardless of height—that is, the 16- and 17-year-olds possessing F and denied a break under the height-sensitive policy—are female. And, conversely, almost all the false positives who would have been true positives are male. So, if the height-sensitive policy employs a better proxy for F it is because gender is relevant to the distribution of F by age. What this shows is that a true defense of the objection to the Proxy for Culpability argument—a true defense of the problem of empirical dependency—is aided by a showing that our resistance to the gender-sensitive policy, and not just the height-sensitive policy, is itself reflective of the fact that our implicit rationale for giving kids a break is not captured by the Proxy for Culpability argument.

A premise in the problem of empirical dependency is the claim that our implicit rationale is not empirically dependent in the way that the rationale summarized in the Proxy for Culpability argument is. This premise can be resisted. While it cannot be denied that we would not, in fact, give up our policy of giving all kids a break, regardless of gender, even were it shown that the gender-sensitive policy offers superior classifications to the policy of giving all kids a break, there are a few different ways of explaining our attachment. First, perhaps our attachment to our policy in the face of such a discovery would be irrational. Perhaps, that is, the policy is psychologically stickier than it should be; perhaps our attachment to it is stronger than the rationale for it warrants. Perhaps. But it seems to me at least methodologically dubious to appeal to this idea at this point in the argument. It amounts to insulating a rationale for a policy against moral objection by asserting that moral qualms about those policies that it rationalizes can be dismissed as irrational. Rather, it seems to me that appropriate methodology requires us to assume, until we have no choice but to deny it, that the discovery that a proposed rationale for a policy supports seemingly morally dubious policies is to be taken at face value.

But perhaps our qualms about the gender-sensitive policy, even if it does offer superior classification, are both rational and consistent with the Proxy for Culpability argument. Perhaps there is something else wrong with the gender-sensitive policy that drives our moral intuitions, something that does not speak against the policy of giving all kids a break regardless of gender. In fact, one might bolster this thought through appeal to the well-known Supreme Court case of *Craig v. Boren* (97 S.Ct 451 (1976)) which struck down a statute that allowed girls to purchase alcohol provided they were over 16, while boys were barred from doing so until 18. Under one natural reading, the court is allowing that age by itself is a less good proxy for the quality of being a responsible drinker than is age conjoined with gender. But the court strikes down the law despite this because of the law's broader, harmful effects: it helps to propagate harmful stereotypes. Perhaps we recoil at the idea of the gender-sensitive policy for giving breaks for the same reason: it has, or we suspect that it has, broader negative effects, either through the perpetuation of stereotypes of girls as relatively docile rule-followers, or through some other mechanism.

However, it is very important to see the difference between the policy that the Supreme Court rejected in *Craig v. Boren*, and the gender-sensitive policy for giving breaks to those who commit crimes. The reasons that we seek to keep alcohol away from those who are not responsible drinkers is purely consequentialist: irresponsible drinkers harm themselves and others to a degree that outweighs the benefits to themselves and to sellers of alcohol. Given this fact, we are licensed in assessing a policy for distributing the entitlement to buy alcohol by weighing the value and disvalue of *all* of the consequences of such a policy, including those, such as stereotype perpetuation, that are not direct effects of the distribution of alcohol purchases. And, in general, when a policy's rationale is purely consequentialist, as is common, the fact that a proxy argument in its favor is empirically dependent is no objection at all to that argument. But, and here is the crucial point, *the reasons that we have policies aimed at distributing punishment in accordance with culpability are not purely consequentialist*. It is not the case that we punish people in accordance with their culpability because good things happen that way. For one thing, good things frequently do not happen that way; sometimes the world would be better in many ways if we punished a culpable wrongdoer not at all, or in some other way that mismatches with culpability. For another, even when good things do happen thanks to matching punishment to culpability, this is not what makes it worth doing. And so we cannot justify a choice in favor of a policy that results in a less good mix of hits and misses, in our effort to conform punishment to culpability, on the grounds that it has better collateral consequences than policies employing better proxies. The consequences just are not what matters, whether they are good or bad.

To say this much is to evince a commitment to only a very weak form of retributivism. It does require a non-consequentialist, retributivist justification of a comparative proportionality principle: a principle according to which punishment P1 is more easily justified than punishment P2, if P1 involves a closer match to criminal culpability than P2 does. But such a justification does not entail that punishment is the right response to crime because it is deserved.[14] Why we are justified in punishing is a different question from why we are required to adjust punishment to culpability.

If I am right, then the consequentialist disvalue of a gender-sensitive policy for giving a break—its potential role, for instance, in the perpetuation of stereotypes—is not the source of our aversion to it. But perhaps there is another explanation for our aversion that is consistent with the Proxy for Culpability argument. Why do we recoil at the idea of having different age standards for getting a break depending on gender? It is plausible to answer that such a policy would introduce gender-based inequality in the distribution of benefits and burdens. One plausibly ought to be opposed to such inequalities of distribution for non-consequentialist reasons; even if the pie gets bigger, one might think, there is something wrong in giving different-sized slices to girls and boys, men and women. But notice that the policy of giving kids a break regardless of gender also introduces inequality of this sort: those above 18 are burdened differently from those below that age threshold. The Proxy for Culpability argument justifies this inequality in treatment with the claim that there is a genuine, morally significant difference between the groups: feature F is more frequently found in those above 18 than those below it, and at rates thanks to which the classifications that result when the threshold is set at 18 are optimal (or closer to optimal than any other implementable policy). So, an advocate of the Proxy for Culpability argument cannot object to the gender-sensitive policy, which involves giving breaks to 16–18-year-old boys that are denied to girls in that group, on the grounds that it involves inequality per se. If the gender-sensitive policy is superior in its classifications to the policy of giving all kids a

---

[14] H. L. A Hart famously claims that a rationale for "principles of the distribution of punishment," such as the comparative proportionality principle offered here, are independent from accounts of punishment's "general justifying aim"—accounts, that is, of the point of responding to crimes with punishment, rather than something else. I think Hart is right about this. See H. L. A. Hart (2008) "Prolegomena to the Principles of Punishment" in *Punishment and Responsibility: Essays in the Philosophy of Law*, John Gardner (ed.), Oxford: Oxford University Press.

break, then the advocate of the Proxy for Culpability argument is committed to the view that the resulting gender inequality in the distribution of burdens and benefits is justified in the very same way that the age inequality is justified when we give kids a break. In fact, if the 16–18-year-old girls, as a population, are more similar in distribution of feature F to the general population of people over 18 than they are to the boys between the ages of 16 and 18, then the policy of giving kids a break regardless of gender *involves gender inequality*. The advocate of the Proxy for Culpability argument, therefore, is even more strongly committed to the gender-sensitive policy under those empirical assumptions.

Perhaps the problem with the gender-sensitive policy is that it improves classification by predicating a difference of treatment on *gender*, period. Perhaps, that is, governments should not do that even if things would be better that way, and even if there would be no problematic inequalities in the distribution of burdens and benefits that way. After all, we might be able to improve our classifications by predicating who we give a break to on race or on religion. But we would recoil at the idea thanks to the special status of those properties. It's an empirical question whether older adolescents who are regular churchgoers are more likely to have feature F than are those lacking such structured guidance in their lives. Perhaps, for instance, 16-year-olds who are regular churchgoers are more likely to have the capacity to appreciate the difference between right and wrong, and perhaps that *is* feature F—the feature that is necessary for full responsibility. If so, then we could improve our classifications by denying a break to regular churchgoers between the ages of 16 and 18, a break that we would give to those in that age-range who are not regular churchgoers. We might not want to adopt that policy *even while recognizing that we would have an improvement in our classifications* simply because we do not think that the government should be in the business of predicating differences in treatment on religiosity. Perhaps gender is like that too.

As attractive as this idea is, it is overstated, and in ways that undermine its capacity to support the Proxy for Culpability argument. We can see this by reflecting on the fact that when gender is a job qualification, differences in treatment can be predicated on it. The government is allowed, in certain circumstances, to disproportionately reject male applicants for jobs working the airport security lines. The reason is that some proportion of travelers will need to be patted down and will have a strong preference about the gender of the person who does the task. If the Transportation Security Administration (TSA) has fewer women on staff than are needed for this purpose, then they can preferentially choose women over men. But why? To bar the government from giving preferential treatment to women in hiring would make it impossible for the government to fulfill one of its essential functions, namely providing airport safety in a way that does not cause offense. The government must not just provide airport safety, but must do so respectfully, and so must give preference to women TSA applicants. But punishing is also an essential government activity. And the government must not just punish, but must do so respectfully by punishing in a way that is constrained and guided by offender culpability. By the same reasoning, if the gender-sensitive policy, that denies a break to the female 16–18-year-olds, really does offer significantly better classifications overall than the policy of giving a break to all kids, then this one essential government activity is better pursued through its adoption. We can accept that the government ought not predicate differences in treatment on gender, period...except when an essential government function requires it to do so. And so it follows that the case for allowing the government's adoption of the gender-sensitive policy is just as strong as the case for allowing the government to give women preferential treatment sometimes in hiring.

Yet, still, perhaps we have not yet gotten to the source of the objection to the gender-sensitive policy. Perhaps there is a ground for aversion to that policy that is consistent with advocacy of the Proxy for Culpability argument. After all, even if race were a good proxy for a difference in distribution of feature F, there would be something abhorrent about predicating differences in government treatment on race in this context. We might say that it is better to adjust our conception of what government functions are essential than to demand that the government engage in an activity that requires it to predicate differences in treatment on race. Still, before fully acquiescing to this thought, it's important to distinguish between a policy that gives more breaks to those of a race traditionally and historically favored, on the one hand, in comparison to a policy that gives more breaks, instead, to those of a race that has been traditionally and historically oppressed. Say we give breaks to White kids and not to Black kids. While it could be doubted, it seems to me that the value of the true positives resulting from this policy is not race-sensitive; there is just as much value in convicting fully responsible White people as fully responsible Black people. But the disvalue of the false positives is, indeed, race-sensitive. The reason is that even if the policy had exactly the same false-positive rate for Black people as it has for White people, Black false positives solidify and extend historical systems of oppression.

But this fact is something which can be accommodated by an adequate account of the overall value of the classifications produced by a social policy. That is, if there is a significant class of false positives, under one sorting method, that are of much greater disvalue than the false positives under another, then it will be that much less likely that the former method will outperform the latter. I suspect that the powerful feeling that a system that gave breaks to White kids and not to Black kids would be abhorrent *even if it offered superior classifications in comparison to a race-blind policy*, and *even if the government will necessarily perform its essential functions significantly less well by declining to adopt it*, is rooted in a failure to appreciate what is involved in calculating the overall value of a policy's true and false positives and negatives. False positives in a race-sensitive system are so damaging that the improvements in true positives would have to be enormous to outweigh them—so enormous that we can be almost certain that any race-sensitive system would be far worse than a race-blind system. Perhaps it is better that one hundred guilty Black people go free than that one innocent Black person be convicted; or perhaps the right ratio is 1000:1, even though 10:1 does just fine for the population as a whole. The history of racial oppression, that is, implies that the relevant ratio of values here is race-dependent. But this is to say that a race-sensitive system is very unlikely to actually offer superior classification, all things considered, in comparison to a race-blind system. Fair enough. But this fact is consistent with the further claim that the advocate of the Proxy for Culpability argument is committed to favoring even the race-sensitive system *if, in fact, its classifications are better.*

To me, this is a powerful argument against the Proxy for Culpability argument. It would be unacceptable to adopt a race-sensitive system *even if it offered better classifications than the system of giving kids a break regardless of race.* And not just that: it is a mistake to even characterize the increases in true positives under a race-sensitive policy *as improvements*. What this shows is that there is more involved in the rationale for the policy of giving kids a break than is captured by the Proxy for Culpability argument. But given the powerful temptation to buck the hypothetical here—can we *really* think of any plausible, implementable race-sensitive policy that has better classifications than the policy of giving all kids a break?—the point is limited in its rhetorical power. But notice that there is much less reason to buck the parallel hypothetical about the gender-sensitive system. After all, it is not women, but men, who have traditionally suffered much more under problematic criminal justice policies. Traditional oppression of women, for whatever reason, has not manifested in excessive criminal punishment of women in comparison to men, for instance. This is not to say that the criminal law has always been good to women; far from it. A quick glance at the history of rape law belies that claim. But it would be false to say that women have been more oppressed by the criminal law overall than men have; the reverse seems much more likely. The result is that the false positives of women in a gender-sensitive system, damaging as they are, are not nearly as damaging as the false positives in a race-sensitive system. And, further, there is an empirically grounded reason to think that girls between the ages of 16 and 18 are more likely to be fully responsible for their behavior than boys, while there is no reason at all to think that Black kids in that age group are more likely to be fully responsible than White. Hence the gender-sensitive policy is likely to promise real improvements in true positives, and much less damaging losses in its increases in false positives in comparison to other systems.

Is there a different reason to recoil from the gender-sensitive policy that is consistent with adherence to the Proxy for Culpability argument, a reason not yet considered? While in the end it is probably just a different label for an idea already canvassed, one might say so by drawing on Joseph Raz's notion of an exclusionary reason.[15] Perhaps the reason to favor the gender-sensitive policy—an improvement in the overall balance of correct and incorrect classifications—is one that there is reason not to act on when choosing a social policy. If this is right, then one might accept the Proxy for Culpability argument while also granting that the policy one ought to select is not the policy that employs the very best proxy for culpability; it is instead the one that employs

---

[15] Raz defines the term in several places. See, for instance, Joseph Raz (1990) *Practical Reason and Norms*, Princeton: Princeton University Press, p. 37ff.

the best proxy for culpability *where one can, consistent with one's exclusionary reasons, choose the policy for that reason*. If there really is an exclusionary reason not to act on the reasons favoring the gender-sensitive policy over the gender-neutral policy, then that would explain why the advocate of the Proxy for Culpability argument would recoil from the gender-sensitive policy despite the improvements in hits and misses that it might promise.

The problem is that there is no reason to think that there is an exclusionary reason of the sort that the advocate of the Proxy for Culpability argument would need. In fact, that is the lesson of the discussion of the last few pages. There is no shortage of contexts in which it is perfectly permissible to choose a policy based on the reasons in its favor provided by facts about gender. The TSA hiring example illustrates the point. There are also contexts in which it is not permissible. This is so when, for instance, there is a history of closely related policies being used as instruments of oppression against those of a particular gender. But this is not such a case; criminal punishment has not been disproportionately heaped on women. The claim that there is an exclusionary reason in this case appears to be without positive support.

But, to emphasize the point, my point is not that all this shows that we ought not to give breaks to girls between the ages of 16 and 18. Far from it. I think the gender-sensitive policy should be laughed out of contention. My point is that the advocate of the Proxy for Culpability argument *cannot laugh at it*, but must instead entertain the serious possibility that it is more justified *by the standards informing the Proxy for Culpability argument in the first place*. This is an objection to the Proxy for Culpability argument because the gender-sensitive policy is *unjustified even if it offers superior classification than the policy of giving all kids a break regardless of gender.*

If there are lingering worries about the possibility that the intuitions about the gender-sensitive policy are distorted, note how easy it is to launch the same argument by appeal to examples of policies that are sensitive to age and other properties distinct from gender, properties that are not even proxies for gender (as height is). For instance: For all we know, some childhood deprivations might increase the rate at which people acquire property F. After all, we know that tough circumstances speed other kinds of learning, why not learning to be a fully responsible person? If that turned out to be true, then a policy that denied a break to, say, 16- and 17-year-olds, provided they grew up in poverty, or with few adult role models, might offer a better mix of true and false positives and negatives. It could be that enough of those kids have responded to their tough circumstances with fast development to make the increase in hits worth the increase in misses. But no one would or should prefer such a policy to the one we have, in which kids are given a break regardless of the presence of such factors. The result: the Proxy for Culpability argument fails to capture the correct rationale for the policy of giving kids a break. The policy's appropriateness is not empirically dependent in the same way that the rationale for it is, under the Proxy for Culpability argument. What that shows is that the Proxy for Culpability argument fails to capture the policy's rationale.

1.5 A Ground for Ignoring the False Positive Rate?

Let's turn to an assumption of the Proxy for Culpability argument in the form that has been under consideration. The assumption is that there is commensurability between the disvalue of the true and false positives and negatives. What if that assumption is false when it comes to giving breaks to kids who are, or who are not, less than fully responsible for their wrongful behavior? What if the disvalue of denying a break to someone to whom it is owed is not at all offset by another feature of the method thanks to which this happened, namely the value of giving a break to someone to whom it was, indeed, owed? Perhaps the values here do not aggregate, and so cannot be outweighed, at least not in the way in which weights on one side of a scale are outweighed by greater weights on the other.

The very idea of moving forward with conduct that makes sense when the values in play are incommensurable is puzzling. Say that the disvalue of false convictions is incommensurable with the value of true convictions; we get good things out of convicting the guilty, but those goods do not outweigh or diminish the disvalue of convicting the innocent. There is no single scale on which to place these competing forms of value. How can we then be justified in adopting a policy that involves both convictions of the innocent and convictions of the guilty? Given incommensurability, we cannot say that such a policy is justified thanks to the fact that, all things considered, its value is positive. The policy is good in some respects and bad in others. To be sure, a given method is better than one that has both a lower false positive rate and a higher true positive rate; but in the cases of interest to us, by lowering the false positive rate—by, for instance, moving the threshold for breaks from 18 to 16 and thereby denying a break to some who have feature F and so are not owed one—we also lower the true positive rate. So the comparisons of interest are always between methods in which one has a better false positive rate, the other a better true positive rate. If the values here are truly incommensurable, how can we compare methods in such cases?

We can put the question here a different way. Say that it is false that the policy of giving kids a break is *better* than competing policies, such as the policies of setting the age of culpability at 16, or 21, or the gender- or height-sensitive policies described above. There are things to be said for the policy of giving kids a break; there are pros and there are cons, just as there are with competing policies, but the pros and the cons cannot be placed on a common scale. There is incommensurability. Can we, under that assumption, be justified in choosing a given policy *by its pros*? What the policy of giving kids a break has going for it is that there are lots of kids lacking feature F, who are owed a break, and get one under the policy, period. Can it ever be appropriate to cite what's good about a policy, and ignore what is bad about it? Can we ever be justified in adopting a policy just because of the goods it promises, while ignoring its evils?

There are cases in which this is so, for there are cases in which one is barred for some reason from consideration of one set of evaluative factors in choosing a policy, factors that speak to some genuine evaluative properties of the policy. For instance, say that a legislator is considering voting for a policy which would have net benefits for the public, benefits greater than any alternative policy that could be adopted but also which promises the legislator personally a very large financial loss. She is barred from considering her personal financial losses in deciding whether to vote for the policy. She could not justify a decision to vote against the policy by citing the losses she personally would incur were it adopted. And so, conversely, when she votes *for* the policy, she *can* justify her decision simply by citing the good that the policy produces; it's good for the public, period. She bears no burden to show that the good to the public outweighed the losses to herself. She is justified without showing that, even if the goods in question are commensurable—even if, that is, there is an answer to the question of whether the social goods generated by the policy outweighed the personal losses that she suffers thanks to the policy. And so, similarly, her decision to vote for the policy is justified also in the case in which the goods are incommensurable. By being barred from considering the losses to herself, she also gains the freedom to make a decision in the face of incommensurable values; she can make that decision solely on the strength of the good promised by the alternative she chooses.

Perhaps the advocate of the Proxy for Culpability argument can avoid the charge of inappropriate empirical dependency by pressing an analogy between this example and the proffered defense of the policy of giving kids a break. The idea would be that although the values of the false positive and true positive rate are genuinely incommensurable, it is justified to adopt the policy thanks to the positive value associated with its true positive rate—the rate at which breaks are given to those lacking feature F, and so lacking full responsibility—and while ignoring the question of the disvalue of the policy's false positive rate. We would then need an explanation for why it is appropriate, or even required, to ignore the policy's false positive rate when deciding whether to adopt it. In the analogous example, this role was played by the duties of legislators to represent social interests, and to set aside their own. But is there an analogous feature present in the case that interests us? Is there something about considering how we should treat kids who do wrong that obligates us to set aside consideration of the impact of a potential policy's false positive rate?

We might make some progress here through consideration of the parental obligation to put one's child's interests ahead of one's own. When a parent and child are equally thirsty, and there is enough water for only one of them, and it is up to the parent who drinks, the parent does wrong if he drinks instead of giving the water to his child. But there is just as much quenched thirst either way. When the parent is asked to justify his decision to give the water to his child, he can provide a satisfactory account simply by noting that his child was thirsty. This would justify the decision even if the parent were (within limits) thirstier than the child. Or, to put it another way, parental obligation provides a license, at least, and sometimes imposes a requirement, to fall short of maximizing utility. But this isn't to say that the good achieved through acts that fulfill parental obligations are irrelevant to their justification. Not so. The act is justified by the fact that the child's thirst is quenched, period. That the resource could not have been used to generate more good is not a silent premise in the argument for the act. But the good that is produced through it is an essential premise in the justificatory argument, the argument concluding that what the parent did was what he ought to have done.

Notice that the very same would be true if the good that is achieved through the act that favors the child is incommensurable with the good for the parent thereby forgone. If the parent performs the act that favors the child, he can be fully justified by the good that is thereby achieved for the child even if there is no common scale on which to place the good that is forgone through the act. This is why, we might think, making a career sacrifice for the sake of a child's education can be justified even if the child's contribution to the world is incommensurable with the goods forgone through the career sacrifice.

Use of this point to repel the objection to the Proxy for Culpability argument—the objection that the argument is empirically dependent in a way that the claim that we ought to give kids a break is not—requires the further claim that we have some kind of obligation to give kids lacking feature F a break that does not derive from the state's general obligation to give breaks to those to whom they are owed, and to deny them to those to whom they are not owed. There must be some extra, special obligation to give breaks to kids or, at least, kids who are less than fully responsible for their wrongful behavior. But, notice, and this is an essential point, *if the state had such a special obligation to children—and perhaps it does—then we would not need the Proxy for Culpability argument in order to establish its conclusion, namely that kids ought to be given a break.* There is something lost when someone undeserving of a break gets one. But if the act of giving him a break is justified by the good that is thereby produced in a way that does not require establishing that the good in question outweighs this loss, then the act of giving him a break is justified. Put another way: If our obligations to children are such as to license us to shield them from harm, and to ignore the downside of doing so, then we are justified in doing so regardless of the degree to which they are genuinely responsible for their behavior. Under this assumption, that is, we are justified in giving kids a break even if they are fully responsible for their bad behavior. The advocate for the Proxy for Culpability argument, therefore, can defend it from the primary objection here offered against it only at the cost of providing any positive motivation for the argument. *Defense of the argument requires the postulation of moral duties with a structure that makes the argument unnecessary for establishment of its conclusion.*

The result: no matter how the issue is attacked, the Proxy for Culpability argument fails to capture the rationale for our practice of giving kids a break. Even if kids differ from adults in ways that make them, in general, diminished in responsibility in comparison, that is not the reason why we ought to give them breaks.

1.6 Conclusion

Let's return to the beginning. I take it as a fixed point that kids should be given a break. Our question is why. There are a variety of ways of answering the question. Perhaps it is because criminal behavior is normal for kids; perhaps it is because it will stop as they grow older. Or, as was our focus here, perhaps it is because kids lack the features that we find in adults thanks to which adults can be fully responsible for their wrongful behavior. That last thought, as enormously plausible as it is, turns out not to be the thought that is informing our attachment to the policy of giving kids a break. The problem is not, as one might expect, that it depends on an indefensible theory of responsibility, nor that the claims about the psychological features and capacities of kids on which it depends are false. Both of those things might be true, and, if true, they would undermine the proposed rationale. But the problem identified here persists even if the argument draws on a defensible theory of responsibility and on truths about the psychology of kids.

Understood in its most natural form, the rationale summarized in the Proxy for Culpability argument is empirically dependent in ways that our conviction that kids ought to be given breaks is not. That conviction would withstand empirical discoveries which would undermine this rationale. Understood in another way, the proposed rationale is not empirically dependent. Perhaps we labor under duties towards children that license or require us to ignore the downside of the policy of giving them a break. Perhaps, that is, we are insulated by our duties from empirical facts that would, if we were not so insulated, count against policies for fulfilling them. But if that is so, then it is the rationale for that duty that supports the policy of giving kids a break, and would support it even if, in fact, kids were not diminished in responsibility in comparison to adults. We are thus, still, in search of a rationale. The progress here, I hope, has been in making clear part of what such a rationale must be like.

2

Kids Will Be Kids... Until They Grow Out of It

2.0 Introduction

Growth is marked by error. Since learning is learning from mistakes, it inevitably involves many. If childhood is the period in which we learn to be law-abiding citizens, then we should expect it, like any learning period, to be punctuated by failure. And, of course, we have a name for the failure to be a law-abiding citizen: crime. From this point of view, crimes by kids are like their arithmetic errors: an inevitable byproduct of the process of learning to do things right.

It is a short step from this thought to the proposals that this chapter will be spent examining: We ought to give kids a break when they commit crimes for the same reason that we ought to be lenient to any learner who makes mistakes. It is an inevitable part of learning and so not indicative of any special deformity worthy of being shunned. And, in addition, we should be lenient because we have reason to believe that, when the lessons are learned, the problematic behavior will go away, leaving productive people capable of the kind of participation in government that we expect from any citizen.

Gripped by these lines of thought, productive law-abiding citizens are often tempted to point to their own case to explain their leniency to kids: "You won't believe the kinds of things that *I* did when *I* was 16!" In a different context, such a statement would sound like bragging about one's success in escaping justice for past crimes. Imagine saying, in justification of leniency towards a 30-year-old bank robber, "You won't believe the kinds of things that *I* did when *I* was 30!" But in this context the remark is intended, instead, to take one's own status as a law-abiding citizen, who committed crimes as a kid and was treated with leniency, as a reason to persist in lenient policies towards kids. It is to say, "I learned without punishment, or with lesser punishment than is heaped on adults, and so we should take the same approach to kids today who commit crimes." It is the burden of this chapter to show that this line of thought fails to justify the policy of giving kids a break. In the end, it is rooted in irreparably flawed conceptions of the point and purpose of responding to crime with sanction.

As indicated in chapter 1, this line of thought actually consists of two distinct arguments for the claim that kids ought to be given a break:

Kids Will Be Kids: Wrongful, criminal behavior by kids is a product of the way they are. But being that way is developmentally normal for kids. If wrongful, criminal behavior is developmentally normal for people in a certain category, then anyone in that category is owed a break. So: kids should be given a break.

They'll Grow Out of It: Wrongful, criminal behavior by kids is a product of features of kids that they typically grow out of. Any category of people who perpetrate wrongful, criminal conduct thanks to qualities that they will lose through the passage of time, and without special intervention, are owed a break. So: kids should be given a break.

Section 2.1 examines the first of these two arguments, section 2.2 the second.

2.1 Kids Will Be Kids

As in the case of my treatment in chapter 1 of the Proxy for Culpability argument, it will be useful to separate the Kids Will Be Kids argument into distinct premises leading to the conclusion that kids are to be given a break:

(KW1) Wrongful conduct by kids is the product of the exercise of a collection of psychological mechanisms, M.

(KW2) The possession and exercise of M is developmentally normal for kids.

(KW3) If a person's wrongful conduct is the product of the exercise of psychological capacities that it is developmentally normal for him to possess and exercise, then he ought to be given a break.

(Conclusion) ∴ Kids ought to be given a break for their wrongful conduct.

The conjunction of (KW1) and (KW2) might be what is taken to be empirically supported by high-profile work in psychology and neuroscience on adolescents and children. Consider, for instance, the well-known experiments involving driving simulators in which adolescents are found to engage in risky acts when in the presence of peers at higher rates than either adults, or they themselves when alone.[1] Such results seem to support the idea that criminal conduct, at least that involving risky driving, or that involving groups of kids in other settings, is the product of developmentally normal psychological mechanisms. Or consider work indicating that kids tend to have steeper temporal discounting curves than adults.[2] Crimes by kids that seem explicable when performed myopically, without regard for future distant consequences, might, in

---

[1] M. Gardner and Laurence Steinberg (2005) "Peer influence on risk taking, risk preference, and risky decision making in adolescence and adulthood: an experimental study" in *Developmental Psychology*, 41(4): 625–35; see also B. Simons-Morton, N. Lerner, and J. Singer (2005) "The observed effects of teenage passengers on the risky driving behavior of teenage drivers" in *Accident Analysis and Prevention*, 37(6): 973–82. For an overview of work of this sort, see Dustin Albert, Jason Chein, and Laurence Steinberg (2013) "The Teenage Brain: Peer Influences on Adolescent Decisionmaking" in *Current Directions in Psychological Science*, 22(2): 114–20.

[2] Erik de Water, Antonius H. N. Cillessen, and Anouk Scheres (2014) "Distinct Age-Related Differences in Temporal Discounting and Risk Taking in Adolescents and Young Adults" in *Child Development*, 85(5): 1881–97. It is interesting, however, that this study showed a particularly sharp decrease in the steepness of the temporal discount curves around 15 or 16 years of age, suggesting that kids close to adulthood are little different from adults in their temporal discount rates.

light of such results, be thought to spring from developmentally normal psychological mechanisms found in kids, but absent in adults.

Still, the conjunction of (KW1) and (KW2) can be questioned on empirical grounds, and skepticism in this regard seems especially well placed when it comes to horrific, violent crimes. Is there anything developmentally normal about the psychological mechanisms that drove Christopher Simmons? Wouldn't developmentally normal 17-year-olds stop themselves from acting on the impulse to drown a stranger, even assuming that they actually have such impulses? And Simmons' atrocities pale in comparison to some crimes by kids. Consider the following remark by Justice John Roberts in his dissenting opinion in *Graham v. Florida*, the case in which the majority of the Supreme Court deemed execution cruel and unusual punishment for non-homicide crimes by juveniles. Roberts agrees that Graham himself does not deserve the death penalty, but then asks:

[W]hat about Milagro Cunningham, a 17–year–old who beat and raped an 8–year–old girl before leaving her to die under 197 pounds of rock in a recycling bin in a remote landfill?...Or Nathan Walker and Jakaris Taylor, the Florida juveniles who together with their friends gang-raped a woman and forced her to perform oral sex on her 12–year–old son? (*Graham v. Florida*, 130 S.Ct. 2011 (2010) at 2041)

Roberts' point is primarily that juveniles often commit extremely grave offenses, even when they do not kill anyone. But his point also draws attention to the highly aberrant nature of much juvenile crime, even relative to the behavior of their misbehaving age-mates. Is it really possible that these atrocities are the product of developmentally normal psychological mechanisms?

However, I will set aside empirical challenges to the Kids Will Be Kids argument. As in the case of the Proxy for Culpability argument, the Kids Will Be Kids argument will be shown to fail *even if its advocate's empirical claims are granted*. This concession can be made more palatable by the reminder that the advocate of the Kids Will Be Kids argument is not claiming that the *behavior* is developmentally normal but, rather, that abnormal behavior is, in the case of kids, a product of the workings of developmentally normal psychological mechanisms. The idea is that when normal tendencies to, for instance, ignore or radically discount the future consequences of one's behavior, which one might think typical of kids, encounter certain kinds of circumstances—circumstances of great financial need, or circumstances leading to mixing with "the wrong crowd," for instance—crime results. The further thought, which completes the argument, is that crime ought to draw a more lenient state response when it can be attributed to developmentally normal conduct-producing mechanisms, operating in abnormal and challenging circumstances, in contrast to crime that is, in part, the product of abnormal or developmentally aberrant psychological mechanisms at work. Roughly, the thought is that bad behavior by kids is what happens when good people, at an early stage of development, are thrown into tough circumstances. Since their behavior is therefore attributable to their circumstances, and not to them, they are to be given a break.

It is natural to misinterpret this argument by making false assumptions about the grounds on which its advocate accepts (KW3), the claim that the developmental normality of the springs of action suffices for a break. In particular, if the advocate of the argument believes that (KW3) is true thanks to the fact that people are *reduced in culpability* when they act from developmentally normal psychological capacities, then the Kids Will Be Kids argument is just the Proxy for Culpability argument in disguise. Imagine someone, for instance, who, when asked why he believes (KW3) says that people *cannot act contrary* to what is developmentally normal for them. Such a person holds that kids are to be given a break because they can't do better than they do; and this fact about them matters because, it is assumed, people can't be held fully responsible for falling short when they do the best they can. The result is that such a person is just offering a version of the Proxy for Culpability argument in which the property assumed to be necessary for responsibility (labeled property "F" in chapter 1) is the property of having the ability to avoid wrongful conduct, a property thought to be lacking in kids thanks to the fact that their bad behavior springs from developmentally normal exercises of their psychological capacities. But this version of the Proxy for Culpability argument is, still, just the Proxy for Culpability argument and so subject to the criticisms offered in chapter 1.

The more interesting form of the Kids Will Be Kids argument—more interesting because distinct from the Proxy for Culpability argument—buttresses (KW3) with a view to the effect that the full force of the state should be used only against wrongdoing that springs from abnormal, or aberrant conduct-generating psychological mechanisms. For someone who advocates the argument in that form, which is the form in which it will be considered here, the argument vindicates the policy of giving kids a break even if it would be perfectly in kids' power to act better than is developmentally normal for them to act. The possibility of acting better, that is, does not count against a kid who acts from developmentally normal conduct-producing mechanisms. According to the Kids Will Be Kids argument in the form of interest, development normality, that is, provides a ground for giving kids a break independent of culpability.

2.1.1 Distinguishing from the Proxy for Culpability argument

A first crucial difference, then, between the Kids Will Be Kids argument and the Proxy for Culpability argument is that the Kids Will Be Kids argument does not depend on the claim that the special action-generating psychological states and capacities of kids which distinguish them from adults diminish their responsibility for their bad behavior. One might advocate the Kids Will Be Kids argument even while asserting that M is, say, that set of psychological states and capacities that are constitutive of selfishness or any other objectionable quality that is ordinarily inculpating rather than exculpating. A mature adult cannot shield himself from censure, not to mention criminal punishment, by noting that he's callous, or selfish, or generally insensitive to his obligations to treat others with decency. But the thought behind the Kids Will Be Kids argument is that a kid *can* shield himself from censure in this way provided that the facts about himself that he cites are developmentally normal. If it is normal for a kid his age to be callous, or selfish, or insensitive to his obligations to treat others with decency, then those facts count in favor of the kid who does wrong. Even if kids are evil, even if that's "a phase" of development, then, according to the Kids Will Be Kids argument, they should be given a break *on those grounds*. The developmental normality of even very bad qualities, under the Kids Will Be Kids argument, serves to rationalize our policy of giving kids a break.

Another important difference from the Proxy for Culpability argument can be seen by noting the different ways in which the two arguments are empirically dependent. The Kids Will Be Kids argument employs a pair of empirical premises—(KW1) and (KW2)—and so the justification for giving kids a break which is supported by the argument is no more robust than those empirical claims. At first glance, the argument is in this respect very similar to the Proxy for Culpability argument, which tethered its justification to the empirical claim that kids lack feature F, a psychological state or capacity thought necessary for responsibility. Recall that in chapter 1, I criticized the Proxy for Culpability argument on the grounds that under it the justification for giving kids a break would not survive empirical discoveries that would not in fact shake our attachment to the justification that we implicitly accept. This showed that the Proxy for Culpability argument was failing to capture the justificatory grounds to which we are implicitly attached. I called this "the problem of empirical dependency."

A similar objection can be made to the Kids Will Be Kids argument, but it is significantly weaker. The Kids Will Be Kids argument is empirically tethered: if it turns out that crimes by kids are not actually the product of the exercise of developmentally normal psychological mechanisms—either because it turns out that M is not what gives rise to kids' bad behavior ((KW1) is false), or that M is not developmentally normal for kids ((KW2) is false)—then the advocate of the argument must also accept that we are not then justified in giving kids a break. This point can indeed fuel doubts that the Kids Will Be Kids argument captures the justification that we implicitly accept. Say we came up with a reliable method for distinguishing the precocious, who are developmentally advanced relative to what is normal for their age, from those who are developmentally normal. We could thus improve our combined rates of false and true positives and negatives by giving a break to the normal that we deny to the precocious.[3] But I think that nobody would favor such a draconian policy towards the precocious. Imagine the same argument being offered for distinguishing cases of sex with kids into those that are and are not statutory rape; would it really be better for precocious children to be

---

[3] The point is made also in Andrew Von Hirsch (2001) "Proportionate Sentencing for Juveniles—How Different than for Adults?" in *Punishment and Society*, 3(2): 221–36.

unprotected by the criminal sanctions specified, under our current system, for sex with kids? The same point applies to the case of giving kids a break for their wrongful behavior. The break should extend to the precocious, even if our false and true positive rates could be improved by denying it to them.

But it's important to see that this objection is significantly weaker when applied to the Kids Will Be Kids argument than the Proxy for Culpability argument, and for reasons that illuminate the driving idea behind the Kids Will Be Kids argument. The reason is that (KW1) and (KW2) involve empirical claims of very different sorts. (KW1) involves a claim very similar to that involved in the Proxy for Culpability's premise to the effect that kids lack feature F. And, to be sure, the advocate of the Kids Will Be Kids argument is committed to thinking that if we find that bad behavior by a subset of kids is actually driven by psychological mechanisms distinct from M, that are not developmentally normal, then a better policy will deny those kids a break.

But (KW2) involves a different kind of empirical claim and a much less objectionable form of empirical dependency of the rationale for giving kids a break. To see this, start by noting that, arguably, part of *what it is* to be a child is for the evaluative significance of one's psychological states and capacities to be assessed relative to what is developmentally normal for someone of one's age. That is, to be a child is to be subject to evaluative assessment relative to age-defined standards. Childhood is in part constituted by subjection to age-dependent norms. Adults, too, compare themselves to their age-mates, but the comparison is far less significant or appropriate. A 25-year-old adult can take no pride in reading a book that is ordinarily read by 40-year-olds; nor ought he to be ashamed. Age-related differences in reading material are just irrelevant for adults. But a 10-year-old child can take pride in reading a book that is ordinarily read by 14-year-olds, or 20-year-olds. Why? The reason is that part of the normative significance of childhood is the appropriateness of assessment of psychological states and capacities *relative to what is normal for the age*. Past a certain age, what is age-normal matters much less. It is childish, we might say, for the 25-year-old to pay attention to what those younger and older are like psychologically in assessment of him- or herself. He should be thinking about how he ought to be, not how others his age are. This is also why it is condescending to respond to, for instance, a 25-year-old's shallow romantic relationships by saying, "That's what people in their mid-20s do." It's condescending to assess the 25-year-old relative to his or her age-mates because that's a form of assessment suited to childhood, and to at most a much lesser degree to adulthood.

The reason that this is important is that it means that under the Kids Will Be Kids argument, in contrast to the Proxy for Culpability argument, a change in the empirical facts would in many cases be a change in the applicable normative standards. If it turns out that kids (or some identifiable subset of them) have feature F, which is necessary for responsibility, then they are a step closer to meeting a standard of responsibility *that does not change on the discovery*. By contrast, if it turns out that the possession and exercise of M is not developmentally normal—if (KW2) turns out to be false—then it will turn out that we were mistaken to measure kids relative to the standard that we had been measuring them with respect to. The result is that the new empirical discovery will actually change the metric with respect to which policies are to be judged, rather than holding fixed that metric, as under the Proxy for Culpability argument. If it turns out that *it is not normal* for 16–18-year-olds to act from mechanisms like those that guide the wrongful conduct of those under 16, then that will be an argument for lowering the age of maturity that it might be palatable to accept. After all, a 16-year-old wrongdoer, in light of such a discovery, does not paint himself in a better light by comparing himself to his age-mates; on the contrary, he shows himself to be worse than others in his cohort.

The point just offered is subtle and important, and so it is worth expressing again in a slightly different way.[4] Consider the idea of *what can be expected* of someone. What a person *can* do is often different from what he can be expected to do. A person under lethal threat *cannot be expected* to do anything but comply, but he *could* defy the threatener; he *could* choose to die rather than comply. In the case of children, we might say, what can be expected is constrained by what is developmentally normal. A child is exceeding what can be expected of him if he is discounting the future less than is normal for his age. An adult, by contrast, is exceeding what can be expected if he discounts the future in a way that maximizes welfare, even if his age-mates tend to do even better. What can be expected of adults is not similarly constrained by the facts about developmental normality. The Kids Will Be Kids argument implies that kids are to be given a break only for crimes springing from developmentally normal psychological mechanisms. And so it implies that new empirical discoveries about what is developmentally normal ought to affect the boundary around those who are to be given a break. The region might grow, or shrink, depending on the nature of the empirical discovery. Find that it is normal for kids to discount the future less than we used to think, and the region will shrink; more and it will grow, for instance. Such changes alter the normative facts about what we can expect from kids. The very standards with respect to which kids are to be held will change with empirical discoveries about normality. So if we want to check to see if our implicit rationale for the policy of giving kids a break is that identified by the Kids Will Be Kids argument, we have to ask ourselves whether we would favor a change in the policy *if our very standards for judging our policies were to change*. And the answer is likely to be "yes." Or, at least, the advocate of the Kids Will Be Kids argument need not be embarrassed by the fact that he is committed to the answer being "yes."

This is importantly different from the Proxy for Culpability argument. In that case, entertaining the question of what policy we would favor in the face of new empirical discoveries involves assessing how things would look in that case *relative to our current and fixed standards of responsibility for bad behavior*. Those *standards* do not change

---

[4] A point very close to that being made here, and by appeal to the notion of what can be expected of someone, is offered in Andrew Von Hirsch (2001) "Proportionate Sentencing for Juveniles—How Different than for Adults?" in *Punishment and Society*, 3(2): 221–36.

when we discover, for instance, that girls between 16 and 18 have the psychological profile of adults, even though boys in that age cohort do not. What changes is who falls on which side of the same fixed line that we used, and appropriately, both before and after the discovery. The result is that the Kids Will Be Kids argument is in a better position to repel the objection deriving from the problem of empirical dependency than we found the Proxy for Culpability argument to be.

2.1.2 *The problem with (KW3)*

The claim at the heart of the Kids Will Be Kids argument is (KW3)—the claim that those who act wrongly thanks to the exercise of developmentally normal conduct-generating psychological mechanisms are owed a break. Why would someone think this is true? What is the appealing idea behind this premise?

It seems to me that there are two different kinds of arguments that can be given for this premise. The first: Criminal prohibitions are intended to identify for punishment not all and only those behaviors that meet the descriptions they include but only those that meet the descriptions *and are aberrant*. So, when a defendant shows that, although his conduct falls under a criminal prohibition, it is *normal* in some crucial respect, then he shows that it is an imperfect example of the prohibited conduct and so is deserving of a more lenient response. Call this "the aberrant defense" of (KW3).

The second defense of (KW3) runs like this: What is important about kids' developmentally normal psychological mechanisms is that they are essential for something of great value: experimentation. Crime is, in the wrong circumstances, an unavoidable part of this experimentation, but the function of experimentation is to make discovery possible, discovery of a kind that is essential to a flourishing adult life later. Given that we want to celebrate, rather than condemn, experimentation by kids, we must at least temper our condemnation of its natural concomitant, namely crime, by giving kids a break. Call this "the experimentation defense" of (KW3).

I take these two defenses in turn.

2.1.2.1 THE ABERRANT DEFENSE

The aberrant defense of (KW3) is rooted in the idea that criminal prohibitions are intended to identify aberrant, non-normal behavior for the group of people to which they apply. In criminalizing theft, the thought is, we really criminalize takings of people's things without permission *that are not normal for us*. This is why it is not theft, at least not of the kind that the criminal law is concerned with, when your roommate borrows your bicycle, which you have lent to him frequently in the past, without asking you. The formal elements of the crime of theft might be met in that case, but it is no crime, for it is not different enough from things that *we ordinarily do*. The point here is not merely that criminal punishment brands its victim as aberrant, which it often does. It is, rather, an explanation for why that is appropriate: criminal punishment, on the view proposed, brands its victim as an outsider, worthy of exclusion from the group, because for one's behavior to fall under a criminal prohibition is, *by the very nature of criminal prohibitions,* for it to be abnormal for us. If this is right, then anytime we find a form of behavior that falls under a criminal statute *but is actually normal for us* in some crucial respect we have found a form of behavior warranting at least a break, and perhaps full exemption from criminal liability. It is not, in fact, a clear instance of the kind of behavior that is prohibited by the norms expressed in criminal statutes. Add that normality comes in degrees and we can make good on the idea that sometimes a behavior can be sufficiently abnormal to warrant some form of criminal liability, but sufficiently normal to warrant leniency in comparison to those paradigm abnormal instances of the behavior that are criminalized under the statute.

Further, and importantly, even when a person's behavior is aberrant—normal people do not throw strangers from bridges—there is the possibility that it springs from normal psychological mechanisms functioning in abnormal, criminogenic circumstances. Such behaviors would warrant a break for the reasons just given: they are less bad than the paradigmatic behaviors fitting the description given in the statutory prohibition for they are normal, non-aberrant, in at least one crucial respect, namely in the psychological mechanisms that give rise to them. At least, so goes the aberrant defense of (KW3), the claim that where crime springs from developmentally normal psychological mechanisms it is owed a break.[5]

The aberrant defense involves application to the case of kids a line of thought that we can imagine following in other places. For instance, it is sometimes said that normal adults are regularly subject to momentary lapses of attention, while driving, that would suffice for criminal negligence, were such lapses to cause harm. This observation, if true, prompts an impulse towards leniency with respect to any adult charged with crimes of negligence behind the wheel. Why? The answer, it seems to me, is that we are drawn to the idea that statutes prohibiting negligent driving are really aimed at criminalizing the aberrant cases. Maybe everybody *should* be more attentive. But we have not criminalized failures to live up to this ideal that are typical failures; we have criminalized only egregious, aberrant failures. The more normal lapses are, the less it appears that a given lapse falls squarely under a criminal prohibition.

I don't believe that this defense of (KW3) succeeds. A first reason is that the theory of criminal prohibition which underlies it—the theory according to which criminal statutes saying that C-ings are crimes *really say* that abnormal C-ings are crimes—is not true across the board. Perhaps it is true of statutes criminalizing negligent driving. But criminal statutes are perfectly capable of aspiring to change all-too-normal behavior by criminalizing it. Criminal statutes sometimes aim to shape what is normal by influencing, or aiming to influence, the frequency with which people act in the ways they describe. (It is likely *because* drunk-driving was common that it was criminalized.) Or, to put the point another way, if a given set of legal prohibitions are intended to

---

[5] A closely related line of thought is examined helpfully in Douglas Husak (1996) "The 'But-Everyone-Does-That!' Defense" in *Public Affairs Quarterly*, 10(4): 307–34.

apply only to aberrant behavior, that is a contingent fact about a particular legal system, or a particular set of prohibitions within a legal system. But the thought that kids ought to be given a break extends even to systems with more ambitious plans for their criminal law, including those in which the criminal law is intended to prohibit that which is normal, either for the purpose of reducing the occurrence of such behavior, or for some other reason, such as elevating those abnormal few who avoid acting in the ways that are normal for the group.

A second and deeper reason for skepticism about the aberrant defense derives from the idea of "normal *for us*." The "us" in this formulation is that group of people from whom the political authority of the state to punish is derived. In consent-based theories of political obligation and authority, this is the group of people who have consented to be governed by the state that has established the laws. But crimes by kids are not normal *for us*, in this sense of "us," for kids are not among those from whom the authority of the state derives, and their behavior does not spring from psychological mechanisms normal for us, but, instead, normal *for them*. What is normal for kids is not normal for us; and what is normal for us is what is owed a break under the view that criminal prohibitions prohibit aberrant behavior. So it seems to me that the aberrant defense of (KW3) fails.

2.1.2.2 THE EXPERIMENTATION DEFENSE

In an important paper, Andrew Von Hirsch suggests that kids are owed a break because, given the intimate relation between their bad behavior and valuable, developmentally normal experimentation, their crimes call for an attitude of toleration.[6] Von Hirsch is offering a version of the experimentation defense. We are to have greater toleration of crimes by kids than of crimes by adults because we value, and ought to value, the non-criminal, experimental behaviors that have the same psychological source.[7] The picture is of kids' crimes as part of a package that is valuable overall, and in the deepest sense. Adult human beings owe their flourishing in part to what Ogden Nash describes as adolescence's "incandescence."[8]

Von Hirsch represents his point as speaking to what can be reasonably expected of kids. To avoid crime, the thought is, some kids living in tough circumstances would have to give up on developmentally normal experimentation. This would be an enormous price to pay, given how important such experimentation is to later flourishing. And so it is too big a price to demand of them to refrain from crime. But in cases in which the avoidance of crime is possible, but costly, we frequently recognize that a break is warranted. Judges, for instance, often mitigate sentences for those who would have

---

[6] Andrew Von Hirsch (2001) "Proportionate Sentencing for Juveniles—How Different than for Adults?" in *Punishment and Society*, 3(2): 221–36.
[7] Strands of this line of thought can also be seen in Laurence Steinberg (2014) *Age of Opportunity: Lessons from the New Science of Adolescence*, New York: Houghton Mifflin.
[8] Ogden Nash (1947) "Tarkington, Thou Should'st Be Living in This Hour" in *The New Yorker*, September 20.

had to pay significant prices to avoid criminal conduct, even if all things considered they should have refrained and paid those prices. This, Von Hirsch is suggesting, is the ground for giving kids a break.

However, I do not believe that this line of thought succeeds in defending (KW3) across the full scope of cases to which it would need to apply in order to support a policy of giving kids a break. There are, I suppose, some cases in which avoidance of crime, in the circumstances, would have required halting valuable forms of experimental behavior. But this is hardly true of all of them. This rationale explains why it makes sense, for instance, to give a break to a kid who commits a minor theft, or a kid who paints graffiti on a building, in comparison to an adult who did those things. Kids who shoplift should indeed be given breaks in comparison to adults who do the same things. But it does not provide grounds on which to give a break to violent crimes by kids. Whatever valuable forms of experimentation Christopher Simmons would have had to give up in order to refrain from murdering Shirley Crook, if there were any, are things that he was fully required to give up. The case is analogous to a duress case in which a person would have had to give up money in order to avoid seriously assaulting an innocent person. Such a defendant is owed no break for the assault because the price he would have had to pay in order to avoid it was one that he gets no credit for avoiding. He can be expected to pay that price.

The point is that while there is a region of token crimes where the fact that there was a price to avoid them counts in the offender's favor, the region of token crimes by kids that are deserving of a break is much larger than this. Kids are owed a break even when they commit intentional violent felonies of a sort that people are required to pay almost any price to avoid performing. This fact cannot be accommodated by the experimentation defense of (KW3).

2.1.3 Taking stock

As we've seen in this section, the Kids Will Be Kids argument can be developed in various ways. To keep it distinct from the Proxy for Culpability argument, which is essential if it is to avoid the criticisms levied against that argument in chapter 1, it must be understood as involving the claim that *fully culpable* crimes are sometimes the product of kids' developmentally normal psychological mechanisms at work. This leads quickly to the thought that kids are to be held to standards that are in part set by what is normal for them. But what has been suggested in this section is that no matter how we make good on that idea—either by defending it on the grounds that crime is, by definition, aberrant, or, instead, on the grounds that the price of avoiding experimentation in behavior that sometimes gives rise to crime is too high to demand of kids—we encounter serious difficulties. Kids are owed a break even when the statutes that they violate aspire to change what is normal, and so apply to non-aberrant behavior. And kids are owed a break even when their behavior is so awful that they were fully required to pay the price to avoid it and are owed no credit whatsoever for the fact that avoiding it was not, for them, free. The Kids Will Be Kids argument, that is, captures part of our sympathy to some child criminals. But it does not capture all, and so it cannot serve to ground our policy of giving kids a break.

2.2 They'll Grow Out of It

The They'll Grow Out of It argument begins in the same place as the Kids Will Be Kids argument: with the idea that crimes by kids are the product of developmentally normal psychological mechanisms. But the They'll Grow Out of It argument then takes a different turn, holding that what is significant about this fact is that we can expect kids who commit crimes to be law-abiding citizens in the future, once they reach a greater level of maturity, and without the same harsh punitive intervention that we heap on adults. The point is not to emphasize the developmental normality of the mechanisms that issue in crimes by kids but, instead, something that goes along with developmental normality: impermanence. Put more carefully:

(TG1) Wrongful conduct by kids is the product of the exercise of a collection of developmentally normal psychological mechanisms, M.

(TG2) If a person's wrongful conduct is the product of the exercise of psychological capacities that it is developmentally normal for him to possess and exercise, then, if allowed to develop normally, he will stop engaging in such wrongful conduct in the future.

(TG3) When a person will stop engaging in wrongful conduct in the future if allowed to develop normally, he should be given a break for his past wrongful conduct.

(Conclusion) ∴ Kids ought to be given a break for their wrongful conduct.

2.2.1 Learning to walk the line

One might object to (TG2) on the grounds that it simply does not follow from the fact that someone performs in a way that is developmentally normal that we can expect him to perform better, over time, simply by being left to his own devices. Imagine offering that argument about mathematical performance. It does not follow from the fact that a 7-year-old performs well on math tests that are appropriate for her age that she will, in a few years, perform better *if left to her own devices*. Very possibly, she will develop only if *taught more math*. There is no reason to think that moral development is any different. Very possibly, a 7-year-old who is developmentally normal when it comes to her moral faculties will not improve without being taught. Performance on the famous "marshmallow test"—testing the ability of small children to reject present gratification for greater gratification later—might turn out to predict future success only because those who are behind in their development in this respect often *are* left to their own devices, never taught to overcome their deficiencies in this regard.[9] The growing number of schools for "at risk" kids that take explicit steps to teach them to perform better on tasks such as that set by the marshmallow test testifies to the growing recognition that developmental stage is not fate.[10] And for all that has been said, a crucial part of such teaching might be *less lenient* treatment than that inflicted on adults. Perhaps what is needed is "tough love."

(TG2), however, represents less the mistaken view that development is fate than it does skepticism about the possibility that development can be aided by draconian treatment under the criminal law in contrast to other forms of treatment, treatment of the sort that kids who never cross the line into criminality receive. That is, it represents well-placed skepticism about the idea that the kind of treatment that we inflict on adults under the criminal law is rehabilitative or educative, especially when applied to kids. The idea is that kids will grow out of their bad behavior *given whatever forms of treatment are typically given to them*, where, it is assumed, the harsh treatment we impose on adults in the criminal justice system is not what effectively induces people to develop normally.

This idea goes hand-in-hand with the view that the juvenile system should be a rehabilitative system. The idea is that we should reserve for kids the kind of treatment that will help them to grow into people who are not induced into crime by tough circumstances of the sort that too many juveniles face. And from one point of view this idea is not just appealing, or worth considering, *it is obviously legitimate*. And, in fact, it is hard to see any reason why it should be limited to juveniles. If we can help people to be better, and we can do it non-paternalistically, in a way which is consistent with respect for their liberty, shouldn't we? Add that the demand to avoid paternalism is significantly weaker when it comes to kids—if there's anyone to whom it is appropriate to be fatherly, it is children—and it seems that it is that much easier to justify taking steps to help kids to be better.

But it is important to see that the impulse to help kids to behave better, and the impulse to give them a break for their criminal wrongdoing, are at most contingently connected. There is no reason, as a conceptual matter, why it shouldn't be possible to punish and, at the same time and through entirely distinct instrumentalities, to educate. That is, presumably, the point of almost every social program for those convicted of crimes, whether it is court-mandated treatment of some sort, or a voluntary program made available to prisoners, or a post-incarceration re-entry program. All that (TG2) says is that one particular behavioral goal—the goal of inducing wrongdoers not to recidivate—can be achieved without the help of harsh punitive treatment. It says nothing, all by itself, about the appropriateness of such harsh treatment. We surely

---

[9] The *locus classicus* of these famous experiments is Walter Mischel, Ebbe B. Ebbesen, and Antonette Raskoff Zeiss (1972) "Cognitive and attentional mechanisms in delay of gratification" in *Journal of Personality and Social Psychology*, 21(2): 204–18.

[10] Andrew Reiner (2013) "The Education Issue: Believing self-control predicts success, schools teach coping" in *Washington Post Magazine*, April 11.

have, after all, other goals in punishing besides the goal of inducing wrongdoers to walk the line.

(TG2) limits to a particular group of people the claim that ordinary forms of treatment will induce better behavior, namely those whose crimes are the product of developmentally normal psychological mechanisms. And it is a particularly plausible claim when so limited. But, in fact, the more general claim might also be true. It is perfectly possible that were we to compare the success rates of methods for inducing less wrongdoing by given actors we would find that the kinds of things that we do to people under the criminal justice system perform very poorly relative to very simple alternatives that we can envision. It is often noted that prisons are crime factories. Prisoners develop networks of people willing and able to commit crimes and they take advantage of those connections when they leave prison. If this is true, then in many cases a particular criminal might end up committing fewer crimes in the future if simply let free. In fact, this is borne out by recidivism rates, which are enormous—in excess of 50 percent according to a recent study by the United States Sentencing Commission.[11] Of course, we don't know how many crimes would be committed by former prisoners if they had never been prisoners, but, still, these rates do not give us reason to be optimistic about the effectiveness of punishment for causing people to avoid crime later. Relatedly, traffic schools work, I suspect; they probably cause more improvement in driving than fines do.[12] In fact, the success rates of diversionary courts—such as the drug courts, but also domestic violence courts, veterans courts, etc.—speaks in favor of this.[13] If your goal is to make *this* particular offender behave better in the future, there's little reason to think that heaping him or her with hard treatment is the best way to go about it. And there is further reason to think that what the best tool is is a function, in part, of the developmental stage of the agent. You do not need to be a developmental psychologist to know that what we need to do to help a 10-year-old to act better is, of course, different from what we need to do to help a 30-year-old to act better, assuming that both are at developmental stages typical for their age. This is all just to say that (TG2) is very plausible, but amounts only to a claim about the track record of two distinct treatments of the developmentally normal when it comes to causing better behavior: the kinds of treatment that are typically given to the developmentally normal do better than the kinds of treatment typically given to adults in the criminal justice system.

---

[11] United States Sentencing Commission (2016) "Recidivism Among Offenders: A Comprehensive Overview": http://www.ussc.gov/sites/default/files/pdf/research-and-publications/research-publications/2016/recidivism_overview.pdf (accessed March 10, 2016).

[12] The evidence appears to be mixed. See Allan F. Williams, David F. Preusser, and Katherine A. Ledingham (2009) *Feasibility Study on Evaluating Driver Education Curriculum*, Report of the National Highway Traffic and Safety Adminstration, DOT HS 811 108; Wei Zhang (2010) *A Study on the Effectiveness of Iowa's Driver Improvement Program by Gender and Age*, Graduate Thesis, Iowa State University Digital Depository.

[13] Ojmarrh Mitchell, David B. Wilson, Amy Eggers, and Doris L. MacKenzie (2012) "Assessing the effectiveness of drug courts on recidivism: A meta-analytic review of traditional and non-traditional drug courts" in *Journal of Criminal Justice*, 40: 60–71.

But this then raises the obvious question: Why not *both* punish as harshly as we do adults *and* provide the kinds of treatment that will help kids who have committed crimes to behave better in the future? We can grant that criminal punishment does not fix anybody, much less a kid, and grant that there's good reason to fix people (if one can while complying with the demand to avoid paternalism), without concluding that we ought to gives kids a break. Perhaps we can have it all, as it were. This is to shine a spotlight on (TG3), the claim that where the goal of inducing better behavior in a person can be achieved without the aid of the criminal justice system, or with a lighter touch, the person should get a break. Why think this is true? Why think that the recognition that few who are punished thereby learn to walk the line should stay our hand?

2.2.2 *The very idea of special deterrence*

In many instances, getting people to suffer through that which will cause them to act better requires threat. People on probation show up on time for work since they will otherwise return to prison. People go to traffic school in order to avoid the fines that they would otherwise have to pay. People follow the rules mandated by the drug courts because otherwise they would face a criminal sentence for the underlying charge. In many cases, we ought to give breaks to those who can be made better by a certain treatment because the only motivation they have to suffer through the treatment is that they will thereby get a break. However, this cannot be the driving idea behind (TG3). If it were, then (TG3) would amount only to the claim that we ought to give breaks to those who agree to receive the treatments that will make them better in order to get those breaks. This would then support not the policy of giving kids a break, but, instead, the much weaker policy of giving kids a break to the degree that that is necessary to induce them to be subjected to the kinds of treatment that will serve to make them better. But this is not the policy to which we are attached. Among other things, under it there would be no reason to give a break to a kid who was happy, for independent reasons, to undergo the behavior-improving treatment, whatever it is. But, if anything, that group of kids seems *more* worthy of a break, not less. In addition, if this were the idea behind (TG3), then the rationale for giving kids a break would really have nothing fundamental to do with the developmental normality of the psychological mechanisms that issued in their behavior. Even those who are developmentally ahead or behind should be given a break when that's the price of inducing their compliance with a program of treatment that will make them better. So, we need to seek the rationale for (TG3) elsewhere.

Understanding both what is appealing and what is mistaken about (TG3) requires deeper reflection on the notion of special deterrence—deterring future criminal behavior *by the person to whom the punishment is issued*. (TG3) says, essentially, that we should give breaks to a person when special deterrence with respect to that person can be achieved through ordinary interventions of the kind to which we subject the developmentally normal. Now, if you are choosing between two ways of responding to a person's wrongful behavior, P1 and P2, and the two do not differ with respect to special deterrence—the agent's behavior will improve, or not, equally whether he is given P1 or P2—then one must seek other reasons to choose one option over the other. That is, let's assume that the expected degree of special deterrence associated with a given response to wrongdoing provides a *pro tanto* reason in favor of that response—more special deterrence is better—but it is also not the only relevant consideration. There are other reasons to respond in this way or that, and it is to those we must turn to make up our minds when there is no difference in special deterrence.

Notice that if we grant only this much, then the They'll Grow Out of It argument does not support the policy of giving kids a break. Given only this much, (TG3) is not true. Rather, what is true is the related, but significantly weaker claim that *there is a* pro tanto *reason* to give someone a break if his wrongful conduct sprung from developmentally normal psychological mechanisms. But the policy to which we are attached is one of *giving kids a break*, not the policy of *recognizing a* pro tanto *reason*, that very well might be overridden, for giving kids a break. Again, take Christopher Simmons. And consider the two distinct treatments that were on the table in his case: execution, or life imprisonment. Let's assume that there's no reason to expect greater special deterrence from the one treatment than the other. This is to assume that Simmons will commit the same number of crimes in what remains of his life whether he spends it awaiting execution or spends many additional years languishing in prison. There is not much warrant for this assumption—years in prison, after all, provide ample opportunity to engage in criminal behavior behind bars, and so there may be reason to think that there would be greater special deterrence through execution; but let's grant it for the purposes of argument. Under that assumption, from the point of view of special deterrence, there is no reason to choose execution over life in prison or vice versa. But what that implies is that the prospect of special deterrence does not support leniency towards Christopher Simmons. To support leniency, we need to appeal to some other value in play, present in life imprisonment, but not in execution. And so without more, the They'll Grow Out of It argument does not support the policy of giving kids a break.

The advocate of the They'll Grow Out of It argument will, at this point, respond by claiming that (TG3) should not be understood in the weak way just suggested, as a claim merely about the absence of a *pro tanto* reason to be harsh rather than lenient. Rather, (TG3) should be understood as the claim that when P1 and P2 promise equal special deterrence *that is a positive reason in favor of the more lenient of the two*. To take this position is to hold that the only reason to choose a harsher punishment over a more lenient one is that more special deterrence can thereby be achieved. To be sure, such a claim would, indeed, allow the They'll Grow Out of It argument to support our policy of giving kids a break, assuming that the other premises are true. But such a claim is obviously false. Even those who favor a deterrence theory of punishment—a theory according to which the sole function of punishment is the reduction of crime—do not favor a position according to which special deterrence trumps. There is, after all, also general deterrence—the deterrence of people other than the person being inflicted with the punishment. If it turns out that by treating the person before us more leniently, where harsher treatment will make no difference to special deterrence, just one other person will commit crimes that he would be deterred from committing had we been less lenient, then the deterrence theorist will hold that we ought not to be lenient. And, in fact, there is profound pressure on someone who takes it to count in favor of punishment that special deterrence is achieved through it, to also accept that general deterrence is of equal reason-giving weight. Reduction in crime is reduction in crime, whether the crimes eliminated would otherwise be performed by the person punished or by another person entirely. The result is that the view of the import of special deterrence which the advocate of the They'll Grow Out of It argument would have to accept is far too strong to be defensible. Christopher Simmons should be given a break even if greater deterrence, the combination of special and general, would be achieved by executing him.

Is there room for the position that the special deterrence achieved through a punishment provides greater reason to issue it than an equal amount of general deterrence achieved through it? It seems to me that such a position requires identifying some good realized in special deterrence, and not in general, and so it requires identification of some good realized by special deterrence other than the reduction of crime. The most plausible candidate for such a good is improvement of the character of the person punished, or some other advance in his moral education. But making the case for the claim that we morally improve those we punish, while achieving general deterrence without such improvements of others induced to behave better by the punishment of the person before the tribunal, requires accepting a view of the educative benefits of suffering hard treatment that was rejected in defense of (TG2) in section 2.2.1. The advocate of the They'll Grow Out of It argument wants to eat that cake in defense of (TG2) and so can't have it to use in defense of (TG3).

In short, the They'll Grow Out of It argument involves appeal to the value of special deterrence. But when that value is given its place—as one good thing among many that a punishment might achieve, and is outweighed when greater crime reduction is achieved even where it is lost—then the argument fails to support the policy of giving kids a break. As before, our attachment to the policy of giving kids a break outstrips our attachment to that good which is, defeasibly, achieved through giving kids a break. The result is that the They'll Grow Out of It argument fails to capture the grounds of our attachment to the policy.

2.2.3 Life without parole

One might think that even if the They'll Grow Out of It argument does not serve to support leniency towards kids across the board, it might support holding back from permanent and irrevocable punishments of kids. This would be a more limited conclusion, but it would still be a conclusion of importance. If it follows, it would seem to support banning life without parole (LWOP) sentences for kids, even where such sentences would be appropriate for otherwise identical adults. The thought is that the possibility of parole is the possibility of showing oneself to have changed in ways that we have good reason to think kids will, almost inevitably, change. So to deny a kid the possibility of parole is to make an empirical error: it is to judge a particular kid to be fixed in his criminal ways when, given that he is a kid, he is almost certainly not.

Whether the considerations driving the They'll Grow Out of It argument supports a ban on life without parole sentences for kids is difficult to assess. The problem is that we are lacking a normative theory of parole—an account, that is, of what the point or purpose of parole is. Such an account cannot be produced without an account of one of the most elusive of the central concepts in the theory of punishment: proportionality. Parole decisions must be constrained by considerations of proportionality—they must not result in release either so early as to cause the punishment to be disproportionately small, nor so late as to cause it to be disproportionately large. But parole cannot be primarily aimed at adjusting punishment so as to meet the demand of proportionality, which is a backward-looking consideration, since they are intended to be primarily forward-looking, aimed at releasing those who have a good chance of leading a productive and law-abiding life outside of prison. The question is why the possibility of a good future should matter at all. If the offender has served a sentence proportional to his crime, then anything more would be too much and he should be released even if there is good reason to think he'll recidivate. And if he has not served enough time, then proportionality demands that he should continue to be confined, even if there's good reason to think that his life on the outside would be as good as many a law-abiding citizen. What legitimate moral work can parole do, given that considerations of proportionality threaten to swallow it whole?

These waters are treacherous in the absence of an account of what it is for a punishment to be proportional to a crime. But, still, I believe that we can nonetheless make some progress on understanding how the fact that kids who commit crimes will (probably) grow out of their criminal tendencies bears on the question of whether they should have the possibility of parole. As a start, consider the following plausible claim: A person should be denied the possibility of parole only if he is an incorrigible offender, a person whose recidivism is inevitable. Note that regimes that impose *mandatory* LWOP sentences might do so—in fact, *probably* do so—because they assume that this claim is *false*. If the LWOP sentence is mandatory, then even those who the sentencing judge is certain to be capable of reform are denied the possibility of parole. Why? Perhaps because in the judgment of those who support such laws the crime for which LWOP is mandatory is so heinous as to warrant imprisonment even of those who are reformed many years, maybe even many decades, before they die. I doubt that such a judgment is ever true. But say it were; say there was a crime so bad that it would be appropriate to keep an adult imprisoned for it even if he is entirely reformed. For such a crime, a person's capacity to change is necessarily *irrelevant* to the appropriateness of the sentence. But if that's the case, then an otherwise identical kid, who, let's grant, is likely to reform through normal maturation, should also be given a life sentence *without* the possibility of parole. If the possibility of growing out of criminal tendencies is irrelevant to the sentence, then it's just as irrelevant for the kid as for the adult.

To put the point another way, imagine a crime so terrible that an offender who is released before he dies will necessarily have served a sentence that is disproportionately short. For such a crime, there should be no possibility of parole; proportionality demands that there be none. But then proportionality also demands that the likelihood that the offender will be reformed in the future is irrelevant to the sentence. And so when the offender is a kid, the considerations driving the They'll Grow Out of It argument are necessarily impotent to support a lesser sentence than LWOP.

This result is deeply ironic, given the recent Supreme Court case of *Miller v. Alabama*, (132 S.Ct. 2455 (2012)), which established that kids could not be given *mandatory* LWOP sentences. The considerations driving the They'll Grow Out of It argument in fact support the opposite result. Of all the LWOP sentences, the *mandatory* LWOP sentences, assuming they reflect a judgment to the effect that a life sentence is appropriate regardless of the offender's possibility of reform, are necessarily just as appropriate, in that respect, for an adult as for an otherwise identical kid who is more likely to grow out of his criminal tendencies. While I strongly suspect that mandatory LWOP sentences are never appropriate—I accept the claim that there should be no possibility of parole only if the offender is incorrigible, and further suspect that there is no such thing as a truly incorrigible offender—I deny that they could be appropriate for an adult and not for an otherwise identical kid *in virtue of the fact that the kid will grow out of his criminal tendencies*. Rather, to show that we should treat a kid more leniently than an otherwise identical adult mandatorily sentenced to LWOP, we necessarily need to appeal to more than the fact that the kid will grow out of his criminal tendencies.

What about non-mandatory LWOP sentences? Do the considerations motivating the They'll Grow Out of It argument support banning them? The answer is that it depends why an LWOP sentence is appropriate for a given adult, as we are assuming it is in asking whether it makes sense to shield a kid from such a punishment when an otherwise identical adult would be fittingly punished that way. If it's appropriate because the crime is such that anything short of a life spent in prison would be a disproportionately small sentence, then the reasoning above applies again and the offender's reformability is entirely irrelevant to the question of whether LWOP is appropriate. That is, just as the legislature, when LWOP is mandatory, deems the possibility of parole for a *type* of crime to make possible a disproportionately small sentence, a given judge, working in a regime in which LWOP is possible but not mandatory, might elect LWOP on the grounds that the possibility of parole for the offender's *particular* crime would result in a disproportionately small sentence for him. In either case, the offender's reformability does not bear on the sentence, and so the fact that kids are likely to grow out of their criminal tendencies does not support shielding them from LWOP.

However, there is another conceptually possible set of cases: those in which the LWOP sentence is issued because the judge takes the offender to be incorrigible. The thought motivating the They'll Grow Out of It argument is that kids are not only reformable, they will reform without intervention, just through normal developmental processes. If that's true—if, that is, (TG2) is true—then the claim that a given kid is incorrigible is virtually always false, and maybe never sufficiently supported by evidence, even when true, to warrant inflicting such a harsh sentence in light of it. So far, that is, it appears that the considerations driving the They'll Grow Out of It argument do support shielding kids from LWOP sentences that would be appropriate only when accompanied by a judgment that the offender is incorrigible.

While I believe that this is right, as far as it goes, I also believe that it goes less far than one might think. We can see this by reflecting further on the question of why a judgment of incorrigibility would support issuing an LWOP sentence to an offender who would be worthy of a life sentence *with the possibility of parole* were the judge uncertain about his incorrigibility. Imagine that we have three offenders: Incorrigible, Corrigible, and Kid. They commit the same crime, C, while in the same frame of mind and in the same circumstances. And imagine that C is a crime for which life imprisonment would be a proportional punishment. Imagine, further, that for unspecified reasons, a forty-year sentence would be appropriate for C if it is established that after forty years the offender no longer has the dispositions and tendencies that gave rise to his commission of C, but too short if not. It is not possible that Incorrigible will reform after forty years; it is possible that Corrigible will; and Kid, let's imagine, is *certain* to reform after that time, given normal development. Under these assumptions, it is appropriate to sentence Incorrigible to LWOP, and appropriate to sentence Corrigible to life with the possibility of parole after forty years. *But it is not appropriate to sentence Kid to anything longer than forty years.* That is, if we are certain that Kid will reform after forty years, then forty years is the appropriate sentence, and not life. In this case, that is, the fact that kids will reform through normal development undercuts the issuance of a life sentence *at all*, and so does not bear on the question of whether parole should or should not be available. What this shows is that considerations motivating the They'll Grow Out of It argument provides a reason to make parole available only for a kid who is like Corrigible—he might reform, but he might not. It's an empirical question how large a class of people this is. But what's been shown is that that is the only class for which the considerations motivating the They'll Grow Out of It argument provide a reason against an LWOP sentence. Or, to put the point in a truly deflationary tone: What we've learned is that a judge who is preparing to issue an LWOP sentence to a kid should be cautious because normal development often makes possible reform in kids that would not be possible in otherwise identical adults. Fair enough. But this is hardly the kind of sweeping and categorical conclusion that was sought, initially, by the advocate of the They'll Grow Out of It argument.

The results reached here are summarized in Figure 2.1. Here, X is the length of an appropriate sentence for someone who has reformed after that number of years, but where X would be too short a sentence for someone who has not. The yeses and nos in bold in the terminal boxes are the answers to the question in bold in the box at the top.

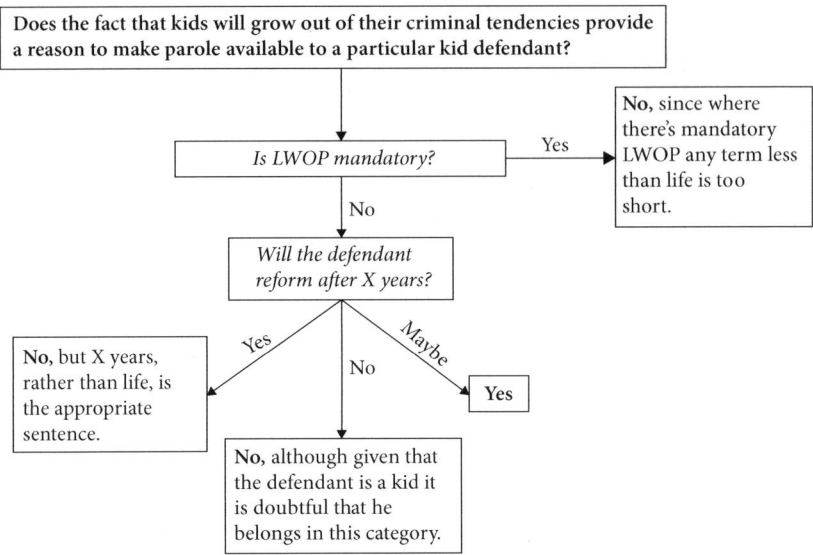

Figure 2.1.

What we have learned, I believe, is that the fact that kids tend to grow out of their criminal tendencies through normal development supports only a judgment that the kid in court will grow out of the dispositions that gave rise to his crime. This provides no shield from an LWOP sentence if, in the view of either the legislature or the judge, any sentence short of life would be too short, as appears to be the case in regimes in which LWOP is mandatory. But it supports some leniency when this is not so. It supports either giving the defendant a sentence just long enough that release would be appropriate for a reformed offender—a sentence less than life—or else giving him a life sentence with the possibility of parole, depending on the judge's degree of certainty that the defendant will reform after that number of years.

But the lesson that we should take from this discussion is not that the considerations driving the They'll Grow Out of It argument are the ones to which we who support leniency for kids should appeal. Quite the reverse. What we learn is that those considerations provide far less leniency than is appropriate. In my view, a kid should *never* receive a life sentence. When that sentence is appropriate for an otherwise identical adult it is *still* inappropriate for a kid *even if the kid is just as incorrigible as the adult*. Kids are owed a break, period. But to make good on this idea we need a different argument for leniency entirely. The They'll Grow Out of It argument will not do.

2.3 Conclusion

I began this chapter by noting the tendency to appeal to one's own bad behavior as a kid in justification of giving kids a break. To do that, I suggested, is to offer either the Kids Will Be Kids or the They'll Grow Out of It arguments, neither of which, it has been shown here, can provide adequate support for our policy of giving kids a break. It is perhaps also worth noting a slightly different tendency, with a similar root: the tendency to appeal to one's own experience *as a parent* in justification for one's leniency to kids. Even the Supreme Court, in reaching its decision about Christopher Simmons, felt the need not just to cite differences between kids and adults but also to note that "any parent knows" of these differences.[14] Of course, it is simply false that every parent knows *anything* about what kids *in general* are like. We are at most experts on our own children, and probably not even them. This is not just true, it's also obvious. So why is it still appealing or plausible to suggest that somehow those considerations that are being offered in favor of giving kids a break merely confirm what parenthood teaches?

The answer, I believe, lies in the fact that parenthood involves a commitment to improving our kids, to making them better. To appeal to what "any parent knows" is to remind one's audience that teachers do not do best by punishing mistakes, but, instead, by responding to them in other ways to induce better behavior in their students. But then the appeal supports the claim that kids ought to be given a break only to the degree to which the Kids Will Be Kids and They'll Grow Out of It arguments are valid. It supports the claim only to the extent that the facts about developmental normality, and, in contrast, the educative impotence of draconian measures, support the policy of giving kids a break. Since these considerations are insufficient, the appeal to the experience of parenthood does no more, in the end, than to remind us of what we all believe, namely that kids ought to be given breaks, a belief the grounds of which we are still seeking.

---

[14] *Roper v. Simmons* (125 S.Ct. 1183 (2005)) at 195.

3

Criminal Culpability

3.0 Introduction

Given the negative tone of the last two chapters, it is worth mentioning again that my aim is to argue that our policy of giving kids a break is justified. In fact, despite arguing in chapter 1 that kids are not to be given a break thanks to the fact that age is a good proxy for culpability-diminishing psychological features, ultimately it will be argued, in chapter 6, that kids are to be given a break because they are reduced in culpability. They are reduced in culpability because of facts about the political meaning of age, a meaning in part constituted by the fact that kids are disenfranchised. But the link between disenfranchisement and diminished culpability remains, at this point, obscure. Ultimately, it will be argued that by disenfranchising kids we weaken their legal reasons to refrain from crime. And by weakening their legal reasons to refrain from crime, we diminish their culpability for crime. And by diminishing their culpability we also cause it to be the case that they deserve lesser punishments. The links here make a chain, as we will see, given independently plausible theories of the nature of criminal culpability, desert for wrongdoing, and legal reasons. This chapter concerns culpability; desert for wrongdoing and legal reasons are the topics of chapters 4 and 5, respectively. Chapter 6 completes the argument.

3.1 Culpability and Wrongdoing

The distinction between culpability and wrongdoing is well known, and important. Wrongfulness is a property of actions. An action is wrongful (or, equivalently, an instance of wrongdoing) just in case it is in violation of a norm; it is not-to-be-done. Wrongfulness is contrasted with permissibility. An action is permissible just in case it is not wrongful, or not in violation of any relevant norm. So the wrongfulness of a wrongful act is a relational property of the act; it is a property an act possesses thanks to its relation to a set of norms. So, wrongfulness is grounded in the properties of the act, the set of norms, and the violation relation. The relation of violation is one of match between the content of the norm and the properties of the act. If the act has properties thanks to which it matches the content of a norm that can be expressed with a statement of the form "You ought not...," then the act violates the norm and is wrongful.

In different contexts, different sets of norms are salient to wrongfulness. Or, put another way, the predicate "...is wrong" involves a tacit reference to a set of norms, where that reference varies by context. Typically, the relevant kind of wrongfulness is moral wrongfulness and so the relevant set of norms are moral norms. (I will not hazard a theory as to the criteria a norm must meet to be a moral norm.) But there are other sets of norms. If you're painting a portrait, it might be wrong to paint the eyes blue. It is not *morally* wrong, but *aesthetically* wrong, or maybe wrong because it violates norms of a particular genre of painting, such as realistic portraiture. The act is in violation of some set of painting norms. And, critically, in many contexts the tacitly referred to set of norms are *legal* norms, particularly norms of criminal law. Actions that are in violation of such norms are *legally* wrongful; they are *crimes*—a term that I take to be synonymous with "in violation of a norm of criminal law."[1] While it is often true that a legally wrongful act is also morally wrongful, a given usage of the term "wrong" might not involve any assertion of moral wrongfulness, but only of legal. If you point to a jaywalker and say, "What he's doing is wrong!" you might be asserting only that what he is doing is in violation of legal norms. Perhaps it is *also* morally wrong because, for instance, it violates moral norms against endangerment of some kind; or perhaps it is also morally wrongful because there is a moral obligation to obey the law. But you need not be saying that the act is in violation of a moral norm in saying the act is wrong. You might be saying only that the act is in violation of a legal norm, such as the norm expressed by saying, "You ought to cross at the crosswalk." You might be saying only, that is, that the act is a crime. In general, to know whether what someone says is true when he says that this or that act is wrong, we need to know what set of norms he is claiming the act violates. Often, context alone supplies the answer, but sometimes it is supplied by some linguistic modifier, as when one says, "That act was *legally*, but not morally wrong," and sometimes there is a special term like "sin" or "crime" that makes explicit what set of norms is referred to in the allegation of wrongfulness.

I intend this account of wrongfulness to be stipulative. In many ordinary contexts, moral wrongfulness is so frequently the sort being ascribed to an act when the word "wrong" is used, that many people will see that as the only correct usage of the term "wrongful." Those, for instance, who assert that murder is wrong are rarely making a claim about the law or about aesthetic norms. Someone who skeptically replied that executions are murders, despite not being illegal, would not typically be contradicting what was claimed in the assertion that murder is wrong. But I'm not concerned to capture what we always or ordinarily mean by the term. I am doubtful that there is any singular meaning of the term. I am, rather, specifying how the term is to be used here, a usage that I take to be typical of philosophical discourse about criminal law.

---

[1] The criminal law is sometimes also thought to concern "offenses" or "violations," where these are less bad than crimes and warrant a different kind of response—perhaps fines but not jail, for instance. I set this designation aside and include these behaviors among the crimes.

And, importantly, it is typical of such discourse because it is useful. It captures a very particular property of criminal acts, namely that they are in violation of the norms of conduct codified in criminal prohibitions.

Culpability is not, like wrongfulness, a property of acts, but, instead, a property of agents. However, agents are not culpable, full stop. Rather, they are culpable *for* acts, and not act types, but act tokens. Culpable agents are culpable *for the things they do*. So, culpability is a relational property of agents: it is a property an agent possesses thanks to the relation in which he stands to a token act. To say that an agent engaged in "culpable wrongdoing," then, is to say that he engaged in an act that was in violation of a norm and he stood in a certain yet-to-be-specified relation to that act, a relation thanks to which he is culpable for the act. *The central goal of this chapter is to offer and defend an account of the relation between agent and token act that is constitutive of culpability, and particularly a species of culpability, namely criminal culpability.*

To say that someone is "culpable for an act" is to imply two things: he is responsible for the act, and the act is wrongful. So culpability is a species of responsibility: it is responsibility for wrongful action. This is why it is not the case that Mother Theresa is culpable for her charitable acts, even though she is responsible for them; culpability implies wrongdoing. In fact, someone who asserted that Mother Theresa is culpable for her charitable acts would ordinarily be called upon to explain in what respect he took those acts to have been wrongful. Perhaps, for instance, he discharges this burden by noting that her charity shined a light on the inadequacy of others. There would still be a question as to whether she was responsible for *that*. But at least the assertion of culpability would be intelligible in that instance since it is, plausibly, wrongful (morally) to shine a light on others' inadequacy.

3.2 Causal Responsibility

To say that culpability is responsibility for wrongdoing is to draw on a slippery concept, namely the concept of responsibility. It is common, and appropriate, to distinguish moral from causal responsibility. While it might be true that the earthquake is responsible for the building falling, the earthquake is not *morally* responsible for anything. In ascribing responsibility to the earthquake, the term is being used to refer to direct, normal causation. The claim is that the earthquake caused the building to fall, and not in some weird, indirect, or aberrant way, but, instead, through a causal route that is typical of earthquakes. If the earthquake caused a person to be distracted, and so forget to take his antipsychotic medication, which in turn caused him to have a psychotic episode in which he destroys a building, then the earthquake caused the building to fall; causation, after all, is transitive. But the earthquake would not, in that case, be causally responsible for the building falling. Causal responsibility is a species of causation, namely the normal, direct kind.

It is not a simple matter to describe exactly what is involved in normal, direct causation in contrast to the abnormal or indirect sort. I will be offering a controversial theory of that below. For now, however, what we need is the following idea:

> C normally and directly causes E *only if* E's occurrence manifests salient features of C.

In other words, to say that the causal route from cause to effect was of the normal and direct sort is not to say something solely about the relation between the two. It is to say something also about the "appearance" or "manifestation" in the effect of certain distinctive and salient features of the cause. I will have more to say about the ideas of "manifestation" and "salient features" shortly. For now, I hope only to draw out an intuition. When the earthquake is causally responsible for the building's falling, as when it causes the foundation to crumble, the falling of the building manifests the typical feature of the earthquake, namely that it involves the earth shaking. To use a metaphor, and nothing more precise than a metaphor, we might say that one can "see" the earth shaking in the fall of the building. This isn't literally true since, given plausible theories of event individuation, the event of the building falling does not include the earth shaking—the very same fall could have occurred thanks to some other precipitating event.[2] But, still, the metaphor is intended to capture an intuition; the building falling is like a perceptual medium through which the earth shaking is perceived. By contrast, when the agent fails to take his antipsychotic medication, thanks to the earthquake, and then causes the building to fall, the building's falling does not manifest the typical or salient features of the *earthquake* but, instead, it manifests certain quite different salient features of the agent who knocked it down. So, whether a particular causal relation is an instance of causal responsibility will depend on what the relevant or typical features of the cause are—which might vary from context to context and from cause-type to cause-type—and on the "manifestation" relation, which I will attempt to elucidate later.

I suggest, then, that causal responsibility is a species of causation: it is causation in which the effect manifests salient features of the cause. But since those salient features might fall into certain typical categories, we find that there are species of causal responsibility that are worthy of their own names, such as "moral responsibility" and, I will be suggesting, "criminal responsibility."

---

[2] The literature on event individuation is complex and there are those who reject the claim that events are not individuated by their causes; most, however, accept it. Although entirely inadequate as a summary of the literature, consider the following papers: Jaegwon Kim (1976) "Events as Property Exemplifications" in *Action Theory*, M. Brand and D. Walton (eds.), Dordrecht: Reidel, pp. 159–77; Donald Davidson (1969) "The Individuation of Events" in *Essays in Honor of Carl G. Hempel*, N. Rescher (ed.), Dordrecht: Reidel, pp. 216–34; Myles Brand (1977) "Identity Conditions for Events" in *American Philosophical Quarterly*, 14: 329–37; C. Cleland (1991) "On the Individuation of Events" in *Synthese*, 86: 229–54.

3.3 Modes of Transaction with Reasons

I suggest that in at least the paradigm case of moral responsibility,[3] moral responsibility is a species of causal responsibility in which a certain set of morally relevant features of the agent are manifested in the act. It is possible to be causally responsible without being morally responsible because causal responsibility is a genus of which moral responsibility is just one species. The reason that the earthquake is not morally responsible, even though causally responsible, for the building falling is that the feature of the earthquake that is manifested in the building's fall—namely that it involved the earth shaking—is not morally salient. So, in order to give an account of what moral responsibility is, we need an account of the salient moral features. What features of that which is causally responsible for the effect must be manifested in the effect, for the cause to be morally responsible for the effect? In the cases of interest, the effect is an act, or a consequence of an act, and the cause is the person whose act it is. Further, in searching for an account of the morally relevant features manifested in the effect in such cases, we should be open to the possibility that which features of the agent are morally relevant might vary depending on whether the act is or is not wrongful. Since our concern is with culpability, and hence with responsibility for wrongful acts, this allows us to focus our question: What features of the agent are manifested in a morally wrongful act when the agent is morally responsible for that act?

The answer, I suggest, is this: the agent's modes of recognition, weighing, and response to moral reasons. Put more carefully, I propose the following theory of moral responsibility for wrongful acts, or, equivalently, moral culpability:

To be morally culpable for a morally wrongful act is for the act to manifest an imperfection in the way in which one recognizes, weighs, or responds to the reasons generated by the properties of the act in virtue of which it is morally wrongful.[4]

This formula requires explanation. First, modes of recognition, weighing, and response to reasons consist in dispositions of the agent to display patterns in deliberations, or exercises of practical reasoning. Deliberation starts with beliefs about the facts, notably beliefs about what will and will not be true if one acts in this way or that. But the distinctive feature of deliberation is the way in which those factual beliefs lead to conceptions of prospective acts as supported or unsupported by reasons, and, in turn, to choices to act. It is in those guiding conceptions of facts as reason-giving that we find the agent's modes of recognition and weighing of reasons. Modes of recognition

---

[3] It is possible that there are non-paradigm cases, such as those involving complicity in which the aider is morally responsible for what the person he aids causes, but he is not himself causally responsible for that. But I set such complexities aside for now.

[4] It could be that, in the end, there is no difference at all between the position I am here proposing and that offered in Nomy Arpaly and Timothy Schroeder (2014) *In Praise of Desire*, Oxford: Oxford University Press, esp. chapter 7. If so, then the view I am offering in this chapter should be understood as extending their position to the case of criminal culpability, in contrast to moral. Alex Sarch adopts a position close to mine in forthcoming work.

of reasons are dispositions to display patterns in the facts that the agent takes to provide reason for and against actions, as opposed to those facts that are ignored in deliberation because the agent takes them to be irrelevant to the rational calculus. An agent who is disposed to take other people's pain as a reason against performing a particular action has a salutary mode of recognition of reasons. Another agent who is disposed, instead, to take the pain of a certain class of people—those of a particular race, or those of a particular religion or nationality—as providing no reason for or against acts that will involve such pain possesses, by contrast, a highly objectionable mode of recognition of reason.

Modes of weighing of reasons are dispositions to display patterns in the weight—a notion about which more will be said in chapter 5—of the reasons that the agent recognizes certain facts to provide. We learn about such modes primarily from ordinal rankings among acts possessing various features that drive deliberation. The agent takes there to be more reason to do things that will enhance reputation, for instance, than things that will yield greater profits. But perhaps there is also meaning to be given to the idea of cardinal reason-giving weight.

Modes of response to reasons are dispositions to display patterns in the way in which the agent translates her conception of the facts as reason-giving with various weights into choices to act. I leave open the possibility that an agent will conceive of one act as most supported by reasons while choosing a certain kind of competitor in a systematic way. An agent might conceive of work as more supported by reasons than play, and yet choose play. When he does, he evinces a distinctive mode of response to reasons that is different from that evinced either by the person who chooses work instead, or by the person who chooses sleep over work, but not play, even when work is conceived by him to be most supported by reasons.

For purposes of simplicity, let's use the term "modes of transaction with reasons" to refer to the agent's modes of recognition, weighing, and response to reasons. The proposal is that to be morally culpable is to be causally responsible for a wrongful act, where what is manifested in the wrongful act is an objectionable mode of transaction with reasons.

3.4 Culpability as Manifestation of Modes of Transaction with Reasons

Moral culpability for an act is a function of two things: what an act manifests about the agent's modes of transaction with reasons, on the one hand, and what morality demands of agents when it comes to such modes, on the other. To be morally culpable for a wrongful act is for the act to manifest modes of recognition, weighing, or response to reasons that fall short of what morality demands. In fact, more can be said than this, given our account of wrongfulness as possession of features thanks to which the act is in violation of a norm. Let's assume that the combination of features of the act thanks to which it is in violation of a norm provide, given the norm, a reason to refrain from performance of the act. (More will be said about this in chapter 5. As we will see there, this is true only if the norm is "valid," in a sense I will explain in chapter 5.) This is just to say that certain facts about the act—e.g. that it causes pain, or that it involves disregard of another's freedom—provide moral reasons of a certain weight. To be morally culpable for a wrongful act, then, is to manifest modes of transaction with reasons that are discordant with the moral reasons in virtue of which the act is morally wrongful. Manifesting a failure to appreciate a moral reason that does not bear on the moral wrongfulness of the act, for instance, does not speak to moral culpability *for the act*. We can put the formula above, then, equivalently like this: *Moral culpability involves manifestation in one's conduct of a failure to properly recognize, weigh, or respond to the moral reasons provided by the wrong-making features of the conduct in which one is engaged.* Or, to put the same view yet more carefully:

> D is morally culpable for C *if and only if* (1) D is causally responsible for C, (2) C is morally wrongful, (3) (1) is true because C manifests D's modes of transaction with reasons, and (4) the modes of transaction with reasons manifested in C are discordant with the reason-giving force of the features of C in virtue of which C is morally wrongful.

Notice that if it is granted, as I think it should be, that there are multiple distinct domains of norms—there are moral norms, legal norms, aesthetic, etc.—and it is granted that a feature of an act in virtue of which it is in violation of a norm generates a reason to refrain from the act (as is true, I will argue in chapter 5, when the relevant norm is valid), then we have before us a recipe for distinguishing types of culpability. Criminal culpability, for instance, differs in a significant way from moral culpability. While criminal culpability, like moral culpability, concerns modes of transaction with reasons, criminal culpability, in contrast to moral, concerns only the way the agent transacts with *legal* reasons, and, in fact, only a subset of those, namely the legal reasons in virtue of which the relevant token act is in violation of a criminal legal norm. The idea of a legal reason will be elaborated in chapter 5, but for now the idea is simply parallel to the idea of a moral reason. A feature of an act provides a reason to refrain from conduct provided that the act is in violation of a valid norm in part thanks to the fact that it possesses that feature. An agent who fails either to recognize the reason-giving force of that feature of the act, or fails to grant sufficient weight to the relevant reason, or fails to respond properly to the fact that the act has that feature, manifests a defect in his modes of recognition, weighing, or response to reasons. When the relevant norms are criminal legal norms, such a failure is a failure bearing on criminal culpability. The fact that an act will involve a bodily movement to which another does not consent, for instance, often provides a legal reason against performance of that act. An agent who fails to take that feature of the act as a reason to refrain from the act, and manifests this faulty mode of recognition of reasons in a theft, is criminally culpable for that theft. *To be criminally culpable for a prohibited act is for the act to manifest modes of recognition, weighing, or response to legal reasons discordant with the legal reasons in virtue of which the act is in violation of a norm of criminal law.* Or, again, to parallel the formulation given above of moral culpability:

> D is criminally culpable for C *if and only if* (1) D is causally responsible for C, (2) C is legally wrongful, (3) (1) is true because C manifests D's modes of transaction with reasons and (4) the modes of transaction with reasons manifested in C are discordant with the reason-giving force of the features of C in virtue of which C is legally wrongful.

This is the theory of culpability to be defended in what remains of this chapter, and on which I will be drawing in the remainder of this book.

3.5 Faulty Modes of Transaction with Reasons

More needs to be said about the nature of the kind of faultiness, or objectionableness, that an agent's modes of transaction with reasons can possess. What is critical to see is that the relevant norm, namely the norm that the act violates, sets two standards: a first, primary standard with respect to conduct—certain things ought not to be done and so would be wrongful if done. And, second, a secondary standard with respect to modes of transaction with reasons. The secondary standard is set automatically in setting the primary. When it is true that any act with a certain set of features is wrongful, it is also true that there is something bad about modes of transaction with reasons that discord with the reason-giving weight of those features. If the norm expressed by "You ought not X" is valid, then it is also true that one's modes of transaction with reasons fall short of an evaluative standard if one does not grant a certain amount of reason-giving weight to the fact that an act is of type X, and respond to that reason.

Under the account of culpability just offered, culpability consists in a distinct kind of wrongfulness. If an act violates a primary norm on conduct (e.g. "Don't lie"), and is thus wrongful, then it is culpable only if the agent further violates the associated secondary norm requiring certain modes of recognition, weighing, and response to reasons (e.g. "Don't fail to grant reason-giving weight to the falsity of one's utterance."). Violation of the secondary norm is, itself, a kind of wrongfulness, albeit of a different sort from violation of the primary norm on conduct; after all, it violates a norm, and possession of features thanks to which there is a violation of a norm is all there is to wrongfulness.

This observation invites a further question: Does culpability for wrongful conduct require *culpability* with respect to the wrongful modes of transaction with reasons manifested in that conduct? If the answer is yes, then we have regress; and the existence of such a regress would point strongly towards skepticism about culpability. How could it be that any finite creature managed to be culpable for anything if culpability for conduct requires culpability for something else, which in turn requires culpability for yet something further, and so on?

The answer, I believe, is to stop the regress at the first step. A finding of culpability shows that the wrongful conduct manifests aspects of the agent (namely, modes of transaction with reasons) that are the root of censurability for the wrongful conduct. An agent who is not culpable for the fact that he has faulty modes of transaction with reasons—as, for instance, when that fact about him does not manifest any failure on his part to take there to be a reason to have different modes of transaction with reasons—cannot be censured *for having the modes of transaction with reasons that he has*. But he can still be censured *for engaging in wrongful conduct that manifests those modes of transaction with reasons*. This is why someone can be fully culpable for heinous conduct even when his monstrous modes of transaction with reasons were instilled in him through a combination of genetic vulnerability and childhood trauma, for instance. Culpability for conduct does not require culpability *for being culpable* for that conduct.[5]

Are there cases in which we treat people differently depending on whether they are culpable for the fact that they possess the modes of transactions with reasons manifested in their wrongful behavior? Are there cases, that is, in which two people can be exactly alike in what is manifested in their wrongful conduct and yet differ in culpability thanks to how they got there? If there are, then the account of culpability I propose needs to be amended. After all, for the reasons offered in the previous paragraph, on my view, one's degree of culpability for the fact that one manifests certain modes of transactions with reasons in one's wrongful conduct is irrelevant to one's culpability for that conduct; what matters is only what modes of transactions with reasons are manifested. This might appear a decisive objection to the account as it stands. Consider, for instance, our differential responses to the voluntarily and involuntarily intoxicated. The intoxicated often manifests faulty modes of transaction with reasons in their wrongful conduct. But we think it matters to the appropriate degree of censure for such conduct whether the intoxication was voluntary or involuntary. Why? My answer is that the voluntarily and involuntarily intoxicated manifest *different* modes of transactions with reasons in their wrongful conduct; the modes manifested by the voluntarily intoxicated are worse. So the two differ in culpability under the account I propose, but not for reasons that would warrant amending the account. I argue for this claim at length elsewhere.[6] The disagreement between myself and those who deny it is, in the end, a difference in our views of what "manifestation" amounts to. I take manifestation to be a relation that can be sensitive to past conduct leading to the possession of certain modes of transactions with reasons, while my opponent denies this. I will return briefly to this issue, then, in defending my account of manifestation below.

---

[5] For what is, perhaps, the starkest statement of an opposing view, see Galen Strawson (2010) *Freedom and Belief*, revised edition, Oxford: Oxford University Press.

[6] See Gideon Yaffe (2012) "Intoxication, Recklessness and Negligence" in *Ohio State Journal of Criminal Law*: 545–82; Gideon Yaffe (2016a) "The Point of Mens Rea: The Case of Willful Ignorance" in *Criminal Law and Philosophy*.

3.6 Objection: Culpability for *Mala in Se* Crimes

It is important, at this point, to quiet a worry about the theory of criminal culpability I have offered, a worry that, if just, would sink the argument of this book for leniency towards kids who commit crimes. The worry is that talk of failures to properly recognize, weigh, and respond to *legal* reasons—reasons of a sort that might, plausibly vary in strength with an agent's degree of say over the law—does not seem to capture the kind of failure that is manifested by fully culpable commission of a *mala in se* crime. When 17-year-old Milagro Cunningham beat and raped an 8-year-old girl, and piled her body with rocks, did his act really manifest a failure to properly recognize, weigh, or respond to *legal* reasons? Of course. But that hardly seems to be the significant fact about his behavior that warrants us in punishing him. Far more significant is the fact of his disregard of the humanity of another, a consideration the import of which does not vary at all with any facts about the law.

In response to this critic, let's first consider a hypothetical under which this same terrible act is not illegal. Perhaps, for instance, this hypothetical monstrous society gives 17-year-olds a year-long license to perform acts of this sort, like James Bond's license to kill. And let's stipulate that this license is not just an immunity from prosecution for what is still criminal, but instead the law establishes that behavior like Cunningham's is not criminal provided that it takes place between the seventeenth and eighteenth birthdays. In that case, Cunningham would have had no legal reason to refrain from the act, although he would have continued to have powerful moral reasons to refrain. Criminal punishment of him would have been, in that case, a violation of the Principle of Legality, according to which punishment requires the illegality of the act for which punishment is issued. So, assuming the imagined critic adheres to the Principle of Legality, he will admit that it would be wrong to punish in this instance.

Presumably, the critic's view is that punishment in this hypothetical would be *morally* wrong; it would be morally wrong to violate the Principle of Legality. But why? After all, punishment would give this hypothetical Cunningham what he morally deserves. Here is one answer that the critic *cannot* give: Criminal punishment necessarily expresses a judgment of criminally culpable wrongdoing; since Cunningham committed no crime, he engaged in no criminal wrongdoing, and was not criminally culpable. Since it's morally wrong to issue a punishment expressive of such a judgment *when the judgment is false*, there is a decisive moral objection to criminally punishing Cunningham in this hypothetical. The critic cannot give this answer since it amounts to giving up the objection according to which criminal culpability cannot be disjoined from moral culpability in the way that the theory I offer implies.

By itself, without more, this does not amount to a satisfactory reply to the critic. After all, he might offer some other explanation for why it is morally wrong to violate the Principle of Legality; perhaps it has something to do with the special moral obligations of governments. Perhaps. But it is important to see that precisely the explanation that I suggest for why the Principle of Legality bars punishment of deeply wrongful, fully morally culpable *violent* behavior that happens to be legal is the most natural explanation for why it bars punishment of morally impermissible but legal behavior that is not violent. Consider harmful but truthful gossip. X knows something about Y. It would be great fun for X to tell it to Z but would also hurt Y's feelings badly. When X relays this gossip to Z, he's done something morally wrongful. It would be morally impermissible to criminally punish him for this, however. Why? Because what he did was not illegal. But why should that matter? The answer must be that from the point of view of the state, X has done nothing wrong. But given that he has done something wrong, what does "the point of view of the state" even mean? What it means is that he hasn't done anything criminal and so is not criminally culpable for what he has done. If there's a moral objection to the state punishing what is not, "from its point of view" wrongful it must be because there are moral reasons for the state not to issue punishments expressive of false judgments about the culpability and wrongdoing of those to whom punishment is issued.

A further point: In cases in which morally permissible behavior is criminalized, there can still be good reason to grade the relevant offense by culpability. It's morally permissible but illegal to publish articles unflattering to Kim Jong-un. Such conduct should not be criminalized, although it is. But *given that it is*, it would be even worse if North Korea issued an equal punishment to the person who published such an article knowing it be unflattering as to the person who published it believing it falsely to be flattering while negligent about the article's unflattering nature. To give the same punishment to these two people would be to add moral insult to moral injury, as it were. To explain the moral requirement to treat differently two people who do not differ at all in moral culpability—since the conduct is not morally wrongful, neither the intentional nor the negligent actor is morally culpable—we need to appeal to a difference in criminal culpability, as something distinct from moral, and a moral principle requiring the state to punish differently where there are differences in criminal culpability. But if there can be legal reason to refrain from behavior even when there is no moral reason to do so, then that very same fact can be appealed to in explanation for why Cunningham, in the hypothetical in which his heinous conduct is legal, is not permissibly punished by the state.

The point, put simply, is this: Consider the collection of cases in which there is mismatch between the facts about morally culpable moral wrongdoing and the facts about criminally culpable criminal wrongdoing. There is morally culpable moral wrongdoing without criminal wrongdoing at all, as in the hypothetical Cunningham case, and the gossip case, or there is criminally culpable criminal wrongdoing but no moral wrongdoing at all, as in the Kim Jong-un case. When we turn attention to what punishments it is morally permissible for the government to issue, we find that the facts about *criminal* culpability and *criminal* wrongdoing control. The best explanation for this is that criminal culpability is distinct from moral culpability, despite what one might think when struck with abhorrent, violent, *mala in se* crimes.[7]

3.7 Reasons-responsiveness vs. Quality of Will

It is common for theorists of responsibility to contrast quality of will views of responsibility with reasons-responsiveness views. P.F. Strawson is often identified as the standard-bearer of the quality of will position.[8] John Fischer and Thomas Scanlon are often identified as expressing paradigm versions of reasons-responsiveness positions, albeit views that are importantly different from one another.[9] Quality of will theorists hold that culpability for wrongdoing is found when the wrongful act manifests an objectionable attitude towards others. Reasons-responsiveness theorists hold that culpability is found when wrongful action manifests something problematic about how the agent transacts with reasons. So described, the view of culpability offered here is a reasons-responsiveness view. And I am happy with that label.

But it is worth noting that there is far less light between quality of will theories and reasons-responsiveness theories than is typically suggested, and there is a purely formal distinction between the two views with respect to many sets of norms with respect to which wrongfulness is measured. To see this, note that the views collapse into one another when the relevant set of norms proscribe conduct thanks to the fact that that conduct is other-affecting in bad ways. Say, for instance, that an act is wrongful thanks to the fact that it causes pain. Someone's pain-causing act manifests a failure to grant sufficient reason-giving weight to the act's pain-causing feature just in case it also manifests bad quality of will towards those whose pain is caused by the act. To fail to grant the right degree of reason-giving weight to that fact *is* to manifest bad quality of will; and one cannot manifest bad quality of will of the relevant sort unless one also fails to grant appropriate reason-giving weight to the relevant fact about the act, namely that it causes pain. That is, a faulty mode of transaction with reasons is at most formally distinguishable from an objectionable quality of will, provided that the relevant reason-giving features of the act are other-regarding.

However, quality of will theories and reasons-responsiveness theories have importantly different implications when the norms in question proscribe conduct thanks to features that have nothing to do with the bearing of the conduct on others. Imagine that there is norm against saying critical things about the film *The Godfather*. This norm, let's assume, is a norm of reverence. It has nothing to do with the effect that such statements have on anyone. The norm in question is not other-regarding, in the

---

[7] Ideas in the neighborhood of those explored in this section are very helpfully discussed in Douglas Husak (forthcoming) "What's Legal About Legal Moralism?" in *San Diego Law Review*.
[8] P.F. Strawson (1962) "Freedom and Resentment" in *Proceedings of the British Academy*, 48: 1–25.
[9] Compare, for instance, John Fischer and Mark Ravizza (1998) *Responsibility and Control: A Theory of Moral Responsibility*, Cambridge: Cambridge University Press; and Thomas Scanlon (2000) *What We Owe to Each Other*, Cambridge: Harvard University Press.

way that many norms, possibly all moral norms, are. The thought is, merely, that aesthetes ought not to speak ill of the film. An aesthete who violates this norm does wrong—not moral wrong, but wrong, still, of a different sort. Assuming the norm is indeed a valid norm—imagine that it is part of the Code of the Aesthete—then there is also such a thing as culpable violation of that norm *under the reasons-responsiveness theory of culpability offered here*. To culpably speak ill of *The Godfather* is to manifest in one's speech a failure to grant sufficient reason-giving weight to the fact that one's speech does indeed involve speaking ill of the film. Someone, for instance, who spoke ill of the film while falsely and reasonably believing that he was speaking well of it would violate, but not culpably violate, the norm against speaking ill of the film. But there is no bad quality of will expressed in even a culpable violation of the norm, for culpable acts in violation of it do not, given the nature of the norm, manifest any ill will, or even absence of good will, towards anyone. How could they, given that the conduct in question is not wrongful on the grounds that it is bad for anyone, but on other grounds?

There are two ways for a quality of will theorist to respond to this point. First, he or she might claim that there actually is negative quality of will manifested in the act of speaking ill of *The Godfather*, even under the assumption that that is not a norm valid on other-regarding grounds, but a norm that is valid, instead, on different grounds entirely. To take this line, however, is to collapse the quality of will view into the reasons-responsiveness view. On the proposed view of quality of will, failure to grant sufficient regard to any feature of an act thanks to which it is in violation of a norm is to have bad quality of will. But this is true just in case one has an objectionable mode of transaction with reasons. And the result is that there is no light between the quality of will theory and the reasons-responsiveness theory. That's not an objection to either kind of view but merely an observation that should convert to my camp quality of will theorists.

Alternatively, second, the quality of will theorist could respond to the *Godfather* example by denying that there is ever such a thing as culpable violation of a norm that does not have other-regarding grounds. This is to deny that there is such a thing as culpable violation of the proscription against speaking ill of *The Godfather*. However, if that is so, then the quality of will theorist is trying to understand too narrow a sense of culpability to be of interest to those of us who have our eyes on *criminal* culpability. After all, it is perfectly possible to legally prohibit acts in virtue of features that have nothing whatsoever to do with the relevance of those acts to other people. A legal system could criminally prohibit speaking ill of *The Godfather* in an effort to muster the state's power to enforce an aesthetic norm of reverence. Totalitarian regimes that prohibit the distribution of unflattering representations of leaders, such as that of Kim Jong-un, might be aiming to enforce norms of reverence. We would find both people living under such a legal system who violate the norm culpably and others who violate it non-culpably. If the quality of will theorist does not offer us a theory that distinguishes between these two kinds of violation, then the quality of will theory is a theory of something other than criminal culpability. I conclude, therefore, that quality of will theorists are either offering a merely verbally distinct version of a reasons-responsiveness theory, or else they are offering a theory of something distinct from my target here, namely *criminal* culpability.

3.8 A Character Theory? No

The view that I am offering bears a more complicated relationship than one might think to what are sometimes called "character theories" of culpability according to which an act is culpable to the extent that it manifests an objectionable character trait.[10] While it is true that an agent's modes of transaction with reasons are closely related to his character, there is imperfect overlap between the two. To see this, first note that even if a character trait is to be equated with a collection of dispositions, such as dispositions to treat certain kinds of facts as reason-giving and with certain weights, the possession of a set of such dispositions at a time is not sufficient for possessing a correlated character trait. The reason is that someone's dispositions might change for only a moment, while that would not be a merely momentary change in character.[11] Rather, character requires *stable* dispositions of certain sorts, while what needs to be manifested in one's act for culpability, on the view I am proposing, are a certain set of dispositions, whether or not they are stable. Someone whose conduct manifests a highly objectionable mode of recognition of reason, for instance, is highly culpable, on my view, even if he possessed that mode for only a moment, and so never had, much less manifested in his conduct, a correlated objectionable character trait. To be disposed for a moment to run from danger is not to be a coward, but to manifest that disposition in one's conduct is to be culpable for that conduct.[12]

Second, character traits arguably include dispositions that might have no bearing on the person's modes of transaction with reasons. For instance, the trait of bravery certainly has something to do with one's dispositions to feel, or not to feel, fear. But two people could differ in dispositions to feel fear while having exactly the same modes of transaction with reasons. Feelings, like fear, are at best imperfectly evidential of particular modes of transaction with reasons. The result is that two people could differ with respect to the trait of bravery while not differing in ways that matter, on my view, to culpability. So, the view I am proposing is not a character theory, given a defensible theory of the nature of character.

---

[10] For examples, see Michael Bayles (1982) "Character, Purpose, and Criminal Responsibility" in *Law and Philosophy* v. 1: 5; Kyron Huigens (1995) "Virtue and Inculpation" in *Harvard Law Review*, 108: 1423; Kyron Huigens (1998) "Virtue and Criminal Negligence" in *Buffalo Criminal Law Review*, 1: 431.

[11] Could a character trait be manifested in a lapse? Say that in a moment of weakness a brave person panics and runs from danger. Is his lapse a manifestation of his bravery? It seems to me that it is not. This claim is consistent with the positive theory of manifestation developed below since the lapse does not evidence bravery, even if the person is indeed brave.

[12] Victor Tadros holds a conflicting position. See Victor Tadros (2007) *Criminal Responsibility*, Oxford: Oxford University Press, esp. chapter 1.

3.9 Two Kinds of Excuse

The result of the view of criminal culpability proposed is that an agent's criminal culpability for engaging in legally prohibited behavior is a function of two things: what the agent's wrongful act manifests about his modes of recognition, weighing, and response to legal reasons, on the one hand, and what the law—specifically the law that prohibits the agent's behavior—demands of agents when it comes to such modes, on the other. For instance, an agent's criminal culpability for a prohibited act might derive from a mismatch between the degree of reason-giving weight he gave to refraining from the act that was manifested in his behavior, and the strength of his legal reason to refrain from such acts. When it comes to modes of weighing of legal reasons, then, the greatest criminal culpability is found when the agent granted very strong positive reason to engage in the act and there is a very strong legal reason to refrain. Much lesser culpability is found when, for instance, the agent took there to be a strong reason to refrain from the act in which he engaged, a reason that he took to be outweighed by competitors, and where there is an even stronger legal reason to refrain, a legal reason that outweighed the legal reasons to engage in the act.

This account of criminal culpability goes hand in hand with an account of excuse. To give an excuse from criminal liability is to show that one recognized the reason given by the relevant facts, and weighed and responded to it in a way which aligned with the actual strength of the legal reason provided by those facts. Here, the "relevant facts" are those in virtue of which the behavior being excused was criminally prohibited; typically, this set of facts is identical to the non-mental elements of the crime. So, to offer an excuse is to show that the appearance of a mismatch in the way in which one recognized, weighed, and responded to one's legal reasons, on the one hand, and their actual strength, on the other, is merely an appearance. It is consistent with one's behavior that there is no mismatch in fact.

To illustrate, consider the following California statute:

Any person who knowingly...provides false verification as to...the person's authority to sell property in order to receive money...from a pawnbroker...and who receives money...from the pawnbroker...is guilty of theft.   (Cal. Penal Code 484.1(a))

This statute picks out a very distinctive set of lies for criminal punishment. They are distinctive in content: they are lies about one's authority to sell a piece of property rather than, for instance, lies about the value of that property. They are motivated in a particular way: given to receive money. They are issued to a particular type of person: a pawnbroker. They have certain specific effects: they cause the agent to receive money from the person to whom he lies. Someone who, for instance, tells a pawnbroker that the owner of a ring he aims to pawn has given him permission to sell it, and thereby induces the pawnbroker to give him money for the ring, has violated this statute.

In addition, since the statute also establishes a distinct, secondary norm about modes of transaction with reasons, the statute creates room for distinctive excuses. Someone, for instance, who shows that he had no idea that the person to whom he lied was a pawnbroker provides an excuse for violation of Cal. Penal Code 484.1(a). (Of course, this fact might not excuse him from criminal liability for violation of some other, distinct prohibition, such as a prohibition of fraud.) He thereby shows that his behavior is consistent with his granting special weight to refraining from lying *to a pawnbroker*, the kind of special weight the law requires of him. It is consistent with the evidence to hold that he would have recognized reasons to refrain from the lie he issued if he had known that the lie he was issuing was *to a pawnbroker*. He therefore shows that he was not criminally culpable for violating the statute, for his lie did not manifest the faulty modes of transaction with reasons that it would need to manifest if he was to be culpable for it.

However, it follows from the view that I am proposing that there are two kinds of excuse. A defendant can show, as in the example just given, that it is at least consistent with his behavior that he actually granted more reason-giving weight to the facts than it appeared and so granted them weight in accordance with their actual legal reason-giving force. Or, alternatively, a defendant can show that there was actually less legal reason-giving weight to the facts than it might have at first appeared. One can either show that one met a higher standard than it seemed, or that the standard was in fact lower than it seemed. *Both* are forms of excuse because both involve defending oneself by showing that the modes of transactions with reasons manifested in one's conduct were like those of the law-abiding citizen who grants appropriate reason-giving weight, and responds to the facts in a way that accords with the legal reason-giving weight that those facts have.

Excuses of the second sort are rarely labeled as such because they are typically found in the presence of more obvious shields to criminal liability. Imagine, for instance, that D is somewhere near the border between state S1 and state S2 when he engages in conduct of type C. C is not a crime in S1, although it is in S2. By producing evidence that he was in S1 when he C'd, D provides *two* forms of shield from criminal liability. The first, more obvious of the two, is a shield through the Principle of Legality: he shows that his conduct was not in fact illegal. The second, however, is an excuse: he shows that his failure to grant reason-giving weight to refraining from C was not a criminal fault.[13] In S1, the fact that an act is of type C is not a legal reason to refrain from it and so someone who manifests in his conduct a mode of recognition of reason under which that fact is not recognized to be reason-giving is not thereby criminally culpable.

This account of excuse makes room for the idea of a partial excuse. A person has a partial excuse if he recognized that a fact provided a reason and granted that reason some weight, but less weight than the actual weight of the legal reason provided by that

---

[13] One might think that he is shielded by the Principle of Legality *because* he is shielded in this second way. One might think, that is, that the Principle of Legality gives legal force, in this kind of case, to the moral demand not to punish the excused. But I do not insist on this point.

fact. A partial excuse of the first sort is found in one natural interpretation of the standard common law doctrines through which murder is mitigated to manslaughter. According to such an interpretation, the fact that the defendant was very upset thanks to the provocative behavior of the victim demonstrates that his act manifested a disposition to grant significant reason-giving weight to *refraining* from killing the victim, albeit less than he should have granted it. A partial excuse of the second sort is found when the defendant shows that the legal reason he failed to sufficiently weigh has less weight than it seemed, although, still, more weight than he granted it. Imagine, for instance, that, in our example in which the defendant commits C near the border of states S1 and S2, C is prohibited in both states, but is punished much more heavily in S2 than in S1. By showing that he was actually in S1, the defendant does not show that he granted the reason to refrain from C the weight it deserved, but only that he was less culpable than he would have been had he been in S2, in which the reason to refrain from C is weightier. (This line of thought depends upon the claim that where the sentences are greater, *ceteris paribus* the legal reasons to refrain are weightier. This idea will be elaborated in chapter 5.)

As we will see in chapter 6, kids have a partial excuse of the second sort. It will be argued there that the legal reasons to refrain from crime under which kids labor are weaker than the legal reasons that adults have to refrain from crime. The result is that the modes of transaction with reasons manifested in kids' crimes are less bad than the very same modes of transaction with reasons manifested in adults' crimes. They are less bad, because the standards applicable to kids are less stringent. Given the account of criminal culpability offered here, it follows that kids are diminished in culpability in comparison to adults *even if they do not differ psychologically from adults*. But we should not get ahead of ourselves; this argument will be presented in detail in chapter 6.

It is important to emphasize the innovation in categorizing excuses that this section is offering. It has been thought by many different philosophers that Aristotle's two categories of excuse—compulsion and ignorance—are not exhaustive.[14] Gary Watson's important paper "Responsibility and the Limits of Evil: Variations on a Strawsonian Theme" brings out the issue forcefully.[15] Although it is very difficult to explain why, Watson notes that we feel under powerful psychological pressure to weaken our resentment towards a person for bad behavior that was neither compelled nor performed in ignorance when we are confronted with the fact, for instance, that he suffered horrible childhood deprivation and abuse of a kind that seems to explain why he engaged in such behavior. Victims of such mistreatment seem to be, to use Watson's term, *exempted* from the exacting standards that apply to the rest of us. We might say that the temporally extended agent has not had the life of *a person* but,

---

[14] Aristotle (2012) *Nicomachean Ethics*, Robert C. Bartlett and Susan D. Collins, trans. Chicago: University of Chicago Press, book 3, ch. 1, 1110a, p. 42.

[15] Gary Watson (2004) "Responsibility and the Limits of Evil: Variations on a Strawsonian Theme" in *Agency and Answerablity: Selected Essays*, Oxford: Oxford University Press, pp. 219–59.

instead, at least in part, the life of something else, something less than a person. The temptation to describe those who abuse children in such profound ways as "animals" is, perhaps, no accident. A further thought is that a necessary condition of holding someone to the most stringent standards is *personhood*, in this elusive sense thought to be missing where there has been terrible childhood deprivation, not to mention mental disorder of a kind that produces neither compulsion nor ignorance. Given this idea, we might follow Michael Moore in labeling as a "status excuse" an excuse deriving from the absence of an important status such as personhood (whatever exactly that is).[16] The reason that we ought to temper our resentment to the mentally disordered, for instance, who do terrible things, knowing full well what they are doing, and without being compelled to do so, is that they are not fully persons.

What I am proposing are two substantial extensions in our understanding of the "status excuses." First, I believe that at least some large category of the status excuses, and perhaps all, work by demonstrating that the relevant class of reasons are weaker for an agent lacking the status than they are for those possessing it. So, the reason that status excuses are *excuses* is that, in light of the diminished status of the agent, his modes of transaction with reasons, manifested in his conduct, fall less short of what they should be than those very same modes would fall short for an agent possessing the relevant status. I am providing, in other words, an independent theoretical framework that provides for an explanation for the excusing force of certain diminished statuses. To truly make good on this idea, we need an account of the strength of reasons under which two people who differ in their relevant status, differ in the strength of the reasons for them to refrain from bad behavior. Chapter 5 tries to provide the needed account.

Second, I do not believe that the only relevant status that is necessary for responsibility is that enjoyed by persons. Just as there is a difference between criminal and moral culpability corresponding to a difference in the kinds of reasons of relevance to assessment of the agent's manifested modes of transaction with reasons, there are different statuses that matter to criminal culpability and not to moral culpability. In particular, one's status *as a citizen* does not bear on the question of how strong the moral reasons are for one to refrain from wrongdoing, and so does not bear on the question of whether one has a partial or full status excuse from moral culpability. But citizenship is of central relevance, I will try to show in chapter 5, to one's degree of *criminal* culpability. Full citizenship is a presupposition of application of the most stringent standards of criminal culpability. If this is true, as I aim to establish in chapter 5, and develop further in chapter 6, then there are at least two kinds of status excuse: those deriving from diminished personhood, and those deriving from diminished citizenship. Where only the former are relevant to moral culpability, both are relevant to criminal culpability. So, in essence, kids are owed leniency because they have a

---

[16] Michael Moore (2015) "The Quest for a Responsible Responsibility Test: Norwegian Insanity Law After Breivik" in *Criminal Law and Philosophy*, v. 9: 645–93.

citizenship-based status excuse. In light of their diminished status as citizens, the legal reasons for them to refrain from crime are weaker than for those who are not diminished in citizenship status. And so they are to be held to lower standards of culpability than are fully enfranchised adults. At least, this is the argument to be developed over the course of the next few chapters. It is an argument that depends crucially on the recognition of a new and distinct form of exemption, or status excuse, of a kind that falls out naturally from the account of criminal culpability offered in this chapter.

3.10 An Evidentialist Theory of Manifestation

Let's turn now to the idea of "manifestation." What is it for a property of a cause to be "manifested" by the effect? As indicated above, this relation is not merely a causal relation. The earthquake that causes the delusional disorder patient to forget to take his medication also causes the damage that the patient brings about in his resulting delusional state. Causation is transitive. But the things that the delusional patient causes do not *manifest* the property of the earth shaking, even though they are indeed caused by something that has that property, and even though the possession of that property by the earthquake is causally crucial; but for the earthquake having that property those further events would not have taken place (since the patient would have remembered to take his medication). To manifest, therefore, is narrower than to-be-caused-by.

There is a strong temptation to appeal to notions like "normal" and "non-deviant" in order to unpack the idea of manifestation. And this is fine, as far as it goes. In fact, those who find the notion of normal, non-deviant causation to be unproblematic, who do not feel the need for an analysis of it, might skip now to the end of this chapter. If you are happy with the idea that to be culpable for behavior is for appropriate modes of transaction with reasons to cause that behavior non-deviantly, as on the analysis of criminal culpability offered here, then feel free to use that view of culpability from here forward. In fact, it is my view.[17]

But it seems to me that we should not punt on the question of what direct, non-deviant causation of the kind that I am here referring to as "manifestation" is. In part I believe this because I believe that to the extent that obscure notions can be analyzed, they should be. But I also believe this because a worry about circularity needs to be quieted and can only be quieted by the production of a theory of manifestation. The worry is, in short, that "manifest" just means "culpably cause." And if that is right then to assert that culpability consists in the manifestation of something is to make no progress in understanding the nature of culpability. We can answer this challenge by offering a theory of manifestation that does not draw on the idea of culpability.

---

[17] It is not uncommon to find theorists in this domain who draw on the idea of non-deviant causation without offering an account of the necessary and sufficient conditions for a causal transaction to be non-deviant. See, for instance, Michael Moore (1993) *Act and Crime*, Oxford: Oxford University Press, esp. chapter 6.

I believe that the feature of manifestation, and the closely related features of normality and non-deviance, are not metaphysical features of causal transactions, but, instead, epistemological features. Where there is manifestation, I will suggest, a relevant party is authorized to draw an inference, from the occurrence of the effect, to the conclusion that the manifested quality is present. This idea should appear at this point exactly as it is: dark. But it will be illuminated.

3.10.1 Evidencing

Start with the idea of evidencing. Precisely what the necessary and sufficient conditions are under which one fact counts as evidence for another is elusive. It is an important and disputed issue in epistemology. However, let's work with a theory according to which evidence is that which raises the probability of a hypothesis. Or, in other words:

e is evidence of h *if and only if* $P(h|e) > P(h)$

Very little reflection on this appealing, Bayesian idea leads one to the conclusion that whether a particular fact will or will not count as evidence of a particular hypothesis depends on background information in just the way that probability depends on background information. If, for instance, it is in the background that the election will be decided by vote, then the fact that I voted for the Democrat provides evidence that the Democrat will win. The hypothesis (namely, that the Democrat will win) is a bit more likely given the proposition that I voted for the Democrat than it is independently of that. By contrast, if it is in the background that the election is fixed, and so decided by the rich fat cats, no matter what the vote, then the fact that I voted for the Democrat (and have no influence over the rich fat cats) is no evidence at all that the Democrat will win. The prior and conditional probabilities of the hypothesis that the Democrat will win are different in the two cases; they are affected by the background information.[18] So, this allows the following refinement:

e is evidence of h relative to background B *if and only if* $P(h|e) > P(h)$ relative to B

Here B is a set of propositions that are taken as given for the purposes of assessing whether e is evidence of h. (Some of these propositions, or even all, may themselves be probabilistic, such as the proposition that there is an 80 percent chance that the election is fixed.)

I have been careful in this formulation not to associate the background information with a set of *believed* propositions. It is an open question, for our purposes, exactly what the relationship is between any real or hypothetical person's beliefs and the background set of propositions with respect to which an evidence claim is made. In many cases, a person who asserts that e is evidence of h, or relies on that in his theoretical reasoning, takes the background information to be the set of propositions that he believes. But there is nothing essential to the concept of evidence about this. It is

---

[18] David Christensen (1997) "What is Relative Confirmation?" in *Nous*, 31(3): 370–84.

perfectly possible to classify a fact as evidence for a hypothesis relative to a narrower, larger, or entirely distinct set of background propositions from those that are believed by the person who so classifies it.

3.10.2 Norms structuring the background

Epistemologists have considered the question of which epistemic norms govern the choice of background information with respect to which an evidence claim is made. You cannot include the existence of unicorns in your background information set, ordinarily, at least not if your interest in evidence is grounded in an interest in the truth. (This is why the fact that the animal before you has a mane and hooves does not count as evidence that it is a unicorn.) And perhaps an evidence claim is false if, for instance, the probability of h is unchanged in light of e, given background propositions that *a reasonable person* would believe, even if the person making the evidence claim does not. Perhaps. There are many important questions about the epistemic norms governing the background information, and I do not claim to give the topic anything like a full treatment here.

However, some things of use can be said. A crucial point for our purposes is that the boundary of the background is in many contexts governed, in part, by *non-epistemic norms*. At least, this is true in contexts in which we are inquiring about the evidence because we intend to predicate decisions with significant effects on others on the conclusions that we make on the basis of the evidence. Say that you are an elementary school teacher trying to decide if your students' scores on a math assessment test provide evidence for the hypothesis that your curriculum is too difficult. If included in the background is the proposition that girls are less good at math than boys, and there are a lot of girls in your class, then, let's imagine, the scores raise the probability that the curriculum is too hard; and if not, then not. Put that proposition in the background, and you can expect slower progress from your students, and so tolerate a lesser shortfall from perfect scores on the test. So whether the scores count as evidence for the hypothesis depends on this bit of background information. But it might be that your role as a teacher precludes you, as a normative matter, from making evidential inferences with this proposition in the background *regardless of its truth, and regardless of your evidence for it*. The thought is that you're not allowed to make inferences from propositions about the distribution of talent across genders; your commitment to conceiving of the girls and the boys as equals precludes you from doing so. The claim about math talent distribution is probably false, but that's not the point. The point is that you, the teacher, are under normative pressure not to make inferences that affect your students from a base of information that includes that proposition, regardless of the proposition's epistemic merit or demerit. The role of teacher, that is, imposes a norm governing the background information from which you can reach conclusions about what is and is not evidence for student-affecting hypotheses that you have. At least, this is true within certain limits. If it would be sufficiently harmful to your students to leave a proposition out of the background, then perhaps you are required to make inferences on its basis, even if acceptance of the proposition is in conflict with other aspects of the teacher's role, such as a commitment to a presumption of independence between gender and intellectual ability. But this observation is consistent with the point of importance for our purposes here: there are non-epistemic norms governing exclusion and inclusion of propositions in the background for the purposes of classification of propositions as evidential, classifications which have direct impact on our inferences from what we believe to conclusions about how the world is.

Nowhere is the prominence of non-epistemic norms governing the structure of the background information more clear than in legal contexts. In fact, the very idea of "admissible evidence" reflects it. Consider, for instance, the rule excluding from evidence a confession when that confession was coerced.[19] This rule is ultimately grounded in the thought that guilty verdicts should not be derived from information brought to light thanks to egregious government misconduct. This has the further implication that propositions cannot be included in the background, and thus determine what does and does not count as evidence, when their inclusion would involve ratifying, or at least tolerating government misconduct. But much that is brought to light by government misconduct *is probative*; many coerced confessions are given by the guilty. And, even when an innocent person gives a coerced confession, that confession provides *some evidence* of guilt. If our only aims were epistemic we would have very different rules for the admission of evidence. The thought driving the rules we have is that the role of the government, or of those, like jurors, who are doing government work, places normative pressure to construct the background in a particular way, to include and exclude propositions in that background on grounds that are independent of their epistemic merit. To say that justice is blind is, in this domain, almost literally true. Justice requires us, sometimes, to blind ourselves to the facts, to make inferences from a background that includes falsehoods, or, at least, excludes well-supported truths.

We are closer to unpacking the assertion, made above, that for an act, or the result of an act, to manifest an agent's modes of transaction with reasons is for it to evidence those modes in a way that licenses a permissible inference to their presence. The point can now be put like this:

Wrongful act C manifests D's modes of transaction with reasons M *if and only if* (1) D's possession of M causes C, (2) the conditional probability that D possesses M, given C, is higher than the prior probability that D possesses M (that is: C is evidence that D possesses M), (3) (2) is true relative to a set of background propositions permissibly employed by those assessing D's culpability for C.

---

[19] The Supreme Court now treats that rule as implicated by the Fifth Amendment's ban on forced self-incrimination. For discussion, see Leonard W. Levy (1968) *Origins of the Fifth Amendment: The Right Against Self-Incrimination*, New York: Oxford University Press.

Unpacking this yet further requires answering the following question: What norms govern the construction of the background by those tasked with assessing culpability? Reflection on this question immediately yields the observation that the answer will vary depending on whether the wrongful act is morally wrongful, legally wrongful, or wrongful relative to some other set of norms entirely. The reason is that the type of norms involved bears on the question of what kind of treatment of the actor will follow from a finding of culpability, and who will administer that treatment. Determining whether your spouse is culpable for flirtatious jealousy-inducing behavior with a stranger might require you to exclude from the background the proposition that your spouse generally gets pleasure out of making you jealous; maybe the role of husband or wife requires charity with respect to such things, even when such charity is not epistemically warranted. But that norm governing the structure of the background is clearly specific to the particular kind of relationship obtaining between, as it were, jury and judge in that case.

I am doubtful that there is a single, context-independent set of non-epistemic norms governing the construction of the background when it comes to assessing moral culpability for moral wrongdoing. In fact, I am doubtful that there is a single set of norms governing the construction of the background for assessment of *criminal* culpability for *criminal* wrongdoing that can be specified independently of examination of the particular legal system under which culpability is being assessed. But, our concern is primarily with criminal culpability for criminal wrongs under mature, current legal systems, and particularly under the American legal system. And in this domain at least two things can be said about the relevant set of norms.

First, there are norms of equality that govern the structure of the background. Ceteris paribus, *we are required to exclude from the background propositions that, if true, would speak to differences in fitness to participate in democratic government of people who we grant equal title to do so.* We cannot include in the background propositions about the differential intelligence, disposition to bad or good behavior, conscience, values, or character of those of one group in contrast to another when those two groups are granted equal rights of participation in governance. This means that we cannot include propositions about, for instance, links between poverty and crime in the background. Such information might imply that criminal conduct is greater evidence of objectionable modes of transaction with reasons on the part of the poor than the rich; or it might imply the opposite. But whatever its implications, we are to leave such propositions out of the background, and so bar them from driving our criminal culpability assessments, regardless of their epistemic merit. The same thing can be said about propositions concerning race, gender, sexual orientation, and party affiliation. We must grant the same evidential status to the fact of bad behavior by Democrats as Republicans, men as women, Black as White, even if there are differences that would be probative as to the modes of transactions of reasons manifested by members of those groups who engaged in just the same forms of wrongdoing.

We can imagine legal systems lacking the kind of commitment to equality that our system possesses. In such systems, these norms of equality will not govern the construction of the background. The result is that there may be differences in criminal culpability under such systems in comparison to ours, even given no differences in either behavior or psychology of those being assessed. Behavior might manifest worse modes of recognition of legal reasons, for instance, in a system that allows into the background propositions about the ways in which a group to which the defendant belongs tends to recognize reasons, propositions which are excluded from the background in systems committed (officially, if not also in fact) to equality. Imagine that those of one political party are significantly less likely to recognize the reason-giving force of a woman's non-consent to their behavior, although they do recognize the reason-giving force of men's non-consent. If that proposition is included in the background, in assessing the criminal culpability of a member of that political party, then behavior by that person to which a woman does not consent would be evidence of that objectionable mode of recognition of reasons. But since we, committed to equality in the ways described, exclude the information about the sexism of members of a particular political party from the background, the relevant mode is not manifested in that behavior here. The relevant objectionable mode of recognition of reasons would be manifested by it in a legal system that allows this into the background. So the norms governing the construction of the background make a difference to what modes of transaction with reasons are manifested by the behavior.

The second kind of non-epistemic norm that governs the construction of the background, when it comes to assessment of criminal culpability under our system, has its root in what is sometimes called "The Principle of Lenity." Broadly speaking, the Principle of Lenity requires legal decision-makers to make decisions, and answer questions, in a way which aids the defendant, when either of two decisions or answers are equally reasonable. The Principle of Lenity is often invoked in connection with statutory interpretation: if two interpretations are equally consistent with the text, and with other constraints on interpretation (deriving from, e.g., *stare decisis* or legislative intent), then the Principle of Lenity requires a judge to interpret the statute in the way that leaves the defendant better off. The principle is also implicated in both the presumption of innocence and the beyond a reasonable doubt standard for a finding of guilt. Both require those tasked with assessing criminal guilt to decide against guilt, and so for the defendant, even in contexts in which a finding of guilt would be epistemically superior to the alternative.

With respect to the question of how to structure the background when making assessments of criminal culpability, the Principle of Lenity requires the positive inclusion in the background of a particular proposition, even if it has very weak epistemic credentials: the proposition that the defendant is disposed to have acceptable modes of transaction with reasons. That is, the Principle of Lenity requires us to determine what the defendant's conduct says about his modes of transaction with reasons under the assumption that he is as little different from the law-abiding citizen as possible, given his behavior.

The Principle of Lenity bars us from being neutral between the hypothesis that the defendant is bad and the hypothesis that he is *very* bad, when both hypotheses are equally consistent with the evidence; instead, we must favor the former hypothesis. The law-abiding citizen grants substantial reason-giving weight to the fact, for instance, of another's non-consent. If it is possible then, consistent with the evidence, to conceive of the defendant as granting *some* reason-giving weight to that fact, even if less than the law-abiding citizen, then the Principle of Lenity requires us to adopt that conception of the defendant. This is true even if there is reason, deriving from information not brought into evidence, for thinking that the defendant is actually much worse, in this respect, than his conduct warrants us in concluding; even if, for instance, there's reason to think he does not even recognize facts about non-consent to bear any reason-giving weight.

In other words, the norms governing the construction of the background, which derive from the Principle of Lenity, require those tasked with assessing criminal culpability to adopt a certain kind of optimism bias. We are required to have a background theory of human behavior under which people are, by default, good. This does not bar us from reaching the conclusion that a particular defendant is not. Rather, it requires that the hypothesis of goodness is sticky, and one from which we can be dislodged only given evidence presented to us through filters that allow the defendant an opportunity of rebuttal.

Armed with these additional pieces of conceptual mechanism, we can build upon the account of "manifestation" offered above like so:

> Criminal act C manifests D's modes of transaction with legal reasons M *if and only if* (1) D's possession of M causes C, (2) the conditional probability that D possesses M, given C, is higher than the prior probability that D possesses M (that is: C is evidence that D possesses M), (3) (2) is true relative to a set of background propositions that is structured in a way that accords with norms deriving from principles of equality and lenity applicable to those assessing D's criminal culpability for C.

3.10.3 Replying to objections to the evidentialist theory of manifestation

I think that most people will grant me that what appears on the right side of the biconditional in the formula proposed at the end of subsection 3.10.2—conditions (1), (2), and (3)—capture something about what is involved in assessing criminal culpability. What they will doubt, I think, is that these three conditions are necessary and sufficient for *manifestation*. After all, how could it be that what an agent's act manifests about his modes of transaction with reasons should be a matter of what *someone else entirely*, who has the hard job of assessing criminal culpability in a way constrained by norms governing the proper use of state power, is in a position to conclude about him? Surely, what a person's act manifests is determined solely by the facts about him, his conduct, and the causal link between the two!

As a first step towards responding to this objection, consider an example. D1 and D2 leave their respective homes in the morning and are both in a hurry to get to work; if they are late again, they are likely to be fired. They both recognize that they will be late if they wait in a long line of cars at a stop light, but can be on time if they swing into the oncoming traffic lane to pass the waiting cars. They both believe that the chance that this maneuver will kill someone else is one in ten. And they both do it. And they both kill another person. Both grant greater reason-giving weight to the chance of saving his job than to the chance of killing another person; that is, in fact, why they drive into the oncoming traffic lane. Are they equally criminally culpable? Of course. After all, I have not specified a single difference between these two people. What we learn from that is that their acts manifest the same objectionable modes of transaction with reasons. In particular, both of their acts manifest a failure to grant sufficient weight to the risk of killing another.

Now imagine that, secretly, D1 takes the risk that another will die to give him no reason to refrain from the act. He does not care a damn about anyone but himself. D2, by contrast, does grant that fact reason-giving weight. He takes the risk to provide a strong reason to refrain, but he takes his reasons to be on time to be even stronger. Given this additional information, should we persist in the claim that they are equally criminally culpable? Before answering, let's assume that reaching the conclusion that there is a difference between D1 and D2 would require violation of norms grounded in our commitments to equality and lenity. We would have to include in the background facts about the groups to which D1 and D2 are members—D1 is in a group that tends to be very hard-hearted, D2 of a softer variety—that is irrelevant to their right to political participation. Under this assumption, there are two possible things to say about the case: (1) D1 and D2 differ in criminal culpability (D1 is more culpable than D2), but we are required by principles of political morality to treat them as though they were the same, or (2) D1 and D2 do not differ in criminal culpability, although they might differ in moral, since moral culpability assessment is not constrained by the principles of equality and lenity that constrain criminal culpability assessments. I favor (2) over (1). The objector, whose concerns I am now trying to address, favors (1) over (2). How can we adjudicate this dispute?

To adjudicate it, return to the irresistible conclusion, reached when the story is told without reference to their differences, *that D1 and D2 do not differ in criminal culpability*. If you favor (1) over (2), then you should hold that that conclusion was rash. The right conclusion would have been that we do not know whether they differ because we do not know whether they grant the same reason-giving weight to the risk of lethal harm, or whether, instead, they differ in how far below the threshold of acceptability in this respect they lie. But I do not believe that conclusion was rash. Rather, what our willingness to reach the conclusion of equal culpability shows is that when making assessments of culpability we constrain our inferences by principles of equality and lenity. Such constraints force us not to remain agnostic about whether D1 and D2 differ in criminal culpability, or are instead the same, when we are told only about their similarities; rather, such constraints force us to reach the conclusion *that they are the same*. And we reach that conclusion *because they are the same*. But what that shows is that the constraints on our inference are actually in part constitutive of the very phenomenon we are trying to uncover. What *it is* to be criminally culpable is for one's act to evidence crucial facts about oneself to those who are constrained by norms of political morality in their conceptions of what evidence is, and in their consequent inferences on the basis of what they conceive to be evidence.

A further point in favor of the evidentialist theory of criminal culpability I am offering, over non-evidentialist variants that attempt to analyze "manifestation" without reference to evidential inference, can be made through reflection on *The Model Penal Code*'s conception of recklessness. Recklessness is defined in the *MPC* as awareness of a risk of the presence of an element of the crime, such as another's non-consent, or the causation of harm by one's conduct, where that risk is some distance[20] above a threshold: it is "substantial," and sufficiently so to make conduct in light of it "unjustifiable" (*MPC §2.02(2)(c)*). While it is difficult to specify with any precision where this threshold lies, for our purposes the point to note is that when a defendant judges the probability to be p, and p is above the threshold set by substantiality and unjustifiability, then p + x is above that threshold, also. The result is that two people who differ greatly in their beliefs about probability will be equally classified as reckless, under the *MPC*, even if one of the relevant probability assignments is far above the threshold required for criminal culpability and the other is just barely over that threshold. The person who thinks the chance is 0.6 that he lacks permission to use his neighbor's car when he borrows it (call him D3), that is, and the person who believes the chance is 0.5 (call him D4), are both reckless, under the *MPC*. Law-abiding citizens do not borrow cars when they think the chances that they lack consent are anywhere near those probabilities.

Should we say that D3 and D4 are equally criminally culpable? Or should we say that D3 is more culpable than D4? It is obvious that D3 is more culpable than D4. Now let's add some information. Imagine that it is worth $100 to borrow the car. And imagine that the act of borrowing the car without permission does $500 worth of damage to its owner. We know from the fact that D3 and D4 borrowed the car that each takes there to have been greater reason-giving weight to the fact of the $100 gain for himself than to the expected loss to the car's owner. Since they differ in their probability judgments, they differ in their expectations of loss to the owner. D3 takes the expected loss to be 0.6*$500 = $300, while D4 take it to be 0.5*$500 = $250. What this implies is that D3's and D4's acts, respectively, manifest different modes of weighing of reasons. D3's act manifests a tendency to take a $100 gain to himself to have more reason-giving weight than a $300 loss to another, while D4's act manifests a tendency to take a $100 gain to himself to have more reason-giving weight than a $250 loss to another. That is why D3 is more culpable than D4. But now let's stipulate a further fact: D4 would have borrowed the car even if he had thought that the probability

---

[20] The distance above the threshold must be great enough to make the conduct "a gross deviation" from that of law-abiding citizens. The implication is that small deviations are not sufficiently large to count as involving criminal culpability.

was 0.6, and neither D3 nor D4 would have borrowed it if the probability had been judged to be greater than 0.6. The result is that, in fact, there is no difference in the modes of weighing of reasons *possessed* by these two actors. Both take a $100 gain to himself to be worth a $300 loss to the other, and both perform the act thanks to this fact about himself. So why is D4 less culpable than D3? The reason is that the Principle of Lenity constrains our judgment about the mode of weighing of reasons manifested in the act. Given what he judged the probabilities to be, and excluding from the background the proposition concerned with what he would have done had he had a different belief about probability, a proposition that paints D4 in a bad light, we cannot infer the presence of a worse mode of weighing of reasons. What matters to culpability, that is, is what the act *manifests*, and that is a function of what the act renders probable given a background constrained by considerations of lenity (and equality). D4's act *evidences* only a tendency to weigh $100 gains to himself more heavily than $250 losses to others, even though, while this is indeed true of him and a fact thanks to which he acts as he does, the relevant modes of weighing of reasons have an even worse quality—they are tendencies to weigh $300 losses to others less heavily than $100 gains to himself. But since that quality is not inferable from the act, given lenity constraints, it is not manifested in the act.

We could, if we wished, continue to resist the proposed evidentialist account of manifestation. Someone who wishes to go this way might insist that D3 and D4 are equally criminally culpable, but they are to be treated *as though* they are not for reasons of lenity. But such a person has trouble explaining why, ceteris paribus, differences in judgments of probability align with differences not just in *the appearance* of culpability, but with differences *in culpability itself*. Hold fixed harmful behavior, and the good pursued through its performance, and vary only the judgment of the likelihood of prior harm, and you vary culpability, ceteris paribus. But judgments of probability have nothing directly to do with culpability. It is not more culpable to think the chances of an event are high than low; it's just a matter of what evidence one happens to have. There is no correlation with the belief that a prospective act has a particular chance of being harmful and culpability. Not even willingness to ignore the prospect of harm is greater where there is greater believed probability. Rather, the strength of the willingness to ignore the prospect of harm *that can be inferred from the act given constraints of lenity* increases as the believed probability increases. What that shows is that what matters is not just the facts about the modes of transaction with reasons that cause the act, but also *what can be inferred* from the act about those modes, given normative constraints on the background.

There is another important objection to the kind of evidentialist view offered here that must be addressed. The basic worry is that culpability judgments do not vary with changes in evidence as robustly as they would if the evidentialist theory of manifestation were true. A clear way to see the issue is with the idea that evidence can be corroborated by things other than the act, which are not excluded from consideration by principles of lenity or equality, but which seem entirely irrelevant to culpability. Say, for instance, that a psychiatrist examines D4 and reaches the conclusion that he would have borrowed the car even if he had thought, as D3 did, that the probability that there was no permission was 0.6. The psychiatrist's testimony, then, provides us with evidence from which to infer that D4's modes of weighing of reasons were just as bad as D3's. But, still, D4 would be reduced in culpability in comparison to D3. The psychiatrist's testimony, that is, is not excluded by principles of lenity or equality, and, in light of it, D4's act evidences the worse mode of weighing of reasons, the one that he shares with D3.

At least as I just stated it, however, the objection misses the mark. Let's use the label "M1" for the modes of weighing of reasons in which a $100 gain to oneself is granted greater reason-giving weight than a $300 loss to another, and "M2" for the modes of weighing of reasons in which $100 gain to oneself is granted greater reason-giving weight than a $250 loss to another. M1 modes are M2 modes, but not vice versa. And let's stipulate that D3 and D4 differ not at all in the modes of weighing of reasons thanks to which they borrow the car. Both myself and the objector agree that both D3's and D4's acts manifest M2, and that D3's manifests M1. And it is being stipulated that D4 possesses M1. The question is whether, in the form of the example in which there is psychiatric testimony pointing to the possession by D4 of M1, that D4's act *manifests* M1. As an intuitive matter, D4's culpability does not depend on the availability of psychiatric testimony, so if the facts about what his act manifests change when such testimony is available, on the view I am proposing, then something is amiss. But, I do not think that the view I am proposing implies that the facts about manifestation change with the availability of such testimony. The reason is that the psychiatric testimony affects the prior probability of the hypothesis that D4 possesses M1; that probability is higher in light of the psychiatric testimony. But there is no boost to that probability *provided by D4's act*. And so while it is true that the chances that D4 possesses M1 are higher, in light of the psychiatric testimony, it is not true that D4's act boosts that hypothesis's probability. And so it is false that the act evidences M1. And so it is false that the act manifests M1, on the evidentialist theory of manifestation on offer.

To come up with the kind of counterexample to my view that the objector seeks, we do not need an example where a fact independently evidences a different mode of transaction with reasons than, intuitively, we take to be manifested in the act; that's what's going on in the psychiatric testimony example. Instead, we need a case in which a proposition has three features: (1) It can be permissibly included in the background, (2) In light of it, *the agent's act* evidences a worse or better mode of transaction with reasons than the act evidences when the proposition is not included in the background, (3) Intuitively speaking, the proposition is irrelevant to culpability. But it seems to me that any case in which (1) and (2) is true will be a case in which (3) is false. In fact, this is illustrated by cases in which we differentially condition our response to agents, and our judgments of their culpability, on past behavior thanks to which they came to have the particular modes of recognition and response to reasons manifested in their behavior. Consider, for instance, the difference in culpability between the voluntarily and involuntarily intoxicated who equally do wrong. As I indicated at the end of section 3.5, in my view, these agents manifest different modes of recognition and response to reasons. The facts about *how* the agent came to be in his intoxicated condition are permissibly included in the background and result in his conduct evidencing different modes of transaction with reasons. If this is right, as I've tried to show elsewhere,[21] then cases of voluntary intoxication, contrasted with involuntary, are cases in which (1) and (2) are true but (3) is false. The facts about how the agent came to be intoxicated make a difference to what is evidenced by his conduct *and* matter, intuitively, to culpability.

My claim that any case in which (1) and (2) is true will be a case in which (3) is false is also demonstrated by our recklessness example. Say we learn that in light of the information that D4 had, the probability that he had permission was 0.6. Then D4 gets on the stand and says, in earnest, that, despite this, he believed the probability to be 0.5. This information about his psychological state can now be included in the background and it makes a difference: in light of it, the act evidences M2 rather than M1. But it's also obviously relevant to his culpability. And, in fact, that is easily explained on the view I defend: in light of it, the act evidences a different mode of weighing of reasons than it would have manifested in its absence. That is, it is precisely because conditions (1) and (2) are met that condition (3) is not met. I believe this will always be true. (1), (2), and (3) cannot be simultaneously satisfied, and so there can be no counterexample to my position of the sort the objector seeks. While this is, to some degree, speculation on my part, I have to confess that I cannot find an example that provides what the objector seeks.

3.10.4 Manifestation of psychological state, rather than modes of transaction with reasons?

A different kind of objection can be raised to the evidentialist theory of manifestation offered here. One might start by accepting the observation offered in the previous section about D3 and D4: people who differ in psychological state, but not in modes of transaction with reasons, differ in culpability. I go on to explain this fact by holding fixed the idea that culpability consists in manifestation of modes of transaction with reasons, and conclude that differences in psychological state provide different evidence of such modes, and so conclude that this is best explained through appeal to the evidentialist theory of manifestation. But one might try to explain this without recourse to the evidentialist theory of manifestation by giving up on the idea that what needs to be manifested for culpability are modes of transaction with reasons. Perhaps what needs to be manifested is *psychological state*. If that were right, we would then

---

[21] See Gideon Yaffe (2012) "Intoxication, Recklessness and Negligence" in *Ohio State Journal of Criminal Law*: 545–82; Gideon Yaffe (2016a) "The Point of Mens Rea: The Case of Willful Ignorance" in *Criminal Law and Philosophy*.

conclude that D3 and D4 differ in culpability for the simple reason that their respective acts manifest different psychological states and they do so because they are caused by different psychological states. The worry is based on the perfectly legitimate observation that my defense of the evidentialist theory of manifestation offered in subsection 3.10.2 depends crucially on another aspect of my theory of culpability, namely that culpability consists in the manifestation of modes of transaction with reasons. Reject that view, and my defense of the evidentialist theory of manifestation falters.

In reply, start with the observation, offered in subsection 3.10.3, that it is not a bad thing to believe this or that, or to be aware of this or that probability. So the objector cannot hold without absurdity that *all* of the psychological differences that we ordinarily take to matter to culpability matter in and of themselves. Rather, the thing for the objector to say is that possession of intentions *accompanied by certain other psychological states* is a bad thing. What's bad is not thinking the chances of killing someone by swerving into the oncoming traffic lane is one in ten; what's bad is *intending to do that* when you have that belief. And then the view is that when that objectionable intention is manifested in behavior, the agent is culpable for the behavior.

But what is bad about such an intention? An adequate answer to this question is going to have to appeal, in the end, to modes of transaction with reasons. What's bad about such an intention is that the person who has it does not grant sufficient reason-giving weight to the fact that his act might kill someone. But if this is true, then where there are differences in psychology but without difference in modes of transaction with reasons, there ought to be *no difference in culpability*. And so the objector is at a loss to explain why D3 and D4 differ in culpability. The psychological difference between the two would only make a difference to culpability if there were a difference also in modes of transaction with reasons; since there isn't, there isn't. The objector can solve this problem by accepting an evidentialist theory of manifestation. Under such a theory, the intention manifested in D3's behavior is worse than the intention manifested in D4's *even though, in fact, there is no difference in the badness of the two intentions*. But, of course, such a move gives up the game by granting the evidentialist theory of manifestation that I have been concerned to defend.

3.11 Conclusion

David Hume famously claimed that causal connections involve two elements: a constant conjunction, supplied by the world, and something more, supplied by, or spread on the world by, the mind. I doubt that this is true of causation. It seems much more likely to be entirely in the world. But if the view offered here is correct, then something like what Hume had in mind is true of culpability. Culpability for wrongdoing involves, first, causation by modes of transaction with reasons, specifically, such modes of transaction with the reason-giving force of the facts in virtue of which the wrongful action is wrong. But the causal relation can be instantiated many different ways, and we do not find culpability in all those cases in which the relevant modes of transaction with reasons cause the relevant behavior. But what distinguishes those causal relations where culpability is found from those where it is not is not something in the world, but something the mind spreads onto the world. Causation is culpability only if it is *manifestation* of the right kinds of objectionable modes of transaction with reasons. But to manifest is to make evident, or to evidence; and what it is to evidence is a function not solely of the relation between the modes that cause behavior and the behavior, but, instead, a function of those two things *plus* facts about those of us tasked with inquiring about culpability.

The result: *Two people can be intrinsic duplicates, duplicates in psychology and in behavior, and yet differ in culpability.* There are, in fact, two distinct ways in which this can happen. First, this can happen thanks to a difference in the information available to, or permissibly draw on, by the person assessing culpability. Intrinsic twins, then, can differ in what modes of transaction with reasons their conduct evidences, and so differ in culpability, since what their conduct evidences is a function in part of the background set of propositions that the judge assessing culpability can permissibly appeal to. If the judge of the one twin can appeal to different things than the judge of the other, thanks to laboring under different norms governing the background, then the twins can differ in culpability. Second, intrinsic duplicates can differ in culpability even when their conduct manifests the very same modes of transaction with reasons, thanks to the fact that those modes are to be assessed for objectionableness by comparison to standards that are not fixed by the intrinsic features of those being assessed but, instead, by other things—in the legal context, things like the actions of legislators and other legal actors, which make a difference to what legal reasons there are, given the facts, and how strong those legal reasons are.

As we will see over chapters 4, 5, and 6, this theory of culpability provides a foundational piece in a justificatory edifice, allowing us to explain why it is that kids deserve a break for wrongful, criminal conduct. As we will see, kids should be treated more leniently than adults who are psychologically and behaviorally no different.

4

Desert for Wrongdoing

4.0 Introduction

I am far from sure what a person would deserve for putting out another's eye. But losing an eye himself seems more likely to be the right thing than, say, being killed, or even losing an arm. It seems to fit better. As a purely introspective matter, it is difficult to identify the source of judgments of this kind. They feel almost perceptually grounded. Or, anyway, the temptation to characterize them that way is almost irresistible. One "sees" a link between putting out an eye and losing one oneself; one "spots" a connection between the two, or "senses" a relation of fitness. But this can't be literally true. The relevant relation, the relation of desert, is very unlikely to affect our senses. Talk of "seeing" and "sensing" such relations is, really, just talk. There is nothing like a visual or tactile link between acts and those harms that seem to fit them better than other harms do. If our intuitions are cottoning on to *something* that is there, when we judge that there's more sense in an eye for an eye than there is in a life for an eye, it is far from clear what, exactly, it is.

And yet desert plays an important role both in life and in many philosophical theories. We both build and dissolve marriages and friendships in light of it; we go to war over it. We build philosophical theories about what justifies our behavior—our infliction of criminal punishment and our distributions of goods, for instance—through appeal to it. And, for our purposes here, one example is particularly important: we give kids a break, and think it appropriate to do so because, we think, *they deserve the breaks we give them*.

The elusive and mysterious nature of desert can lead one to skepticism and despair over all of this. How can we be justified in harming other people, thinking they deserve it, when we do not even know what, exactly, that means? In fact, it can lead to more than skepticism and despair: it can lead to fear. Some of the most consequential decisions that we make, both in our interpersonal relations and as citizens of a state, are predicated on judgments of desert. If there is no there there, then we have reason to shudder at the things we do—and, perhaps more importantly, are done *to* us and to our children—in the name of desert.[1]

---

[1] For a clear statement of an opposing view, according to which there is no there there, but also no reason to shudder, see Derk Pereboom (2001) *Living Without Free Will*, Cambridge: Cambridge University Press.

This chapter concerns the concept of desert for wrongful behavior. It concerns, that is, the idea of deserving something bad in light of and because of the fact that one did something wrongful.[2] A paradigm case falling under the concept is desert of criminal punishment for a "*mala in se*" crime like murder, robbery, or rape. To deserve something in this sense is for there to be a relation of fitness between the wrongful act and the relevant bad thing. A lengthy prison term, one might think, is deservedly issued to those who commit rape. If this is so, then the lengthy prison term fits the crime of rape in a way in which a fine or a caning, or a short prison term, does not. But to talk here of "fitness" is not to illuminate the concept of desert for wrongdoing but, instead, to merely rename it. We still need to know in what this fitness consists. We need to know, that is, why it is that one harm is a fitting thing to suffer in response to a token wrongful act while another is not, or is less so. This chapter aims to provide what is needed. My goal is to produce a *theory*: I will offer an analysis of (one type of) desert by appeal to familiar, independent concepts.

I intend the theory offered here to have implications for more than the central topic of this book, namely the practice of giving kids a break for their criminal conduct. But it is its implications for that issue that are to be explored in subsequent chapters, and particularly in chapter 6. I claim that we are justified in giving kids a break because they deserve a less punitive response than do adults. I think they deserve this because they are reduced in culpability. And I believe that they are reduced in culpability because the legal reasons for them to refrain from crime are weaker than the legal reasons for adults to refrain. Someone who grants that reduced culpability lessens desert for wrongdoing can accept this line of thought while denying, if he or she pleases, the theory of desert for wrongdoing offered here. But, on the other side, I think it a virtue of the view to be offered here that it entails that claim and, thereby, supports the justificatory argument to be described in chapter 6 for giving kids a break. If we are going to give kids a break because we think they deserve it, it is a good thing to know why, exactly, that is. The theory to be offered here helps.

The view of desert for wrongdoing to be offered here can be put, very roughly, like so: *One harm is more deserved for a wrongful act than another if, in light of the one more than the other, the act is supported by reasons for the agent in a way similar to the way it ought to have been supported by reasons for him.* The central task of this chapter is to explain, elaborate, and offer an argument for this theory.

It is striking how rarely philosophers have made an effort to offer a theory of desert, given how much has been written about the concept.[3] Still, this is not, of course, the

---

[2] The chapter does not concern "positive" desert—desert of something good in light of and because of the fact that one did something good. I am uncertain if the account of desert for wrongdoing to be offered here extends to positive desert.

[3] For discussion and an overview, see Owen McLeod (2008) "Desert" in Edward N. Zalta (ed.), *The Stanford Encyclopedia of Philosophy*, http://plato.stanford.edu/entries/desert/. Accessed August 19, 2015. The most important recent book-length study of desert is Shelly Kagan (2012) *The Geometry of Desert*, Oxford: Oxford University Press.

very first effort made to say something illuminating about the fitness relation central to desert. But what I will be proposing here is, as far as I know, different from any other account to be found in the literature. And there is need for a new account.

Some promising accounts to be found conceptualize the wrongdoer as gaining something through his wrongful action which suffering then takes back from him. Perhaps what he gets through wrongdoing is an unearned advantage, or relief from an agreed upon burden of self-restraint. And perhaps what he deserves is that which takes back from him that thing that he achieved for himself through wrongdoing.[4] What all such accounts overlook is that wrongdoing is often positively self-destructive, and not just on balance, but in every single respect. The wrongdoer often gets nothing at all from his wrongful conduct. Worse, he would often have done far better, even taking into consideration only his own good and even ignoring the possibility of punitive response, by not having done wrong. He might not even avoid the burden of self-restraint through his wrongdoing, assuming that that burden can be specified, as it must be to avoid circularity, as something distinct from mere omission of the wrongful act. This is illustrated clearly by cases of failed attempts for which suffering is, still, deserved. The failed attempter often achieves nothing of value for himself *at all*—the attempt itself is of no value to him, when unsuccessful—and yet he can deserve suffering for his attempt.

The fact that even when the wrongdoer gets nothing from his wrongdoing, some harmful responses to it seem more deserving than others is impossible, I believe, for any version of a take-back theory of desert to explain. In such cases, giving the wrongdoer what he deserves cannot involve taking anything from him that he achieved through his wrongdoing, for he may have gained nothing at all, or may even have lost something substantial already. I consider it a virtue of the account of desert for wrongdoing to be offered here that it makes no assumption to the effect that wrongdoing was in any way at all good for the person who engaged in it.[5] Still, it would be misleading to suggest that this chapter succeeds in vindicating a theory of desert *over competitors*.

---

[4] See, for instance: Michael Davis (1986), "Harm and Retribution" in *Philosophy & Public Affairs*, 15(3): 236–66; Herbert Morris (1968) "Persons and Punishment" in *The Monist*, 52(4): 475–501. For illuminating discussion of views that understand desert in terms of some kind of balance between the imposition of burdens and the benefits of wrongful conduct, see Richard Burgh (1982) "Do the Guilty Deserve Punishment?" in *Journal of Philosophy*, 79(4): 193–213 and George Sher (1987) *Desert*, Princeton: Princeton University Press, esp. ch. 5.

[5] The account of desert for blame offered in Michael McKenna (2012) *Conversation and Responsibility*, Oxford: Oxford University Press, esp. ch 6, is distinctively different from those briefly referred to in the main text here. McKenna takes desert to derive from the structure of the conversational relation that he takes to be central to responsibility. For him, roughly, blame is deserved provided that it is a conversationally appropriate response to the meaning expressed by the wrongdoer's wrongful act. McKenna is adamant, however, that this account of desert is distinct from the account that would be needed to understand the conditions under which a criminal punishment is deserved. By contrast, I am centrally concerned with the case of deserved punishment. Still, it is possible that, in the end, the account to be offered here is consistent with McKenna's. The relation between the accounts, it seems to me, will depend a great deal on an adequate account of the relationship between the reasons for a wrongful act, on the one hand, and the act's meaning, in McKenna's sense, on the other.

Very little comparison will be made here between the view I advocate and alternative positions. Instead, a case will be made for the theory I propose, leaving it to others to decide how that case compares to the case that can be made for other theories.

To describe this chapter as providing an account of the fitness that there seems to be, intuitively, between wrongdoing and harm, or setbacks to interests, is to suggest that the account to be offered here is to be tested by its alignment with intuitions about what is and is not deserved. But I am very skeptical of such methodology. An account that fits intuition is only as good as the intuitions it fits. And there is really no reason to think that intuitions about desert are always accurate or even to be relied on as a default. They probably get it right sometimes and get it wrong others. In part, this is a general point about the unreliability of intuition. But the problem is particularly bad when it comes to intuitions about desert. The reason is that doing justice and avenging, while different, do not *feel* much different. Every time that one feels that this or that is deserved for past wrongdoing, there is the possibility that what is really felt is that this or that would avenge the victims of that wrongdoing.[6] So in the case of intuitions about desert we have a candidate class of distinct intuitions that are hard to distinguish from those of interest. And so there is really no way to know whether an account that conforms to intuition is conforming to the right set.

But if conformity to intuition is not the right way to test a theory of desert, what is? The answer, I think, is that while a satisfying account of desert must conform *roughly* to intuition—intuition and the account might come apart, but they will mostly align—it must also serve to illuminate some of the connections that have been thought to exist between desert and other things. And its capacity to do so is, in the end, a far more important reason to accept the account, and even to revise one's intuitions to conform to it, than its capacity to draw lines in the same way as intuition.

Here I will offer an account of desert that illuminates two things, in particular: First, the account to be offered here will explain why what a person deserves for a past act is a function in part of the psychological states that guided that act. It will explain, for instance, why someone who harms intentionally is deserving of a harsher response than someone who inflicts the same harm merely recklessly or negligently. And, second, the account to be offered here will explain why desert is necessary for justified criminal punishment, as retributivists of all stripes hold, even those who take it to be very far from sufficient. The argument, then, for the account of desert to be proposed here is just this: It conforms roughly to intuition and, more importantly, supports two of the most plausible links that have been recognized between desert and other independently specifiable notions, namely culpability and justified punishment. That the account further aids us in justifying our policy of giving kids a break, as subsequent chapters will explain, is another point in its favor.

---

[6] As Robert Nozick famously showed, vengeance, like desert, has a moral logic. It is possible in both cases to both over- and under-shoot. But the logics are different. For discussion, see Robert Nozick (1981) *Philosophical Explanations*, New York: Belknap Press, esp. ch. 4, section III.

4.1 Moving an Act's Place in the Space of Reasons

I limit myself here to offering an account of the concept of desert underlying ordinal judgments of desert. I offer an account, that is, of what goes in the blank in the following schema, where D is an agent, P1 and P2 are by D's lights bad things, and C is a type of wrongful act tokened by D:

For C-ing, D deserves P1 more than P2 *if and only if* _____.

I will assume that the concept of desert underlying ordinal judgments of this kind is the same as that which underlies non-comparative judgments of the form "P1 is/is not deserved for D's C-ing." I will assume, that is, that the non-comparative property possessed by some forms of suffering, the property of being deserved for a past act, is linked to the relational property of being deserved more than something else in the same way that, for instance, being tall is linked to being taller-than, or being smart is linked to being smarter-than. However, there is no reason to think that the truth of an ordinal judgment logically entails the truth of any connected non-comparative judgment. P1 might be undeserved, even though it is more deserved than P2. A one-year prison term for littering is more deserved than a two-year term. But neither are deserved, full stop, since they are both excessive. And P2 might be deserved even though it is less deserved than P1. To do time and pay restitution, for a theft, say, might be more deserved than merely paying restitution. But it is still deserved to pay restitution. Still, despite the absence of entailments of these kinds, to say that P1 is deserved, period, and not just more deserved than something else, is to say that the very same relation is to be found between P1 and C that we find more of when we find that P1 is more deserved for C than P2 is. This is just to say that the concept of non-comparative desert functions like any threshold concept. To be tall is to be taller than a person who is at a certain height threshold. For a form of treatment in response to wrongdoing to be deserved is for it to be more deserved than a form of treatment at a certain threshold. But I will not be making any progress here on a specification of the relevant threshold but, instead, only on a specification of what it is to be more or less deserved than some alternative treatment. So, the view offered here is, admittedly, incomplete.

The idea to be developed here is as follows: *A form of treatment for a wrongful act is more deserved than another just in case, in light of it more than the other, the wrongful act occupies a position in the space of reasons closer to the position it ought to have occupied for that agent.* Putting this idea in the form of the theory to be defended here:

Desert as Isomorphism in the Space of Reasons (ISR):

For C-ing, D deserves P1 more than P2 *if and only if* The form of rational support, relative to the ideal agent, enjoyed by C is more similar in relevant respects to the form of rational support, relative to D, enjoyed by C&P1 than that enjoyed, relative to D, by C&P2.

DESERT FOR WRONGDOING   103

The central task of this section is to explain what this means. Primarily, what is required is elucidation of the notions of "form of rational support relative to an agent," "ideal agent," and "similarity in relevant respects." But before explaining these ideas, a few observations about ISR are in order.

Note first that, under ISR, desert is ultimately grounded in relations of similarity. Imagine that you have two blue-green paint squares and are asked which one is greener. You answer that question by first fixing on a paradigm green—kelly green, say—and then seeing which of the two blue-green squares is more similar to that paradigm. Similarly, under ISR, when asked whether P1 or P2 is more deserved, for C-ing, we identify a paradigm for comparison and see which of two things, C&P1 or C&P2, is most similar to it. If this is right, then desert is no more mysterious than similarity. The trick to understanding it is to identify the right things to compare and to check for similarity in the appropriate respects.

The rough idea behind ISR is that to give someone what they most deserve for past wrongdoing is to attach something to the act thanks to which the act has, for the agent, the very same reason-giving properties that it has, without that thing attached to it, to a better agent. If a year in prison is deserved for robbery, it is because a robbery with a one-year prison term attached to it has for the agent the same reason-giving properties as that same token robbery, with no such consequence attached to it, has for the good person who would not commit it. Under ISR, that is, to give someone what he most deserves is, in a sense, to *correct* something: If we don't respond to the wrongful act, it would occupy a position in the place of reasons for the agent different from the place it should have occupied. By responding, we move the act closer to the position that it should have occupied by moving it closer to the position that it occupies for another, better agent.

We could also describe the central idea here by reference to the *deliberation* of the agent in contrast to that of an agent better than him. From this point of view, the idea behind ISR is that to give someone what he deserves is to attach something to the act such that, in light of it, his deliberations about the act would proceed in just the same way as the deliberations about that act by a good person proceed without that thing attached to it. If a good person takes a robbery to be unthinkable, for instance—he does not include it, in his deliberations, even among the acts he considers, no matter what—then the robber gets what he deserves when the robbery, given a year in prison, would be, for him, unthinkable. Of course, "unthinkability" is just an example of a form of treatment of an act in deliberation. What is important is that the agent treats the act with the putatively deserved thing attached to it, in deliberation, in the same way that the good agent treats the act without that thing attached to it. The metaphor of "the act's place in the space of reasons" can be understood, then, either as the set of, and relations among, the act's reason-giving properties, or as the treatment that the act receives in deliberation.

However, whether we describe this background idea in terms of reason-giving properties, or in terms of proper deliberation, ISR is also motivated by the realistic observation that it is not possible to place the agent's act into the *precise* location in the space of reasons that the act occupies for the ideal agent. Rather, we determine which of two forms of treatment is more deserved—P1 or P2—by comparing how close the act is in the space of reasons to the act of the ideal agent when each of these two things is, respectively, attached to it. The closer is more deserved than the farther. "Closeness" here is similarity with respect to the treatment of the act as a bearer of reason-giving properties.

But, this rough characterization of the idea behind ISR needs precisification.

4.1.1 Rational support relative to an agent

Bernard Williams famously says that a fact provides an "internal reason" for a given course of action just in case there is a "deliberative route" from one's affective and motivational states and dispositions to performance of that course of action, thanks in part to the relevant fact.[7] (Williams called the set of affective and motivational states and dispositions "the agent's *S*.") In the most obvious case, that involving facts about means, on the one hand, and, on the other, desires for ends, the fact that I will build a birdhouse only if I acquire some wood—the fact that one thing will happen only if another also happens—provides an internal reason to acquire some wood, given that I want to build a birdhouse. Deliberation of a certain kind—notably, deliberation that conforms to norms of rationality, such as consistency norms, and involves belief in the relevant fact—will draw on the fact in question combined with my desire in order to provide rational support for the relevant course of conduct; and that is why the fact in question gives me internal reason to acquire wood.[8]

Williams also thinks that all reasons, and particularly moral reasons, are internal. But my purposes here will not require following him that far. Rather, what is important for me is that Williams here identifies a plausible type of reason that is relativized to given agents. The fact that a birdhouse will be built only given the acquisition of wood provides reason to acquire wood to *some* agents, but not to others, since only some and not all want to build birdhouses or have some other element of their set of motivational and affective states which could lead proper deliberation towards wood acquisition. And, in fact, we need not follow Williams even so far as to suggest that the set of features of the agent's psychology includes only the motivational and the affective. We can recognize, instead, that there are a large number of facts that provide reasons because there is a deliberative route from some feature of the agent's psychology to a particular course of conduct, thanks in part to those facts. If an agent believes, for instance, that a course of conduct is his duty, then, perhaps, the agent has a reason to

---

[7] Bernard Williams (1979) "Internal and External Reasons" in Ross Harrison (ed.), *Rational Action*, Cambridge: Cambridge University Press, 101–13.

[8] On Williams' view, does the element of the agent's S provide reason for the act? We need not answer this question. For our purposes, what is important is that the fact provides reason in virtue of the further fact that a certain kind of deliberation engaged in by an agent with the right elements of his S will favor the act in a respect.

engage in that course of conduct that those lacking such a belief do not. In such cases, the relevant facts provide rational support for courses of conduct, *relative* to agents possessing those psychological features from which there is a deliberative route to those courses of conduct, given those facts. They provide reasons for some agents, but not for others, since they provide reasons for agents possessing the right psychological features, and not to agents lacking them.

So far, the observation inspired by Williams is just that reasons can be relativized to psychological states and dispositions, and not just, as Williams thought, to *affective and motivational* psychological states and dispositions. But, depending on how we define the boundaries of the psychological, this too may be too limiting. Consider a sadist. Such a person takes the fact that an act will produce pain in another as a positive reason in favor of that act. This defining feature of the sadist is a fact about the way in which the sadist deliberates (or would deliberate, or is disposed to deliberate). In the sadist, deliberations that draw on the belief that a particular course of conduct will cause pain also generate mental representations of that course of conduct as having something to be said for it, as having rational support. It could be that this is because the sadist gets pleasure out of others' pain, or finds it attractive or amusing, or even fulfilling to know that others are in pain. It could be, that is, that this manner of deliberation on the sadist's part derives from a psychological feature of this kind, *present prior to deliberation*. But the possession of such a prior psychological feature that grounds or explains deliberations of this sort is not what is essential to sadism. Rather, what is essential to sadism is a disposition to engage in *that form of deliberation*, a form of deliberation that involves treating the fact in question as reason-giving.

Further, it is not just modes of *recognition* of reasons of the kind just described—dispositions to display patterns in the facts that the agent takes to provide reason for courses of conduct, like facts about what causes pain—that seem essential to a condition like sadism, but also modes of *weighing* of reasons. (Both kinds of modes of transaction with reasons should be familiar from chapter 3.) The sadist does not just take the fact that a course of conduct will cause pain as a reason in favor of that act, she also grants that reason a certain degree of weight. She is less of a sadist than someone who grants it more weight than she does. She might therefore deliberate to the conclusion that her afternoon is better spent cleaning her dirty house than causing pain, although there is something to be said for spending the time causing pain, while a different kind of sadist, a worse one, would reach the opposite conclusion.[9]

---

[9] There are, also, modes of response to reasons. Imagine a perennially weak-willed sadist: she regularly reaches the conclusion that causing pain is more supported by reasons than alternatives, but nonetheless chooses the alternatives. If she *always* chooses the alternatives that she takes to be less well-supported by reasons than causing pain, then she isn't a sadist. She must at least sometimes *respond* to the reason-giving force of pain-causing in order to be a sadist. And she might differ, both from non-sadists and from other sadists, in her modes of response to reasons; some sadists are more resolute than others. But for now this point is relegated to a footnote for the following reason: where two people differ only in their modes of response to reasons, they do not differ in what reasons they have. Where one sits in the space of reasons, that is, is not determined by how one responds to reasons, but only by how one recognizes and weighs them.

I am uncertain if modes of recognition and weighing of reasons are psychological features of agents, present prior to the deliberations (actual or hypothetical) through which they are revealed. Perhaps they are. But regardless of what kinds of facts they are, they are, indeed, features that vary among people; and, more importantly, where we find variations in these modes we also find variations in what reasons agents have to act. Thanks to the fact that he takes pain-causing to be reason-giving, the sadist has a reason to engage in pain-causing acts that agents who have different modes of recognition of reasons lack. And a similar point can be made about modes of weighing of reasons. Because the sadist grants a certain degree of reason-giving weight to pain-causing he has greater reason to clean the house in contrast to another sadist who grants greater reason-giving weight to pain-causing and so has greater reason to cause pain than to clean the house. Further, where we find differences in psychology of the kind that make for differences in the rational support for actions that are otherwise the same, we also find differences in modes of recognition or weighing of reasons. Someone who wants something recognizes the fact that a given course of conduct promotes it as a reason in favor of that course of conduct. He recognizes reasons differently from the person who does not want that thing.

For our purposes, it is the way in which reasons are at least sometimes relativized to agents' modes of recognition and weighing of reasons that is important. This is the notion of "rational support, relative to an agent" appealed to in ISR. Consider two agents in identical circumstances, differing only in their modes of recognition or weighing of reasons. Actions that each of these two agents might perform, actions that have all of the same intrinsic features and causal powers, might nonetheless differ in their rational support relative to each of these two agents, respectively. If one is a sadist, and the other is not, to continue the example, then pain-causing acts enjoy some rational support relative to one of these agents (the sadist) that they do not enjoy, relative to the other. In general, if a possible action has a feature that figures into the rational calculus for one agent differently than the other, then that action will differ in its rational support relative to the two agents, respectively. So, we can offer the following:

> Fact F provides rational support, relative to agent D, for act C *if and only if* D has modes of recognition and weighing of reasons in virtue of which, thanks to F, he takes there to be a reason of some weight for C-ing.

Or, equivalently (given some assumptions):

> Fact F provides rational support, relative to agent D, for act C *if and only if* If D were to deliberate in accordance with norms of rationality governing deliberation, then D would, thanks to F, thereby come to represent C as supported by a reason of some weight.

These two formulations are equivalent because what it is to possess a given mode of recognition or weighing of reasons is to be disposed to represent acts as supported by reasons, in light of certain types of facts, where that disposition is triggered by deliberation.[10]

The precise *form* that the rational support for the act, relative to the agent, takes is a function of the agent's modes of recognition and weighing of reasons. If a fact provides rational support for a course of conduct, relative to two different agents who differ in their modes of recognition and weighing of reasons, it provides support of different forms, varying with the modes of recognition and weighing of reasons those agents possess.

Under ISR, desert of something bad for an agent, for a past wrong, is a function of the form of rational support, relative to that agent, that there is for the wrong together with the bad thing, in comparison to the form of rational support, relative to an ideal agent, for the wrongful act considered independently of the bad thing. This comparison, then, is ultimately a special form of comparison between the agent's modes of recognition and weighing of reasons, on the one hand, and the modes of recognition and weighing of reasons of the person so far referred to as "the ideal agent."

4.1.2 The ideal agent

Who is this ideal agent? The answer, I believe, varies across domains, because there are variations across domains in how people ought to recognize and weigh the reasons that are generated by given facts. Focus, for now, on the domain of criminal law. Assume that C has a variety of statutorily specified characteristics. For instance, consider robbery in the state of Michigan:

A person who, in the course of committing a larceny...uses force or violence against any person who is present...is guilty of a felony punishable by imprisonment.
(Michigan Penal Code §750.530(1))

None of the characteristics of an act of robbery, as defined here, logically entails anything about the rational support enjoyed by any given token robbery. Some agents will take the fact that an act involves force or violence to be a positive reason in favor of engaging in that act. Others will take that fact to be a reason against performing the act, although they may not grant that reason much weight; they might, for instance, grant so much reason-giving weight to the fact that the act will result in their possession of the victim's money that they see there as, on balance, much more reason to perform the act than refrain from it. And almost unlimited variations are possible. An agent might have a mode of recognition of reason in which the prospect of violence not only is no positive reason in favor of performance, but cancels the reason-giving force of any other qualities of the act, so that for him the fact that he would get rich if he engaged in the act is no reason at all in favor of the act, given that the act also involves violence.

---

[10] Of course, counterfactual analyses of dispositions are notoriously problematic. The hedge phrase "thanks to F" is intended to exclude interpretations of the counterfactual under which it is true even when the agent lacks the relevant disposition. The literature on this issue is large. For a start, see David Lewis (1997) "Finkish Dispositions" in *The Philosophical Quarterly*, 47(187): 143–58.

As these examples make clear, there are better and worse ways to recognize and weigh the reasons, if there are any, generated by the features of robbery.

In the context of criminal law, the ideal agent is the agent who has modes of recognition and weighing of reasons thanks to which he grants as much reason-giving weight to the relevant features as is necessary for the act of refraining from robbery to be more supported by reasons than the act of robbery. By passing the statute above, the Michigan legislature identifies a kind of conduct as not-to-be-done. That is to say, the Michigan legislature makes it the case that citizens are required to take there to be insufficient reason to commit robbery, or greater reason to refrain. A wide variety of agents meet this requirement. It is met by agents who take robberies to be unthinkable, who positively recoil from the very idea so strongly as to exclude it from consideration in their deliberations about what to do. But it is also met by those who see greater reason to commit lucrative robberies than not so lucrative—and so recognize powerful reasons to perform very lucrative robberies—provided they also take these reasons to be outweighed across the board. Since, in criminal law, we adopt the Principle of Lenity—according to which we conceptualize the defendant as as good as he can be consistent with the evidence—the ideal agent to whom he is to be compared is the worst possible agent who nonetheless meets the state's demand. The ideal agent, that is, is the worst agent who nonetheless recognizes greater reason to refrain from the relevant token robbery than to commit it. By comparing the defendant to such an agent, the defendant comes off better, as required by Lenity, than he would come off if any other agent were identified as the one to whom he is to be compared. That is a way of setting the bar as low as it can be set, consistent with the legislature's dictates; this is lenity's demand.

The same recipe for identification of the ideal agent does not apply in other domains. Notably, morality is not governed by a lenity principle. And so in determining what an agent morally deserves, we have no obligation to compare him to someone who is only good enough; we can permissibly compare him to someone much better than that. And, in fact, in some domains the ideal agent may be far better than the ideal agent relevant to judgments of moral desert. Someone might hold her spouse to standards of recognition and weighing of reasons such that when trying to determine what he deserves in response to his infidelity she compares him to an agent who recoils far more violently from the very idea than the agent to whom she would compare him in assessing his moral desert. She may hold that while morality requires only the slightest rebuke in response to marital infidelity, *her* marriage requires much worse.

In addition, morality is often sensitive to more than just the overall evaluation of the wrongful act. Perhaps this is true of law, too, although there is no reason to think that the additional features that matter to morality are the same as those that matter to law. Morality might require, for instance, not just that we take ourselves to have more reason to refrain from taking others' things with violence, but also that we find that idea unthinkable. If that is the case, then a form of treatment attached to a robbery that caused the person who committed a robbery to take the balance of reasons to favor refraining, but did not make the robbery unthinkable, might suffice for law, but it would be far less than the agent deserves morally. What these points imply is that *legal* desert is a different thing from *moral* desert, and there are, probably, yet other forms of desert varying with conceptions of the ideal agent of importance to other given domains.

Putting together the view of rational support relative to a particular agent, sketched in subsection 4.1.1, with the view of the ideal agent, sketched in this subsection, we find the following. According to ISR, judgments of ordinal desert involve, first, a hypothetical agent who conforms to often domain-specific norms concerning modes of recognition and weighing of reasons; call that the ideal agent. The rational support relative to the ideal agent of the token act of C-ing performed by D is then identified; it is a function of the modes of recognition and weighing of reasons adopted by the ideal agent. And this form of rational support is then compared to the rational support relative to D of two things: C together with P1, on the one hand, and C together with P2, on the other. We ask ourselves, that is, how D, given his modes of recognition and weighing of reasons, would characterize the reasons for C-ing, given that C-ing involves P1, and also how he would characterize the reasons for C-ing, given that it involves P2, instead. These two forms of rational support are then compared to the rational support enjoyed by C, relative to the ideal agent. Where there is greater similarity, there is greater desert in the corresponding hardship, P1 or P2, to be inflicted on D in response to his C-ing.

But in this description there was a wave of the hands. Under what conditions, exactly, is the rational support for something similar *in the relevant respects* to the rational support of another? Under what conditions, exactly, is the rational support for a robbery with fifteen years of incarceration (relative to the person who committed that robbery) similar to the rational support of a robbery considered independently of such a sentence (relative to the ideal agent)? Without an account of this similarity relation, ISR is no less shrouded in mystery than the phenomenon it is intended to illuminate, namely desert for wrongdoing.

4.1.3 Similarity in forms of rational support

Part of what is involved in similarity in forms of rational support is captured by overall, all-things-considered rational assessments that we make about courses of conduct. If the ideal agent takes robbery to be unthinkable—ineligible to even be deliberatively considered—and D takes the robbery coupled with a fifteen-year sentence to be unthinkable, then in that respect the relevant forms of rational support are similar. But all-things-considered evaluations of this kind hide information about the form of rational support that the relevant courses of conduct have, given our modes of recognition and weighing of reasons. An agent who considers larceny unthinkable will also take robbery to be, since part of what robbery *is* is larceny. But he might not be above violence for other purposes besides stealing. By contrast, a person who takes violence to be unthinkable might not be above non-violent larceny. Yet neither will grant robbery—violent larceny—any positive reason-giving weight. There is therefore more to the similarity between forms of rational support than is captured by the agent's all-things-considered rational verdict with regard to a particular course of conduct. That is part of the story, but only a small part. It matters, also, how agents get to their final, bottom-line conclusions.

One way to get started thinking about what more there is to similarity in forms of rational support is through using the (possibly fictional) idea of what we might call "rational atoms." Imagine an agent who is short of cash and commits a robbery. We ask him why he did it and he cites, in explanation, the fact that it was lucrative. Further questioning reveals that he also got a thrill out of the violence involved. And yet further questioning reveals that he is perversely attracted to courses of conduct that risk capture by police. What this questioning reveals is that his overall rational evaluation of the robbery—it was supported by reasons more than alternatives—is grounded in the reason-giving weight he granted to several separable features of the robbery. He granted different reason-giving weight to its being lucrative, to its involving violence, to its entailing a risk of capture. If you ask him why he finds violence thrilling, you are likely to move from the realm of reasons to the realm of causes. Maybe it has something to do with his parents. But he doesn't grant reason-giving weight to doing violence because *he grants reason-giving weight* to something about his parents. Parental treatment causes the way in which he assigns reason-giving weight to this feature, but it does not explain by reducing it to some other act of assigning reason-giving weight. The "rational atoms" are features of the act that are assigned reason-giving weight and where such assignments are not reducible or explicable by appeal to the reason-giving weight assigned to yet other features. If violence were not a rational atom for an agent, then we could explain the fact that he grants reason-giving weight to violence by identifying something else to which he grants reason-giving weight, where rationality would thereby require him to grant reason-giving weight to violence. If there is no such explanation, then violence is a rational atom. (As we will see, the argument to be offered here does not require that there actually *are* rational atoms. They are simply a useful device for explaining in what similarity in forms of rational support consists.)

It is worth remarking that sometimes conjunctions of rational atoms are themselves rational atoms. Assume, for a moment, that among the rational atoms pertaining to robbery are (1) taking something of someone else's, (2) without permission and (3) through violence. There may be in general reason to avoid actions that involve taking things of others. Perhaps it's better to use one's own things when one can. Similarly, there might be reason not to do things for which one lacks permission. Perhaps it is generally better to get permission than to act without it. But there is additional and distinct reason to avoid actions of *taking things of others without permission*, that is not exhausted by the reason-giving force of each of the two components of this conjunction. It is the conjunction of (1) & (2) that, for many people, provides distinctive reason against robbery, and not either (1) or (2) considered independently from one another. Recognizing the reason-giving force of the conjunction, after all, is a crucial part of what it is to respect property rights. So, we should not conclude from the fact that two things are rational atoms that their conjunction is not. It might be.

The form of the rational support, relative to an agent, of a particular action can be thought of as a function of the reason-giving weight assigned to each of the individual rational atoms of relevance. Imagine a set of variables, $x_1 \ldots x_n$, one for each rational atom. $x_1 \ldots x_n$ are values of either 0 or 1 assigned to the n corresponding reason-bearing facts, depending on whether they are recognized as giving reason for C under the modes of recognition of reasons possessed by agent D. And now imagine another set of variables, $a_1 \ldots a_n$, which are positive real number values reflecting the weight of the reason D assigns, under the modes of weighing of reasons he adopts, to the reason provided by the corresponding rational atom. The overall, all-things-considered rational support enjoyed by action C is a function of the x's and the a's. A simple-minded, albeit appealing theory of the form of rational support enjoyed by an act, for instance, would employ the following equation:

$$\textit{Overall Rational Support}_D(C) = a_1 x_1 + a_2 x_2 + \ldots + a_n x_n$$

This is a simple-minded theory for three primary reasons. First, it assumes rational commensurability of the reason-giving weight assigned to each of the rational atoms, even though there may be none. It will often be the case that one factor will provide one kind of reason, another an entirely different kind of reason, the weight of which is measured in entirely different "units." In such cases, it is false to suggest that the contribution to overall rational support of the two rational atoms is a sum. Second, the theory assumes that, when there is rational commensurability, the weights assigned to the rational atoms and subsets of them contribute to overall rational support additively when, in fact, they might contribute in some other, much more complicated way. This is illustrated by the earlier example in which the agent takes the fact that an act involves violence to make it unthinkable, and thereby to cancel the reason-giving force of the features of the act that would, in the absence of violence, count in its favor. To characterize the overall rational support enjoyed by a violent act, relative to such an agent, we would need some other tool besides this simple-minded theory. And, third, the theory assumes that there is no difference between, on the one hand, a reason being recognized and given zero weight and, on the other, the reason not being recognized at all: in both cases the $a_i x_i$ term is zero. This is simplistic because deliberation proceeds differently when a person places a feature of a prospective act on the deliberative scales—and so recognizes that the feature is reason-giving—than when the feature is not even given consideration; and this is true regardless of whether the consideration is granted any weight when placed on the scales. Imagine, for instance, that the ideal agent does not recognize the race of a beneficiary of his act as providing any kind of reason, pro or con, for performance of the act. Another agent who grants that consideration a place in deliberation, but gives it no weight, is not duplicating the deliberations of the ideal agent; he is not race-blind. This distinction is lost under this simple-minded theory of how the overall rational support for a course of conduct arises from the rational support assigned to each of the rational atoms.

But for our purposes, the thing to recognize is that there is *some function*, albeit not the simple one just described, that takes as inputs the information encoded in the x's and the a's and outputs the overall rational support enjoyed by the action, relative to a given agent. Exactly what the function *is* is hard to say. In fact, there may not be just one. Perhaps a different function is involved with legal reasons than with moral. Or perhaps each person has a somewhat different function. Who knows? The point is that there is, in each case, some function of this sort.

Mathematically speaking, then, we are looking at a function of 2n dimensions—n being the total number of rational atoms. And like any multi-dimensional function, a lot can be learned by considering the behavior of the function over changes in one variable, while the others are held fixed. What this means is that the function just described determines the answers to a variety of illuminating counterfactual questions. For instance: We can ask of the person who committed a robbery how the overall rational support that the action enjoyed for him would have changed had he granted more, or less, negative reason-giving weight to the fact that the act involved violence? For some agents, there would have been no change, or very little overall change in the form of rational support enjoyed by the act; for others, there would be much. Counterfactual questions of this sort involve consideration of the way in which the relevant function changes while we hold fixed the values of all but one of the x and a variables.

There are, then, 2n potential respects in which two forms of rational support—the one relative to the ideal agent, the other relative to the agent whose desert of harm is being assessed—can be similar or dissimilar. The ideal agent's overall rational evaluation of an act changes in a certain respect with changes in the reason-giving weight that he assigns to, for instance, the violence involved in the act. To say that an agent takes violence into consideration in his deliberation in the same way that the ideal agent does is to say that changes in the reason-giving weight that he assigns to the fact that an act is violent results in the same pattern of changes for him in the overall rational support the act enjoys. Imagine, for simplicity, that the ideal agent takes violence to have a linear contribution to the overall rational support enjoyed by the act. As the negative weight that he grants to violence increases at a constant rate, the overall rational support enjoyed by the act decreases at a constant rate. We can now ask whether D, who committed a robbery, would exhibit the same pattern of change in overall rational support were the robbery to promise fifteen years of incarceration for him. Perhaps that would induce him to treat violence as significant in the way in which the ideal agent does; or perhaps not. The question of similarity is, thus, a 2n-dimensional question. We need to know whether these 2n-patterns of treatment, of which the treatment of the reason-giving force of violence is but one, are similar or dissimilar to that of the ideal agent.

How do we combine these 2n respects of similarity and difference to reach an overall measure of the similarity between the way in which the ideal agent treats C in comparison to the way in which D treats each of C&P1 and C&P2? The answer, I suspect, is that sometimes we don't. Imagine that n = 2. There are just two relevant reason-bearing items corresponding to variables x_1 and x_2 (set aside a_1 and a_2). And imagine that when it comes to C&P1, D is the same as the ideal agent with respect to x_1 and different with respect to x_2. The situation is reversed when it comes to C&P2. There, D is the same as the ideal agent with respect to x_2 and different with respect to x_1. Is P1 or P2 more deserved for D's C-ing? I suspect that the answer is that they are equally deserved. P1 corrects D in one respect, as it were, P2 in another. Both P1 and P2 would be less deserved than a form of treatment that corrected D in both respects. To say, then, that there is greater similarity between the form of rational support enjoyed by C&P1 than that enjoyed by C&P2 is to say that C&P1 is more similar in more of the 2n relevant respects. Where this criterion is not met, as when there is greater similarity in one respect and greater difference in another, we have a tie in the degree to which P1 and P2 are deserved. One is more deserved in one way, the other in another.

Does this account of the relevant similarity in forms of rational support survive rejection of the very idea of rational atoms? Say that we hold that there are cases in which there is no end to the explanation for the fact that the agent grants a certain degree of reason-giving weight to a particular feature. He grants weight to F_1 because he grants weight to F_2; F_2 because of F_3; ad infinitum. If that is the case, then when we imagine changes in the reason-giving weight assigned to F_1 we must also imagine changes to the reason-giving weight assigned to all the F's. And we can find ourselves over-counting important differences between the agent and the ideal agent since we shouldn't count every difference in every one of the F's equally; they are linked. But, still, the primary point I am after survives. What the idea of rational atoms draws our attention to is that it is useful to consider not just how much reason-giving weight an agent assigns to a fact, but also how changes in the weight he assigns to that fact, holding everything else fixed that can be held fixed, would affect his deliberations. If less can be held fixed than the idea of rational atoms assumes, then so be it. Even then forms of rational support need to be compared by looking not just at what the agent recognizes to be reason-giving and how much weight he assigns to it, but also to the way such assignments change in response to changes in others. The calculation of similarity, then, is multidimensional and non-trivial to calculate. But it is calculable, in principle, to the extent that it needs to be to support judgments of ordinal desert.

Similarity judgments are often thought to be interest-driven. If we find, on a given occasion, that the red apple is more similar to the green apple than it is to the red rose, it is because we are making a pie rather than testing for color-blindness. The interest-relativity of similarity is consistent with the proposal here for the relevant respects in which forms of rational support are judged to be similar when we make ordinal judgments of desert. What I have proposed is that desert judgments involve a very particular kind of interest: an interest in the way in which, given one's modes of recognition and weighing of reasons, the overall rational support that an action enjoys changes as single reason-bearing features (whether rational atoms or combinations of them) change. When it comes to desert, that is, the relevant similarity judgments are driven by an interest in the way in which people employ their rational faculties in guiding their behavior. To deserve this more than that, for one's past wrongful act, is for this, more than that, to require one to regard the reasons supporting one's wrongful act in ways that match how one ought to regard them.[11]

4.1.4 *The currency of punishment*

It is an implication of ISR that if a person has idiosyncratic modes of transaction with reasons—if, for instance, he likes prison and so is disposed to grant positive reason-giving weight to a potential act in light of the fact that it promises prison—then what is more deserved than what will be, for him, idiosyncratic as well. For such a person, a year in jail for littering might be as deserved as a reward would be for someone less idiosyncratic. For such a person, a day in jail for petty theft might be less deserved than no penalty at all since he might grant positive reason-giving weight to the fact that the theft promises a day in jail. For him, thanks to the promise of jail, the act will occupy a place in the space of reasons even farther away from the place that it occupies for the ideal agent.

Some will see this observation as an objection. We might think that since any possible harm that we might inflict on someone might, in theory, be one to which he is rationally attracted, or less rationally averse than is even close to normal, it follows that what a person deserves for wrongdoing cannot be a function of his degree of rational attraction or aversion; his particular modes of recognition and weighing of reasons cannot matter to the question of what he deserves. If you do the crime, then you deserve to do the time, we might say, even if you happen to like it.

But I embrace the implication of ISR and do not see it as an objection. I believe that the idiosyncratic *are not getting what they deserve* when we attach to their wrongful acts things in light of which those acts are more rationally attractive to them than they would be to someone whose modes of transactions with reasons are normal. Such consequences attached to wrongful acts are less deserved for those acts than nothing at all. However, there are several reasons for thinking that this is a much less bitter pill to swallow than one might have thought. To see why, consider the case of Jamaine Makepeace.[12] Makepeace was a homeless man in Troy, New York who broke several windows in a government building with the aim of getting a one-year jail sentence that would provide him with a warm place to sleep and save him from begging for his meals. For him, the only reason to do the crime was to do the time. Is a year in jail more deserved, for Makepeace's act, than no penalty at all? Not under ISR. The ideal agent

---

[11] One implication of this point is that creatures lacking in rational faculties cannot be deserving of harm for wrongdoing. This is surely the right result, since there is no amount of hard time for which a lion should be sentenced for killing an endangered gazelle, wrong as it was to do so.

[12] Bob Gardinier (2013) "Homeless and Hungry Man Prefers a Jail Cell" in *Albany Times-Union*, January 23, 2013, http://www.timesunion.com/local/article/Homeless-and-hungry-man-prefers-a-jail-cell-4213734.php (visited December 15, 2016).

recognizes sufficient reason to refrain from the act. After all, the fact that the act involved destroying government property provided a legal reason to refrain from it, and, since there is no necessity defense available for commission of the crime in service of a warm place to sleep, the ideal agent would have granted sufficient reason-giving weight to the relevant facts to refrain from the crime. In fact, Makepeace himself would have recognized such a sufficient reason had the act promised *no* jail time; had that been the case, why bother breaking the windows?

However, there is a further and independent question whether people should be given what they deserve for criminal behavior performed out of desperate need. If not, then providing Makepeace with a warm place to sleep is the appropriate response to his wrongful conduct, even if he thereby fails to receive what he deserves. The point, put more generally, is that an account of what makes one form of treatment more deserved than another does not imply that there are no other considerations besides desert that are relevant to the question of how the state should respond to wrongful behavior. The fact that desperate need led to crime matters to the appropriate state response, although not to what is deserved for the crime; and other things, potentially, matter just as much or more.

Of course, not all cases of wrongful behavior by agents with idiosyncratic modes of transaction with reasons are performed out of desperate need or include some other factor that warrants the state in choosing a less deserved response over a more deserved. We can imagine someone who commits Makepeace's crime out of the desire to spend his days lifting weights and knowing he will have that opportunity in jail. For him, a judge who sentences to a year in jail essentially offers a state-funded gym membership. Or, on the other side, we can imagine someone who is very strongly rationally averse to jail time, far more so than is normal, so that for him the prospect of one minute in jail would suffice to place the crime in the same space of reasons as the act occupies for the ideal agent. For him, it would appear, one minute in jail is closer to being deserved than is a year, or even two minutes.

To respond to cases of this kind, it is important to remind ourselves of what is being assumed about the relevant hypothetical agents in drawing from ISR what can seem to be peculiar implications about them. It is being assumed that there is a rational deliberative route from the peculiar fact of relevance (e.g. that the crime promises the opportunity to lift weights every day) to commission of the crime, and further that the agent is disposed to grant sufficient weight to this factor as to outweigh those factors that matter to normal agents (e.g. that the act also promises significant limitations on liberty). An agent, for instance, who would reach the conclusion that the crime is worth doing for the sake of the opportunity to lift weights *only because he irrationally ignores the awful things that the crime also promises* is not an example of an agent of the kind who currently concerns us. Such an agent does not have modes of transaction with reasons thanks to which there is sufficient reason for him to commit the crime given the prospect of time to lift weights. Rather, his relevant dispositions to recognize and weigh reasons are not activated by the prospect of a year in jail. Put another way, we cannot in his case gauge what his relevant modes of transaction with reasons are by asking him what he would choose, for when he is asked, other features of his psychology drive his answer (such as his tendency not to think straight when beguiled by the prospect of lifting weights all the time). The potentially problematic cases, in contrast, are those in which the agent truly possesses modes of transactions with reasons under which he grants greater reason-giving weight to the prospect of lifting weights every day than to the deprivations of freedom that jail time will involve.

The same point can be made about cases in which the agent is far more rationally averse to something than is normal. The problematic case is not the agent who irrationally panics at the prospect of even a minute in jail and so will rashly reach the conclusion that the crime is not worth performing given that possibility. The potentially problematic case is the agent who would reach such a conclusion even while deliberating rationally. What I suspect is that at least some of the intuitions opposing ISR deriving from reflection on what is deserved by idiosyncratic agents are not actually driven by a conception of what I am calling "idiosyncratic agents" but are driven, instead, by a conception of *irrational* agents whose choices are often the product of mechanisms distinct from the activation of dispositions to recognize, weigh, and respond to reasons. But dispositions to behave irrationally are not dispositions of the kind that bear on what a person deserves, so no counterintuitive conclusions will follow about such agents. I am biting the bullet (if a bullet it is), that is, about a smaller number of cases than one might have imagined. The irrational, who are also disposed to grant the prospect of prison the same reason-giving weight as the rest of us, deserve just what the rest of us deserve, under ISR. And they are easily confused with the idiosyncratic agents.

Note, in addition, that the kinds of considerations that are being put forth here to object to my theory of comparative desert—what is deserved more than what varies among agents to the extent that modes of transactions with reasons vary among agents—are endemic to the very idea of proportionality.[13] Place a very tall person in a jail cell with a short bed and you have inflicted a greater punishment than you inflict when you place a short person in that same cell. Should we say, then, that the degree of punishment, and so what punishment is proportional to a given crime, is a function of height? It seems to me very unlikely that a theory of *proportionality* is going to solve this problem. Examples of this kind, that is, do not demonstrate that what is proportional to what does not vary from person to person. Rather, they show that principles limiting punishments to those that are proportional have limits. The true principle of proportionality does not say "Do not inflict disproportional punishments" but, instead, "Do not inflict punishments that would be disproportional (and excessive) if inflicted on normal citizens." What's proportional to a given form of wrongdoing *does* vary from wrongdoer to wrongdoer, although probably less than one might imagine. But the constraint that the principle of proportionality places on the government does not.

---

[13] Adam Kolber makes the point. See Adam Kolber (2009) "The Subjective Experience of Punishment" in *The Columbia Law Review*, v. 109, 182–237.

It seems to me that the same thing is true of desert. (In fact, the concept of proportionality might, in the end, just *be* the concept of desert.) What is deserved for a given form of wrongdoing *does* vary with variation in modes of transactions with reasons. But the constraint that desert places on the government does not.

In short, then, I embrace the implication of ISR under discussion in this subsection. I believe that the set of cases that can appear counterintuitive in light of it is smaller than one might imagine. I also accept that, with respect to those cases, the right thing for the government to do might well be to issue a punishment that is less deserved in comparison to no punishment at all. It was better, all told, to give Jamaine Makepeace a punishment that was, for him, less deserved than setting him free. I do not believe that this is an implication of ISR for which an apology is needed.

4.2 Criminal Punishment and Culpability

As was suggested in the introduction to this chapter, while a theory of desert ought to conform, roughly, to intuition—it ought to classify cases in roughly the way in which intuition classifies them—it is more important that it illuminate relationships between desert and other properties of interest to life and to philosophical theory. A theory of desert, that is, is to be measured less by its capacity to make explicit the grounds for what we already know through intuition than it is by its capacity to teach us something that we did not already know, even if we suspected it to be true. This section, therefore, is aimed at completing the argument for ISR by demonstrating two things. First, I will show that, under ISR, the psychological states that guided a wrongful act bear on the question of the degree to which a given form of punishment for the act is deserved. Culpability, that is, bears on desert. The argument for this conclusions draws on the theory of culpability offered in chapter 3. Second, I will show that, under ISR, one criminal punishment is more likely to be justified than another if it is more deserved for the crime. This provides a step towards a vindication of retributivist views about punishment. While we might already have thought that these two things were true, ISR helps to explain why they are true.

4.2.1 Culpability

It is obvious that wrongdoers differing only in mental state can deserve different punishments. The person who intentionally runs down his neighbor deserves a much harsher punishment than the one who does so negligently. This is true even if the neighbor suffers no more in the one case than the other; even if the collateral consequences of the death, for the neighbor's children, say, are the same in both cases; and even if both wrongdoers hate the neighbor and stand to inherit from his will. Hold everything fixed other than mental state, and you still find differences in desert.

I believe that theorists have not been sufficiently puzzled by this. Why should small differences in psychology make for large differences in desert? Psychological differences that would be incredibly hard to detect in a psychology lab—to detect them at all would require inventive experiments and equipment for measuring things like reaction times and eye-tracking—make enormous moral differences. Why? The answer is that where there are small differences in psychology there are differences in modes of transaction with reasons. And as we saw in chapter 3, where there are differences in modes of transaction with reasons, there are differences, also, in culpability. But, and this is the crucial point, where there are differences in modes of transaction with reasons there are also differences in the form of rational support that the act has, relative to the agent. The act occupies a different place in the space of reasons, and so a different punishment must be attached to it to move it closer to the place in the space of reasons that it occupies for the ideal agent. Add ISR and we reach the result that where we find differences in psychological states guiding action we find differences in desert.

Further, this simple link between culpability and desert explains why intent seems to be at "the top" of the culpability hierarchy. It explains, that is, why intentional harming is deserving of greater punishment than harming knowingly, inadvertently, or through the conscious imposition of risk. The reason is that those who intend harm grant the fact that an act promises harm positive reason-giving weight in their deliberations about what to do.[14] By contrast, those who know that their act will produce harm, but do not intend that harm, need not. They may grant no reason-giving weight to that fact, but take the act to be worth performing because of other features of it. By contrast, the ideal agent takes the fact that the act will cause harm as a reason *not* to perform it. The result is that we need to attach something worse to the act (by the agent's lights) to move it into the same place in the space of reasons that it occupies for the intending agent than for the knowing. And the same point applies to those who harm knowingly in contrast to those who harm through the conscious imposition of risk. For those who consciously impose risk, we need to attach something to the act that counts against it (by the agent's lights) to the extent that *the risk* of harm counts against it. But since risks of harm are not as bad as guaranteed harms, less aversive consequences need to be attached to the act to "correct" its position in the space of reasons when the act is performed recklessly than when it is performed knowingly.[15]

The point just made is connected to the well-known current debate in ethics and moral psychology as to whether the permissibility of an act depends on the intention with which the act is performed.[16] Those who think that intentions are irrelevant to permissibility should embrace ISR for the reasons just described. After all, the primary datum in support of the claim that intentions matter to permissibility is that they

---

[14] In fact, this is true even if the act is intended merely as a means. The reason is that for those who intend the means, the reasons for pursuing the end are reasons to undertake the act.

[15] I develop this idea in a couple of different places. See Gideon Yaffe (2012) "Intoxication, Recklessness and Negligence" in *Ohio State Journal of Criminal Law*, v. 9: 545–82; Gideon Yaffe (2010) *Attempts: In the Philosophy of Action and the Criminal Law*, Oxford: Oxford University Press, esp. chs 1 & 2; Gideon Yaffe (2014a) "Criminal Attempts" in *The Yale Law Journal*, v. 124: 92–156.

[16] See Thomas Scanlon (2008) *Moral Dimensions: Permissibility, Meaning, Blame*, Cambridge: Harvard University Press, esp. ch 1. For one particularly illuminating discussion see, Dana Nelkin and Sam Rickless (2014) "Three Cheers for Double Effect" in *Philosophy and Phenomenological Research*, 89(1): 125–58.

matter to desert. But if what one deserves turns not just on the nature of the wrongdoing in which one engaged, but also on one's degree of culpability for such wrongdoing, then it is possible to explain this datum without asserting that intentions matter to permissibility. However, the point here is also compatible with the claim that intentions can matter to permissibility. To say that what a person deserves is a function of culpability is not to deny that it is also a function of wrongdoing. Of course, where there is greater wrongdoing greater punishments are deserved. But it is possible that intentions matter to wrongdoing, as well as culpability, and so matter to desert in two ways. In fact, it seems likely that this is the case for any morally relevant act type defined, in part, by the mental states from which it is performed. If lying essentially involves intent to deceive, then there are two reasons why a liar deserves a worse punishment than someone who merely speaks falsely: he engaged in a worse form of wrongdoing, he *lied*, and, second, he took the fact of his utterance's falsehood as a positive reason in favor of making it when the ideal agent, and the person who did not intentionally speak falsely, by contrast, take it to be a reason against.

The central point of this subsection—namely that ISR is given support by its capacity to explain why culpability matters to desert—can be flipped. One might wonder why the property that ISR identifies—the property, possessed by a form of suffering, of providing a greater corrective to the past act's place in the space of reasons than another form of suffering provides—should be thought to pertain to *desert*. That is, one might suggest that it is one thing to say that one form of suffering has this property more than another, and another to say that it is therefore *more deserved* for past wrongdoing than the other. But we now have part of an answer to this objection to hand: changes in mental state result in changes in the property of interest *and also* result in changes in desert. And the two changes align. This should give us confidence that the property identified in ISR *is* desert.

4.2.2 Justified criminal punishment

Retributivists believe that a criminal punishment is justified only if it is deserved. This is, in the first instance, a claim about non-comparative desert. The claim implies, for instance, that a year in prison is an unjustified punishment for littering since it is not deserved, but excessive. This claim is compatible with the further claim that a year in prison for littering is more deserved than two years. But the retributivist's view also has positive implications for ordinal desert. In particular, retributivists will agree to the following: *Ceteris paribus, if P1 is more deserved for D's C-ing than P2 is, then P1 is closer to being a justified punishment for C-ing than P2 is.*[17] Justification, like desert, is a threshold concept. And, as in the case of desert, it is hard to know how to specify the relevant threshold. But, still, there is a meaningful sense in which one form of treatment

---

[17] Those who accept this can also hold (and should) that it might be unjustified, all told, to inflict either P1 or P2 for independent reasons having nothing to do with desert (perhaps the world would end). It is true that some retributivists believe that if a punishment is deserved, then it is justified to inflict it. However, this stronger position is not under consideration here.

can be more justified than another, even if it is not justified full stop, because it is below the relevant threshold, or even if both are justified full stop, because they are both above it. What retributivists are committed to is the claim that when we hold fixed everything besides desert, for a punishment to be more deserved is also for it to be more justified. The goal in this subsection is to show that this claim follows from ISR, given some plausible supporting assumptions.

We can make a step towards that goal by identifying one meaningful sense in which something can be easier to justify than something else. When a person to whom you are doing something cannot complain about it, or cannot offer some particular complaint, it is easier to justify your conduct than it would be if he could offer the complaint. Easier to justify can mean, that is, that there are fewer complaints to respond to, or answer. A person might not be able to offer a complaint because the complaint has no merit at all, not even enough to warrant an answer. He also might not be able to offer a complaint because he lacks standing to offer it, whether or not it has merit. It is easier to justify giving someone a taste of *his own* medicine than it is to justify giving him a taste of medicine that he has not inflicted on others. The reason is that those who have given others bitter medicine lack standing to complain when they too are given that medicine. And this is true whether or not there is merit in administering the bitter medicine. The result is that if X does the same thing to Y as he does to Z, where there is equal merit or demerit in X's doing it, respectively, it can nonetheless be easier to justify doing it to Y than to Z, for Y might lack standing to make a complaint that Z has every right to make. This simple observation is the key, I believe, to understanding why it is easier to justify criminal punishments that are more deserved, under ISR.[18]

Imagine that X is considering doing A, and Y does not want him to do it. Ordinarily, Y has every right to raise the following point in favor of X's refraining: If X A's, then there will be less reason for Y to have pursued some past course of conduct he undertook than he rationally thought, at the time, that there was. This matters because if X A's, he interferes in an important way with Y's autonomy. He does not interfere by preventing Y from doing something that he wants to do. This might be true, but it is not what Y is complaining about. Rather, he interferes by transforming Y's past act from one that was supported by reasons, and autonomously performed in light of that fact, into one that actually runs counter to what Y himself would have pursued, had he known what X would go on to do. The fact that I made a reservation weeks ago for us at a sushi restaurant tonight provides a reason for you not to give up eating fish this morning. The problem of interest isn't that I want to have sushi with you tonight. The problem is that by giving up fish, you undermine the sense in which my past act was supported by reasons. And in so far as part of what it is to act autonomously is to act in ways supported by reasons, by giving up fish you interfere with the autonomy of my

---

[18] I take the point here to be compatible with the approach to the justification of punishment, and the role of desert in such a justification, offered in Mitchell Berman (2008) "Punishment and Justification" in *Ethics* 118(2): 258–90.

past act by weakening the rational support for its performance. This does not mean that you ought to stick to eating fish. This is only one reason, after all. But it is a reason. Or, put another way, if you give up eating fish, and I complain that I made plans for us to eat sushi tonight, part of what is required for you to justify your act is to answer this complaint. Perhaps you can do that easily: you are acting on doctor's orders, or have had a crisis of conscience about supporting the fish industry, or, just, let's face it, the reservation isn't that important. But still, it is a task you need to perform. Ordinarily, that is, the preservation of the rational support that each agent took there to be for his projects provides a defeasible constraint on the behaviors of others. The constraint is defeasible in the way in which any reason is defeasible; there can be, and often are, stronger reasons pointing the other way.

Let's assume that an agent who offers this kind of complaint is speaking the truth. He speaks the truth when he says, "If you A, then that will weaken the reasons I had to B in the past." Still, you should only take this complaint seriously—you should only see it as providing a reason for you not to act—if you also think that he is entitled to the perspective from which his past behavior, B, had the rational support he took it to have. If you think that he *ought to* have had modes of recognition and weighing of reasons thanks to which the rational support for B was quite different from what he took it to have been, then his complaint requires further scrutiny before it is honored. Even in that case, however, you would still have to take the complaint seriously if the rational support he would have assigned to B, knowing that you would A later, is no closer to that which he ought to have assigned to B in the absence of that knowledge. To ignore his complaint, you need to think, that is, that the rational support he would have assigned to B, given that you would A, was closer to what he ought to have assigned B considered independently of your A-ing. You need to think that by A-ing you place B in *a better* place in the space of reasons than you would by refraining. If you think both that he shouldn't have recognized and weighed reasons in the way that he did, and also that were you to act then the form of rational support he assigned to his act would have been closer to what it should have been, then you can ignore his complaint. But, of course, this is precisely the state of things if your act gets closer to giving him what he deserves for his past act, under ISR, than refraining would have done. The result: if you are contemplating giving him what he deserves for his conduct, under ISR, it is easier to justify your act than it would be if this were not true. One complaint that he would ordinarily be able to make, given that he doesn't want you to treat him that way, is silenced.

The argument of the last paragraph is the central point of this subsection and so it is worth offering it again, less abstractly. Imagine that D committed a robbery yesterday and the question is whether we are more justified in incarcerating him for fifteen years or, instead, in letting him walk. Imagine that he offers the following complaint: "If I had known that the robbery promised fifteen years in prison, that would have radically altered the rational support that I took it to have; in fact, it would have had substantially less rational support. So, if you now incarcerate me for fifteen years you are interfering with my autonomous agency by radically altering the rationality of my past act of robbery." This is a lame complaint. But why? After all, the parallel complaint in cases in which the past act is not wrongful, much less legally prohibited, has some force; it needs to be answered. Why does this complaint need no answer? The reason is that D should have refrained from robbery *even if there was no prison term attached to it*. That is, D should have taken there to be insufficient reason to commit robbery. So if he would have taken there to be insufficient reason to commit robbery *given that it has a prison term attached to it*, then he lacks the standing to complain about the prison term. To validly complain about the prison term on the grounds that it alters his reasons to commit robbery, the agent needs to be able to show that the alteration would not be an improvement. But *if a prison term is deserved under ISR*, then this condition is not met. What follows is that under ISR, when a punishment is more deserved, a certain kind of complaint about it is weakened or undermined. And when complaints about a punishment are undermined or weakened, it is easier to justify imposing the punishment.

The same point can be seen with a different kind of example. Imagine that D litters and the question is whether to give him a $100 fine or, instead, a year in prison. About the year in prison D has a valid complaint: if he had known that littering promised a year in prison, he would have taken it to be far less choice-worthy, far less supported by reasons, than the ideal agent would have taken it to be. And so he can validly complain that a year in prison would involve an inappropriate incursion on his autonomous agency. By contrast, the parallel complaint about the $100 fine is either completely inept, or, at least, far weaker. Had he known that littering promises a $100 fine, he would have taken littering to have had a form of rational support much closer to that that the ideal agent would take littering to have. Again, the result is that those punishments that are more deserved, under ISR, are easier to justify because this particular kind of complaint about them is weakened or undermined.

The result of the last few paragraphs is that ISR accounts for something that a theory of desert should account for. It explains why punishments that are more deserved are easier to justify. This is an argument in ISR's favor, far stronger, I believe, than ISR's alignment with intuitions about ordinal desert.

A further point can be made here: ISR sheds light on an important issue in the philosophy of punishment. Opponents of deterrence theories sometimes note that few people who comply with the law do so out of fear of punishment. Each of us has many opportunities to kill others in the course of an average day. Why do we decline these opportunities? It is very rarely out of fear of punishment. Most of us never even seriously consider committing murder, it never even crosses our minds, much less consider it deeply enough to make some kind of calculation of the pros and cons. And even those who become riled up enough to really think about killing another usually refrain out of recognition of what an awful thing it is to do. They never have, nor would they be praiseworthy for having, the extra thought that it would be terrible to be punished. On the flipside, it is only rarely that those who commit crimes do so after making a calculation that involves consideration of the expected value of punishment. Such calculations may take place for some crimes, such as, perhaps, property crimes, more than others, but it seems very unlikely that they take place as a rule even with respect to those crimes. And there are some crimes (think about rape, for instance) where such calculations seem anathema to the mental state that ordinarily gives rise to them. Deterrence theorists, then, seem to want to justify punishment through appeal to the way in which it engages psychological mechanisms of action-generation *that are almost never involved in generating either law-abiding or criminal behavior*. This is like justifying leaching by appeal to the bad-bile theory of disease; since the theory is false, as an empirical matter, the justification that appeals to it falls flat.

This seems to me to be a decisive reason to reject deterrence theories, in their baldest forms. But, still, the deterrence theorist is right that there is something superior about punishments that make it more rational to refrain from the crimes to which they attach than to follow through with them. A slap on the wrist is an insufficient punishment for grand theft precisely because someone who thinks grand theft is worth committing will also think it worth committing when conjoined with a slap on the wrist. The deterrence theorist thinks that this simple insight is best explained by the further claim that the point of punishment is to deter. But then the deterrence theorist falls afoul of the following undeniable fact: punishments that make the crimes to which they attach not worth doing do not, thereby, cause people to refrain from them. The simple reason for this is that hardly anyone refrains out of fear of punishment. But ISR provides an alternative explanation for the simple insight that punishments are better when they make crimes irrational: punishments that alter the rational support for crimes in such a way as to make them not worth doing move them closer to the position in the space of reasons that they occupy for the ideal agent. And, given ISR, this means that they are more deserved than nothing. Add that it is easier to justify more deserved punishments than less, and we are able to explain *on retributivist grounds* the simple insight motivating many deterrence theorists.

4.3 Conclusion

This chapter began with the idea of *lex talionis*, an eye for an eye, and so it is fitting to return to that idea briefly. I suspect that the reason that losing an eye seems a particularly fitting response to putting out another's eye is that we assume that selfishness is the source of the distortions in the modes of transactions with reasons of the person who puts out another's eye. This is to assume two things: first, that the agent grants appropriate reason-giving weight to all the features of the act thanks to which *he* is affected by it, and, second, he grants inappropriate weight to those features thanks to which *others* are affected by it. But if selfishness of this kind is the source of the problem, then a perfect corrective is one in which the agent would have inflicted on himself precisely what he inflicts on others. Such a treatment would induce him to engage his self-regarding modes of recognition and weighing of reasons when deliberating about other-affecting aspects of his act. Since, by hypothesis, his self-regarding modes are just like those of the ideal agent, such treatment would therefore induce him to have other-regarding modes that were also similar to those of the ideal agent. This is why, also, that when a blind man puts out another's eye, he does not receive what he deserves when he has his eye put out (assuming that sight is the only thing lost in the loss of an eye). Even if selfishness was the source of the distortion in his modes of recognition and weighing of reasons, being blind, he does not grant the same kind and degree of reason-giving weight to the loss of an eye that the ideal agent grants to the other's loss of an eye. Ultimately, that is, the kinds of intuitions that are supported by *lex talionis* have their source, I suggest, in acceptance of ISR together with simplifying moral assumptions about the pattern in distortion in the wrongdoers' modes of recognition and weighing of reasons.

The idea of desert for wrongdoing—an idea that entails that what a person has done can make it fitting for him to suffer something that anyone would do anything to avoid—is sometimes characterized as primitive, and unenlightened. Toddlers strike back at those who take their toys. Of course, the fact that a concept emerges early, much less that it takes very little experience to learn to apply it, should not count against it. In fact, those very facts about some concepts count in favor of their claim to importance and fundamentality; think of the concept of number.

Desert is with greater justice sometimes characterized as mysterious. Talk of desert, it is sometimes thought, is like talk of bad karma: such talk is evocative but, in the end, it is talk about nothing. Sometimes the thought that desert is a fundamentally mysterious notion is expressed by coupling it with a claim to the effect that people deserve this or that only given some non-naturalistic view—dualism about the mind and body, or agent-causalism about free will, for instance. But whether a derogatory attitude towards desert is justified depends entirely on what desert is. If, when we figure that out, we find that the concept is not just intelligible, but domestic, then we should rest easy in our use of it. And that, it has been suggested here, is precisely what we find. To predicate our behavior, and the behavior of the state, on desert, it has been argued here, is to predicate it on something familiar. Ultimately, to give someone what they deserve for bad behavior is to give them that which would induce them to conceptualize the rational support for that behavior in the way they should. There is nothing strange about that, nothing mysterious, and nothing that commits one to metaphysical excess. To stop fearing desert, we need only see it for what it is.

As we will see in the chapters to come, by seeing desert for what it is, and by seeing its link to culpability, as culpability is characterized in chapter 3, we are able to ground our leniency towards kids *in* desert. We are justified in giving kids a break, as we will see, because they deserve it, in the very sense of desert described here.

5

The Weight of a Legal Reason

5.0 Introduction

The last two chapters offered a pair of positions, one concerning the nature of criminal culpability, the other the nature of desert for criminal behavior. These two positions are closely linked and draw on a common concept: the concept of legal reasons for action, and, particularly, legal reasons for refraining from conduct prohibited by a criminal statute. In addition, the two positions depend on the idea that the legal reasons to refrain from conduct differ in strength or weight. It is more culpable to manifest in one's conduct a mode of transaction with reasons that involves disregarding a weightier legal reason than a less weighty one. And, a person deserves to suffer to a greater degree for her wrongful conduct if she had a weightier legal reason to refrain from the conduct, than if she had a less weighty reason.

As we will see in chapter 6, the accounts of criminal culpability and desert offered in chapters 3 and 4, respectively, imply, together with some supporting ideas to be developed there, that kids are to be given a break because they are reduced in culpability relative to adults, and deserve a more lenient response to their wrongful behavior. This is true despite the fact that they are not to be given a break for the reasons proposed by the Proxy for Culpability, Kids Will Be Kids, or They'll Grow Out of It arguments, rejected in chapters 1 and 2. They are reduced in culpability and deserving of leniency not because of anything going along with youth that gives rise to crime—such as psychological dispositions distinctive of the young, developmental normality of criminogenic psychological dispositions, or the impermanence of the condition—but because they are subject to less demanding criminal culpability standards than adults. The bar is lower for them thanks to the limited role we have granted them to contribute to the creation and authority of law. We should give kids a break because of the political meaning of age.

But behind this argument for giving kids a break, an argument to be developed in chapter 6, lies a jurisprudential theory, a theory about the nature of legal reasons, and particularly a theory of what it is for legal reasons to have weight or strength. The disclosure of that theory is the aim of this chapter.

To describe the aim of the chapter this way, however, is grandiose in one important respect. The chapter makes no original contribution to the variety of debates among the various strains of positivism or natural law theory, whether of the Austinian,

Hartian, Razian, Dworkinian, or Finnissian variety.[1] Rather, I accept and do not defend a legal positivist position that allows for the possibility that moral features and facts can give legal reasons for acting and refraining in various ways. Section 5.1 explains what, exactly, this commitment amounts to. What I say there will be familiar to anyone who has taken or taught a course in the philosophy of law. The modest contribution of this chapter is in its canvassing of the various senses in which legal reasons can differ in strength or weight. Section 5.2, and its subsections, identify three different kinds of weight that a legal reason can have. What really matters for the argument to be developed in chapter 6, however, is another observation offered in section 5.2: how strong a legal reason is *for a particular person* is a function both of the legal reason's weight, in one of the three senses identified, *and also* the degree to which the person enjoys a full share of, or has a full say over, those facts in virtue of which the relevant fact provides a legal reason of a particular strength. The final subsection of section 5.2 says a word about the way in which this account of a legal reason's weight for a particular citizen informs our standards for criminal culpability, and desert for wrongdoing, given the accounts of those notions offered in chapters 3 and 4. The purpose of this chapter, then, is not the grand one of building a jurisprudential foundation for the view to be offered of the grounds for giving kids a break, but, rather, the more modest one of supplementing, with some remarks about the weight of legal reasons, a foundation built in the last century or so by the defenders of legal positivism.

5.1 Legal Positivism and the Incorporation of the Moral into the Legal

The discussion to follow is framed around the idea of a "legal reason." The starting point is the idea that there are many facts, and many fewer reasons. Some facts provide reason for a particular action, but most do not. If I cover my eyes, many, many things will be true. But very few of them provide me with reason to cover my eyes. So to say that there is a reason to do A is to imply that there is some fact that provides a reason to do A. We can also speak of features of acts, rather than facts, as providing reason. But this is shorthand. If an act has a certain reason-providing feature, then what provides reason is the fact that the act has that feature.

Further, we are familiar, in other settings, with modifiers of the term "reason." We speak of prudential reasons, and moral reasons, and religious reasons, among others. These modifiers imply something about the source of the fact's reason-giving power. If there's a moral reason, then there is a fact that provides reason in virtue of the body of moral facts, facts about what is morally permissible, impermissible, obligatory, and so

---

[1] John Austin (1832) *The Province of Jurisprudence Determined*, London: Weidenfeld & Nicolson; H.L.A. Hart (1961) *The Concept of Law*, Oxford: Clarendon Press; Joseph Raz (1979) *The Authority of Law*, Oxford: Clarendon Press; Ronald Dworkin (1986) *Law's Empire*, Cambridge: Harvard University Press; John Finnis (1980) *Natural Law and Natural Rights*, Oxford: Clarendon Press.

on. If there's a prudential reason, there is a fact that provides reason in virtue of the facts about what is in people's interests. And the same thing is true of aesthetic reasons, religious reasons, and other sorts. In all these cases, to say that there is an x-reason is to imply that there is a fact that provides a reason in virtue of a body of x-facts. The same is true of legal reasons. To say that there is a legal reason to do this or that act is to imply that there is a fact (perhaps the fact that this or that act has such-and-such feature) that provides a reason to do this or that in virtue of the body of legal facts.

Note that to say this much is to imply nothing one way or the other about whether there is a reason—moral? prudential? legal?—to obey the law. The question of whether there is such a reason is the question of whether the fact *that a particular type of act is legally prohibited* (for instance) provides a reason to refrain from engaging in an act of that type. That is a different question from the question of whether, for instance, the fact *that the act is a taking of something of someone else's without his permission* provides a reason to refrain from the act. Illegality is just one kind of feature that some acts possess and so we can ask about it, just as we can ask about any other feature of an act, whether it provides a reason—moral, prudential, legal—for engaging in, or refraining from engaging in, the act. The very idea of a legal reason provides us with no answer to that question.

The view of the strength of legal reasons propounded in section 5.2 presupposes a positivist view of the nature of law, a view that nonetheless allows for the possibility that moral features of acts (such as the feature of being morally wrongful) and moral facts (such as the fact that a particular act is morally wrongful) can provide legal reason for action. The first subsection says a word about positivism, the second about the idea that law can incorporate morality.

5.1.1 *Positivism*

Legal positivists believe that there are distinctive legal reasons for action that supervene on social facts, such as the facts about the social practice of creating a constitution and following the procedures specified by it for enactment of law. I take the claim of supervenience to be neutral with respect to competing conceptions of the metaphysical status of the "higher-order" properties that supervene on those of a "lower order." One who holds that mental properties supervene on physical might believe that there are no mental properties, or that mental properties exist but are reducible to physical, or that mental properties have no subordinate metaphysical status relative to physical but just happen to exist if and only if certain complexes of physical properties exist. Similarly, the positivist claim that legal reasons supervene on social facts will be taken, for our purposes, to be neutral with respect to all the various positions that one might hold as to whether the furniture of the universe includes legal reasons. What matters is only that what legal reasons there are is a function of what the social facts are.

The idea that the legal reasons are *distinctive* is important to the kind of positivism with which I am associating myself. The belief is that reasons fall into various categories.

There are, uncontroversially, both moral and prudential reasons, for instance. There are reasons to do what is morally obligatory, for example, and reasons to do what is in one's best interests. And while these two kinds of reasons have a complicated relationship—it might turn out that the moral reasons are a special subset of the prudential, or vice versa, or not—there is no denying that there are these *two kinds of reasons*. A presupposition of positivism, and, also of its opponents, is that there is a third kind of reason also, namely legal reasons, that, in turn, bears a complicated relationship to moral and prudential reasons (not to mention other sets of reasons, such as aesthetic reasons).[2] The further claim, distinctive of positivism, is that the facts about legal reasons depend, supervene on, a certain set of social facts, although there is, of course, substantial disagreement among positivists about which social facts are constitutive of the facts about legal reasons.

One of the interesting things about law is that it plays a substantial role in determining what facts are included in the supervenience base for the facts about legal reasons. The law often tells us what facts constitute legal reasons. It is not just that what the law is varies with what the social facts are, but also that what social facts determine what the law *is* is, in part, determined by the law. Say that an act I am considering would be one of taking something of someone else's without his permission. I have a legal reason not to perform that token act. The relevant legal reason supervenes on (among other things) the features of the act, namely that it is a taking of something that does not belong to me, and without permission. But the act has many other features: it's the act of a body at 98.6 degrees Fahrenheit, for instance. But *that* feature of the act is not relevant to my legal reason to refrain from it; it's not in the supervenience base. Why does the legal reason to refrain supervene on the features of being a taking without permission of something that does not belong to me, and not on other features of the act? Answer: Because there is a statute that prohibits theft, and that statute was passed by the legislature and signed by the president. If we ask why it is that a statute passed by the legislature and signed by the president generates a legal reason to refrain from the behavior that it identifies, while a statute that I scrawled on the back of an envelope (or even published as a model in a law review) generates no legal reason for anyone to do anything, the answer is that passage by the legislature, followed by signature by the president, is what is specified *by law* as law-creating; scrawling on an envelope (or publishing in a law review) is not a legally authoritative procedure for creation of law

---

[2] It is this presupposition that both Scott Hershovitz and Mark Greenberg take themselves to be attacking. See, for instance, Scott Hershovitz (2015) "The End of Jurisprudence" in *The Yale Law Journal*, 124(4): 1160–204; Mark Greenberg (2014) "The Moral Impact Theory of Law" in *The Yale Law Journal*, 123: 1288; Mark Greenberg (2011) "The Standard Picture and Its Discontents" in *Oxford Studies in Philosophy of Law*, Leslie Green and Brian Leiter (eds.), Oxford: Oxford University Press. However, both Hershovitz and Greenberg grant that there are reasons to which the label "legal" properly attaches and reasons to which it does not attach. They also think that the legal reasons are merely a subset of the moral. But that is not to deny that there are distinctive legal reasons in the sense in which I have in mind. In just the way that those who think that moral reasons are just a subset of the prudential reasons do not deny that there are moral reasons, the view that the legal reasons are a subset of the moral is not a denial of the view that there are distinctive legal reasons. Eagles are distinctive, even though they are birds.

according to the law. The reason, that is, that features of the act I am considering together with facts about legislative votes and presidential signatures are in the supervenience base for legal reasons, and facts about what was scrawled on envelopes are not, *is because the law says so*.[3]

This is importantly different from morality. It is in the hands of legal actors to determine what the content of the law is, and so it is sometimes in the hands of legal actors to determine what facts are and are not in the supervenience base of legal reasons. Legal actors can adopt direct democracy, thus causing it to be the case that that for which the majority of citizens has voted is included in the supervenience base of the legal reasons. Or legal actors can reject direct democracy, thus excluding those facts from the supervenience base. By contrast, it is not in the hands of people to determine what facts are in the supervenience base for moral reasons. People can decide whether, for instance, to cause pain. But they cannot decide whether the fact that an act will cause pain is included in the supervenience base for the facts about what moral reasons there are to engage in or refrain from the act. In the case of legal reasons, and not in the case of moral, the very boundaries of the supervenience base are, at least to some degree, in our hands. They are in our hands to the extent to which the law is in our hands, including laws about how to make and change law.

There is, of course, a famous problem in jurisprudential theory about how, exactly, the law acquires the power to cause certain sets of facts to be legal-reason-generating. Legislators have the power to place features of a potential act (e.g. the taking of something of someone else's without permission) into the supervenience base of legal reasons only thanks to the fact that they have been elected. But elections supply legal authority only because the law says so. And the statements that say so only have legal authority because those who wrote them had legal authority. And so on. At the bottom, as it were, there must be something that gets legal authority not thanks to the fact that something else has legal authority, but for some other reason. Positivists hold that the supervenience base of these fundamental legal facts does not include anything normative, anything about what people ought or ought not to do or how things ought to be.[4]

This can seem puzzling; a derivation of an "ought" from an "is." John Austin's idea of habitual obedience was intended to be a solution to the problem: some people have legal authority just because they are habitually obeyed. H.L.A. Hart's idea of "the internal attitude" was also intended to be a solution to the problem: the law's rules for specifying what facts constitute legal reasons, what Hart called "the rules of recognition," succeed in aiding the specification of the boundaries of the supervenience base, thanks to the fact, Hart thought, that people take the "internal attitude" towards those rules.

---

[3] I take the point of this paragraph to be just the same as H.L.A. Hart's point that the law includes not just primary rules, but secondary rules as well. See H.L.A. Hart (1961) *The Concept of Law*, Oxford: Clarendon Press, esp. ch. 5.
[4] As Scott Shapiro puts it, "[L]egal positivism is necessarily committed to the [thesis that legal facts are ultimately determined by social facts alone]." Scott Shapiro (2011) *Legality*, Cambridge: Harvard University Press, pp. 270, 269.

These theories probably fail.[5] And I will not propose an alternative theory. Rather, what I assume is that the problem admits of positivist solution. I assume, that is, that there is some set of legal facts that supervene on non-normative facts, probably social facts, and, further, in light of these special legal facts it is possible for human actors to specify the further boundaries of the supervenience base for legal reasons to refrain from certain forms of behavior. There are social facts thanks to which a particular set of rules of recognition, when followed, affect the boundaries of the supervenience base while competing rules of recognition do not. Perhaps these are facts about what conventions people have adopted, or perhaps they are facts about citizens' master plan; I am not sure. What matters, for our purposes, is that law's capacity to set the boundaries of the supervenience base is itself constituted by certain social facts.

In short, what I am here committed to is legal positivism—but no particular brand of it. What matters for our purposes is that the proposition expressed by the sentence "D had a legal reason not to take his neighbor's car" can be true thanks to the fact that there is a set of true propositions that do not concern what legal reasons there are but concern, instead, facts about what statutes say, and what legislatures did to cause it to be the case that statutes say those things, and other social facts thanks to which the rules that were followed were themselves such that, by following them, the supervenience base of the legal reasons has certain boundaries.

5.1.2 Moral incorporation

Despite what has just been said about the nature of legal positivism, legal positivists also hold that it is possible for legal reasons to supervene in part on moral facts. This is possible because the law's power to draw the boundary of the supervenience base for legal reasons can be exercised to include certain sets of moral facts within that boundary. This happens when, for instance, a statute identifies what it prohibits as *morally wrongful* behavior of a certain sort, but it also sometimes happens when the law invokes standards of "reasonableness," and through other less obvious means too.

Consider, for instance, the following California statute, mentioned also in chapter 3:

Any person who knowingly...provides false verification as to...the person's authority to sell property in order to receive money...from a pawnbroker...and who receives money...from the pawnbroker...is guilty of theft.   (Cal. Penal Code 484.1(a))

There is at most imperfect overlap between the features of the action of someone who violates this statute thanks to which his act is morally wrongful (considered independently of the moral import of legal prohibition) and the features of his act thanks to which it is prohibited by this statute. The fact, for instance, that the lie is issued *to a pawnbroker*, rather than an ordinary potential buyer, is surely irrelevant from a moral

---

[5] The literature on the topic is not small. For overviews, see Scott Shapiro (2011) *Legality*, Cambridge: Harvard University Press, esp. chs 3 & 4; Andrei Marmor (2011) *Philosophy of Law*, Princeton: Princeton University Press.

point of view. But that fact about the act provides a legal reason not to engage in the act. Pawnbrokers are given special protection under the law—they are protected by Cal. Penal Code 484.1(a)—in a way that other people are not. Morality, considered independently of law, protects pawnbrokers no more than it protects the rest of us. So, the fact that the lie is told to a pawnbroker is in the supervenience base of the legal reasons to refrain from the lie; but the fact would not be in the supervenience base of the moral reasons to refrain, considered independently of law. *Given* that it is legally prohibited to lie *to a pawnbroker*, perhaps the fact that the lie is issued to a pawnbroker has some moral significance; I do not want to rule out the possibility that there is a moral reason to respond to one's legal reasons. But what matters for our purposes is that the legal reason generated by the recipient of the lie's pawnbroker status does not depend, one way or the other, on that fact's antecedent moral import, if it has any.

But notice that the statute also, arguably anyway, requires that the wrongdoer lacks "authority" to sell the relevant property.[6] The statute is thus incorporating standards for authority to sell property that are established elsewhere. And, for all the statute says, those standards might be established by morality. If so, then the statute is giving legal force to a certain set of moral facts, namely the facts about who has authority to sell a piece of property. Of course, the law has a lot to say about that. But morality does too. Say that Finders Keepers is a true moral principle; if you find something that has been abandoned, you have a moral right to it. It would thus follow that a finder has the moral authority to sell that which he finds. Say that a finder is accused under this statute and offers the fact that he found the object in his defense, as a rebuttal of the prosecution's claim that he lacked the authority to sell the object. Such a defense amounts to an effort to show that this statute, the statute under which the defendant is charged, provides no legal reason for him to refrain from the conduct in which he engaged. And the defense establishes this, in this case, only if the law has incorporated what is, by hypothesis, a truth of morality, namely Finders Keepers. Under the kind of legal positivism presupposed here, the law very well may have incorporated this truth, for the law's rules for drawing the boundary of the supervenience base of legal reasons may allow that when the legislature uses the word "authority," as they did in Cal. Penal Code 484.1(a), they thereby cause it to be the case that the supervenience base for facts about the legal reasons to refrain from certain lies includes the moral facts about authority to sell certain objects. This is not to say the *only* facts in the relevant supervenience base are such facts—there are also many arbitrary legal methods for acquiring such authority that have no independent moral import. But the legal positivist holds that it is perfectly possible that the moral facts are included. When we place our focus on the question of what is and is not included in the supervenience base for the facts about legal reasons, and we recognize law's capacity to place it in the hands of people to set the boundaries, it is close

---

[6] This is only "arguable," and not obviously true, because the statute might be interpreted to ban acts of providing false verification of authority even by those who have authority. But set this interpretation aside.

to obvious that moral facts are, potentially, included: people might include them through conduct that, thanks to law, has the power to do so.

The question arises here of what light there is between the legal positivist's view of a legal system in which various moral facts (such as the facts about what objects people have the moral authority to sell) are part of the supervenience base of the legal reasons, and the non-positivist's view of such a legal system. They agree in the observation that what legal reasons there are is a function, in part, of the moral facts. They disagree only in their view of *why* this is so. The positivist believes that the explanation is ultimately rooted in social facts—certain people followed certain procedures for including the moral facts in the supervenience base, procedures that succeed in this respect thanks to having been anointed by law, and the acts of anointing succeeded thanks to certain social facts in virtue of which the anointers had anointing authority. The non-positivist has an alternative explanation. There is an open question as to whether this difference matters to our central purposes here. It may not. But the aim here is to show that there is a plausible jurisprudence that provides what we need, not that it is the exclusive jurisprudential theory that could do so.[7]

5.1.3 Moral reasons, legal reasons

One important thing that sets the jurisprudential position I am presupposing apart from that of some other positivists is that for me the primary object of analysis is *legal reasons* rather than law. Many positivists seem to hold that the question of what the law requires of us—refraining from taking things of others without permission, for instance—and the question of what reasons there are to conform one's behavior to law are separate questions. Sometimes this view falls out of the theorist's positivist position. Joseph Raz, for instance, holds that in light of the law there is reason to act, or refrain from acting, *on* the reasons that there are (moral, prudential, etc.) for engaging in various forms of activity.[8] On this view, then, if the fact that another is a pawnbroker provides no moral or prudential reason (or, anyway, non-legal reason) for or against defrauding him, even taking into consideration the moral and prudential (and other non-legal) reasons that there are to abide by California law, then it is just not true that

---

[7] I believe that the point made in this section—positivists allow that the moral features of acts can be included in the supervenience base of facts about legal reasons—is independent of the debate between inclusive and exclusive legal positivists. (The distinction is first drawn by Jules Coleman (1982) "Negative and Positive Positivism," in v. 11 *Journal of Legal Studies:* 139–64.) Inclusive legal positivists think that rules of recognition (or, more generally, any legally mandated criterion for membership in the supervenience base of legal reasons) can include moral features and moral facts, while the exclusive legal positivist denies it. Whatever's passed by the legislature and signed by the president is law. Could "the president" be defined to be, for instance, "the most virtuous person in the community," where "virtuous" is a moral predicate? The inclusive legal positivist thinks this is possible, the exclusive denies it. But both agree that the legislature could pass a law, and the president could sign it, under which virtuous people need not pay taxes, for instance. So moral incorporation is possible, whether it turns out that inclusive or exclusive legal positivism is correct.

[8] See, for instance, Jospeh Raz (1994) "Authority, Law and Morality" in *Ethics in the Public Domain*, Oxford: Clarendon Press, pp. 210–37.

there is a legal reason provided by the fact that another is a pawnbroker. By contrast, I claim that the fact that the other is a pawnbroker gives one a (legal) reason to refrain from defrauding him that one does not have with respect to neighbors or shopkeepers who do not happen to be pawnbrokers *even if* that fact is of no relevance prudentially, or morally (or in any other non-legal way).

Someone holding the kind of view I reject can agree that the passage of the statute protecting pawnbrokers might *cause* the fact that another is a pawnbroker to be rationally relevant by, for instance, attaching additional penalties to the defrauding of a pawnbroker that there is prudential reason to avoid. There can be deliberative routes from the fact that another is a pawnbroker to refraining from defrauding him. But such deliberative routes are necessarily of a sort that we recognize from reasoning outside of contexts in which there are legal facts to contend with. They are deliberative routes that exhibit the fact in question to generate a prudential reason, or a moral reason (or a reason of some other non-legal sort). What I insist upon, by contrast, is that there is a kind of deliberative route from a fact to an act in light of which it is true that the fact provides a legal reason for or against the act. And I further hold that when Cal. Penal Code 484.1(a) was passed it became the case that there was such a deliberative route from the fact that another is a pawnbroker to the act of refraining from defrauding him. The passage of that statute also made it the case that there were *other* deliberative routes from that fact to that act; a new prudential route emerged, as well, since there is now an additional penalty attached to the act in light of the fact. But the route that I care about is the route in virtue of which the fact provides a legal reason.

I cannot here offer a full defense of my position over competitors, such as Raz's. It would be disingenuous to suggest that the obstacle to offering a full defense is that I do not have space on these pages. Rather, I cannot offer a full defense because I do not have a full defense to offer. I do, however, want to note one important feature of my position that counts in its favor over competitors: my position explains why someone who defrauds another person whom he does not know to be a pawnbroker is not criminally culpable for violation of Cal. Penal Code 484.1(a), and, conversely, why knowledge of that fact counts against a claim that a particular person is not criminally culpable for violation of that statute. The absence of knowledge demonstrates that the act of defrauding the other did not manifest a failure to grant reason-giving weight to the fact that the victim was a pawnbroker. But this shows the actor not to be criminally culpable *only if he should have granted reason-giving weight to that fact*. And he should have granted reason-giving weight to that fact *only if the fact did indeed provide him with reason to refrain from defrauding the other person*. Since the absence of knowledge does indeed undercut the claim that the actor was criminally culpable for violating the statute, it follows that the fact that the other is a pawnbroker provides reason to refrain from defrauding him. And, since this would all be true *even if there were no deliberative route of a moral, prudential, or any other non-legal sort* from the fact to the relevant act, it follows that the fact in question provides a legal reason even if that were so. The result is not that the competitor position (such as Raz's) is mistaken, full stop. The result is, rather, that it is inconsistent with the theory of criminal culpability offered in chapter 3, a theory for which there is independent support. Put more forcefully: The very idea of criminal culpability, if the account offered in chapter 3 is correct, presupposes a jurisprudential theory according to which facts can provide legal reasons even when they do not provide reasons of any other familiar sort.

Some will find it counterintuitive to say, as I am, that in cases in which the criminal law demands things that are out of line with morality—either because the law requires morally impermissible conduct or prohibits morally permissible—that there is *any sense* in which there is a reason to do as the law specifies. They balk at the idea that even in cases in which disobeying the law is morally required, much less morally permissible, that there is a reason (a legal reason, but still) to obey generated by the features of the act in virtue of which it is prohibited. They imagine, for instance, that if the law requires one to submit to being raped—as it did under the notorious "droit du seigneur" laws thought to have been in force in Medieval Europe, and perhaps in other times and places, under which a landowner had the legal right to have sex with a tenant's wife against her will—then we have a case in which the law requires something that there is no reason at all to do, and in fact strong reason to refrain from doing, independently of the harms to be inflicted through enforcement.

But there are two things to be said here that should quiet this concern. First, often efforts to enact laws that are in manifest conflict with morality fail to be enacted simply because regimes that would make such demands lack legal authority and so cannot make law. This is true, when it is, because relevant moral facts have been incorporated into the criteria for legality. This is, arguably, the case with the droit du seigneur. Arguably, that is, the legal criterion of validity was not that whatever the monarch demands is law, but, instead, that whatever the monarch demands, *provided that the opposite is not stringently demanded by morality*, is law. So at least some cases in which it appears that the law makes a demand that there is no reason to comply with are better understood as cases in which there has been a failed effort to make law and so a failed effort to make it the case that a given fact generates a legal reason for action. This is not to say that this will always be so—it is perfectly possible for there to be immoral laws—but only that in some of the more intuitively problematic cases, such as many in which the law *seems* to demand morally egregious conduct, it is so.

Second, to claim that there is a legal reason to do something is not to claim that that is what one should do, all things considered. There are aesthetic reasons to pollute the air—it makes for prettier sunsets—but there is insufficient reason to do it. We need not insist that there is *no reason* to pollute the air in order to agree with the claim that we shouldn't. Similarly, often what one should do is to act contrary to one's legal reasons. Or, to put the point in the language of culpability, often morality requires one to engage in criminally culpable criminal wrongdoing. So, if the droit du seigneur were laws, then they did indeed generate legal reasons to submit to rape. These were cases in which the thing to do, all things considered, was to commit the crime of wholehearted resistance. Although I know that some find this characterization of justified civil disobedience to be strained, it does not seem to me to be more strained than the alternative characterization under which the legality of a norm makes no difference to the degree to which action in compliance with it is supported by reasons.

The advantage of a positivist position is that it allows for conflicts between law and morality. This is attractive since the traditional slogan that an unjust law is no law at all seems to define away the all-too-common phenomenon of morally bad law. Such a natural law view insists on law-morality alignment despite the fact that we often find discord. But to accept the positivist insight while insisting on the claim that there can be no legal reasons where there are no reasons of other sorts, is, again, to insist on law-morality alignment (or, anyway, an alignment between law and other sources of reasons) and so, essentially, to reintroduce the natural law theorist's error. Rather, what we should recognize is that where there is law there are legal reasons, which may or may not align with reasons of other sorts, including moral reasons.

5.2 The Weight of a Legal Reason

The goal of this section is to offer an analysis, or, rather, multiple analyses, of the idea of the ordinal strength of a legal reason. Our question is this: What are the necessary and sufficient conditions under which one legal reason to refrain from doing something is stronger than another? I put the question here in terms of "refraining" from action because the case of interest to us is the case of legal prohibition in which the criminal law specifies that certain acts are not-to-be-done, and are to be punished, if done. One question of relevance is whether the legal reason to refrain from one type of prohibited action is stronger or weaker than the legal reason to refrain from another type of prohibited action. But it is also important to know the conditions under which one feature of an act provides a stronger or weaker legal reason for refraining from it than another feature of that act, or another feature of another distinct act.

So, in short, what we seek is a way of filling in the blank in the following schema, where Q1 is a feature of acts of type C1 and Q2 is a feature of acts of type C2:

> Q1 provides a stronger legal reason for refraining from C1 than Q2 provides for refraining from C2 *if and only if* _____.

This is to represent strength as an ordinal relation. What we are after is what makes one legal reason stronger than another. The target of analysis, then, is not the cardinal strength of a legal reason. This is not to say that I deny that there can be such a thing; I am agnostic. But like many agnostics, I am also doubtful. I strongly suspect that legal reasons are only stronger and weaker than other legal reasons. They have no strength considered in themselves. But I do not want to insist on this point. It will suffice for our purposes to have accounts of the conditions under which one legal reason is stronger than another, and so there is no need to consider what it is for a legal reason to have a non-comparative strength.

As we will see, I do not believe that there is a single, non-disjunctive sense of the strength or weight of a legal reason. Rather, I think there are three meaningful scales on which strength of a legal reason can be measured, useful for different purposes. There may be others, too. I label the three I identify here the *statutory*, the *expressive*, and the *institutional* conceptions of the strength of a legal reason to refrain from conduct prohibited by criminal statute. What we will further see is that the weight that a legal reason has *for a particular person* is (often) a function not just of the legal reason's weight, in one of the three senses identified, but also the degree to which the person has a say over that from which the reason's weight derives.

5.2.1 *The strength of a legal reason: three types*

Those who hold some species of natural law theory, according to which a type of conduct is criminal only if morally wrongful, are likely to find the idea of the strength of a legal reason to refrain from a legally prohibited act to be, if not unproblematic, then at least as unproblematic as the idea of degrees of moral wrongdoing. There is a stronger legal reason to refrain from stealing someone's car than from painting graffiti on it because it is a more grievous moral wrong to steal than to deface another's property. Or, put in the terms of the schema above, Q1 provides a stronger reason than Q2 just in case it makes a greater contribution to the moral wrongfulness of C1 than Q2 makes to the moral wrongfulness of C2.

But an advocate of any form of positivism should pause before accepting this account of the strength of a legal reason. After all, an act's degree of moral wrongdoing is in the supervenience base of the legal reason to refrain from the act only if something in the law has placed it in the supervenience base. And only if the degree of moral wrongdoing of the act is part of what generates the *legal* reason to refrain from performance of the act can degree of moral wrongdoing contribute to the *strength* of the legal reason. A positivist who denies that moral qualities could be given legal force thinks nothing could cause it to be the case that a moral property, like degree of moral wrongfulness, could be in the supervenience base of a legal reason. And so such a positivist cannot allow that degree of moral wrongdoing is part of what constitutes the strength of the legal reason to refrain from the wrongful act.

A positivist who believes in the possibility that moral features can themselves be made to provide legal reason for action can be a bit more liberal on this point. But such a positivist should hold that the degree of moral wrongdoing dictates the strength of the relevant legal reason only if acts in conformity with relevant legal rules have established that this is so. In some legal systems there will be such acts, and in others there will not. In this way, there is nothing special about degree of moral wrongfulness when it comes to the strength of legal reasons to refrain from prohibited acts. A legal system might peg the strength of a legal reason to that in the same way in which it might peg the strength of a legal reason to any other property in virtue of which there is a legal reason to refrain from the act. It is conceptually (albeit only conceptually) just as possible that the strength of a legal reason to refrain will vary with the actor's height as with the relevant degree of moral wrongdoing. It is just a matter of how the legal system in question constructs the boundaries of the supervenience base.

However, the degree of moral wrongdoing involved in a particular act is, often, relevant to the strength of the legal reason to refrain from the act. It is often included in the relevant supervenience base thanks to the machinations of legal actors. But this is because it bears on three different measures of the strength of a legal reason.

Consider, first, the idea that the strength of a legal reason to refrain from an act is a function of the severity of the punishment specified by statute for the act. Put more carefully:

> Q1 provides a *statutorily* stronger legal reason for refraining from C1 than Q2 provides for refraining from C2 *if and only if* The statutorily specified punishment for C1 is, thanks to C1 having Q1, more severe than the statutorily specified punishment for C2, thanks to C2 having Q2.

An implication of the concept of the statutory strength of a legal reason is that the conjunction of all of the features of C1 provides a statutorily stronger legal reason to refrain from C1 than the conjunction of all the features of C2 provides to refrain from C2 *just in case* the statutorily specified punishment for C2 is less than that for C1. Still, it can be useful to consider, also, the statutory strength of the legal reason provided by given, individual features of an act, insufficient, by themselves, for its criminality. Determining this requires determining what portion of the punishment for the act is assigned to it thanks to the fact that it has the specified feature. Absence of permission to take another's property provides a weaker legal reason to refrain from taking it than absence of consent to sex provides for refraining from sex. Both facts account for a sizeable portion of the punishment assigned to theft and rape, respectively. But since the punishments for theft are less than those for rape (let's assume), the severity of the punishment *due to the absence of consent in theft* is less than the severity of the punishment *due to the absence of consent in rape*. Of course, no statute actually *says* this. But it is, nonetheless, a plausible interpretation of the relevant statutory prohibitions.

It is possible for the statutory strength of the reason provided by Q1 to be less than that provided by Q2, even though C1 is punished much more heavily, by statute, than C2. This is obvious when it comes to so called "jurisdictional elements." Consider, for instance, the federal crime in the United States of crossing state lines with intent to have sex with a child (18 U.S.C. §2423(a)). The element of crossing a state line functions to place an attempted child molestation into federal jurisdiction. What portion of the punishment for the crime is *due to its involving a crossing of state lines?* One might think that the answer is "all of it." After all, if the act did not involve a crossing of state lines, it would not be federally prohibited. But this is a mistake. The reason is that the right question is this: why has the state elected to punish *this* as heavily as it has? And the right answer appeals not at all to the fact that it involves a crossing of state lines, and entirely to the fact that the act involves an attempt to molest a child. The federal government takes itself to have the right to punish any crossings of state lines, if it so chooses. Why it chooses to punish *those performed with intent to molest a child*, and not others, is not because crossing state lines is of different significance in some cases than in others. In this way, the crossing of state lines is importantly different from the absence of consent. The absence of consent bears on prohibition and punishment differently depending on whether the act is a taking of property or having sex. But the crossing of state lines is not like that. Rather, the government chooses to punish intending child molesters (who happen to cross state lines) because they are attempting to molest children, period. So the right answer is that *none* of the punishment for the act specified by statute is due to the fact that it involves a crossing of state lines. So: the fact that the act involves a crossing of state lines provides a statutorily weaker reason to refrain from the act than any of the act's other features provide. In fact, the fact that the act involves a crossing of state lines provides a statutorily weaker legal reason than any of the features *of littering* provide to refrain from littering. And this is true even though crossing state lines with intent to molest a child is a far more serious crime than littering.

The degree of moral wrongdoing involved in an act can bear on the statutory strength of the legal reason to refrain from it. Consider a set of statutes that place the act's moral wrongdoing in the supervenience base for the legal reason to refrain from the act. Imagine, to use a toy example, that a statute bans "morally wrongful uses of other people's property." We can then ask what portion of the punishment is assigned to acts falling under this description thanks to the degree of moral wrongfulness of the relevant acts. And we can compare this to the contribution of other features of either this act, or other prohibited acts, to determine whether the statutory strength of the legal reason to refrain provided by moral wrongfulness is greater or less. That is, moral wrongfulness is just another feature of an act which, if legal-reason-providing, can be assessed for statutory strength relative to other legal-reason-providing features of prohibited acts.

So, the statutory measure of the strength of a legal reason provided by a feature of an act involves determining the contribution, under statute, of the feature *to punishment* for the act. The greater the contribution, the stronger the reason. But statutory prohibitions are often thought significant not only because of the punishments they attach to behaviors, but also because of the way in which they both express, and even to some degree constitute, the community's condemnation of the relevant kind of behavior. This observation supplies a second measure of the strength of a legal reason:

> Q1 provides an *expressively* stronger legal reason for refraining from C1 than Q2 provides for refraining from C2 *if and only if* C1 is, thanks to C1 having Q1, more socially condemned by the law than C2 is, thanks to C2 having Q2.

"Condemnation" here is thought of not merely as an attitude, but as a meaningful public display expressive of disapproval. In this sense of "condemn," the community can condemn something even though nobody thinks particularly ill of it, provided that the community displays behavior expressive of thinking ill of it. Further, the expressive measure of the strength of a legal reason draws not on every form of socially condemnatory display but only on the social condemnation displayed *in the law*. If, for instance, a kind of behavior is perfectly legal but condemned loudly by the community, there is no legal reason to refrain from it, and so no weighty legal reason by any measure of weight. What matters is that *the law* displays disapproval of the act. The greater disapproval the law displays, or expresses, the stronger the legal reason to refrain, under the expressive measure of a legal reason's strength.

There is no necessary connection between the statutory strength of a legal reason and the reason's expressive strength. But the two do tend to go together. Often, that is, the reason for thinking that a certain portion of the punishment for a crime is due to its having a particular feature is that the law displays a certain degree of community disapproval of the act in light of the act's possession of that feature. And, further, how much disapproval is displayed by the law is a function of the magnitude of the punishment assigned to the act in light of its having a particular feature. But the two can come apart. The expressive strength can be far lower than the statutory strength, and vice versa. When Attorney General Eric Holder instructed federal prosecutors to stop prosecuting simple possession of small amounts of marijuana, he substantially weakened the legal reason to refrain from such possession under the expressive measure of a legal reason's strength.[9] The act had the effect of making the law expressive of at most very minor disapproval of simple possession. But his act had no effect on the statutory strength of the relevant legal reason. There was, after all, no change in the punishment specified for the crime by statute. Conversely, the expressive strength of a legal reason can be high even when the statutory strength is low. In the state of Vermont, for instance, it is a crime to fail to provide reasonable assistance to someone in grave need. But the penalty for violation of the statute is a fine of at most $100.[10] By criminalizing failures to provide assistance, the law expresses substantial condemnation of such conduct, even if the statutory price imposed is low. The point is that what our body of law displays about the community's degree of condemnation of a particular form of behavior is a function of more than what its statutes say, while what its statutes say, and the reasons they say what they say, is what is relevant to the statutory strength of our legal reasons.

An act's degree of moral wrongfulness, when included in the supervenience base for the legal reason to refrain from the act—when, that is, it is part of "the law"—can bear on the expressive strength of the legal reason to refrain from the act. When the law expresses the view that a form of behavior is morally wrongful, it expresses community

---

[9] Deputy Attorney General James Cole's August 29, 2013 memo to all of the U.S. attorneys is widely thought to have expressed this policy. http://www.justice.gov/iso/opa/resources/3052013829132756857467.pdf (accessed February 25, 2016). Cole wrote, "[T]he Department of Justice has not historically devoted resources to prosecuting individuals whose conduct is limited to possession of small amounts of marijuana for personal use on private property."

[10] 12 V.S.A. §519.

condemnation of that behavior, and it typically expresses greater condemnation the greater the wrongfulness. But since the social condemnation of relevance is that *expressed by the law*, moral wrongfulness is not relevant in the absence of inclusion of moral wrongfulness in the relevant supervenience base. And, even then, it is only when moral wrongfulness has expressive significance that it bears on the expressive strength of the legal reason. If the attorney general announces that there will be no prosecutions for violation of a statute prohibiting morally wrongful behavior, he thereby weakens the expressive import of the relevant act's moral wrongfulness and thereby also weakens the expressive strength of the legal reason to refrain from the act.

The final measure of interest of the strength of a legal reason is a function not of statutes, or legal expression of social condemnation, but, instead, of the degree to which legally authoritative power is in fact directed against the act. Strength, so measured, is a function of the degree to which legal institutions are using their law-given power to push back against an act, or against people who perform the act. More carefully:

> Q1 provides an *institutionally* stronger legal reason for refraining from C1 than Q2 provides for refraining from C2 *if and only if* A greater amount of legally authoritative power is exercised against C1, thanks to C1 having Q1, than is exercised against C2, thanks to C2 having Q2.

The kind of power that I have in mind here is coercive power, aimed against those who engage in criminal behavior, and against the behavior itself. Sometimes, for instance, the institution directs coercive power against a form of conduct not by exercising coercive power directly against those who engage in such conduct but, instead, by exercising it against those who give safe harbor to those who engage in such conduct, or by making it harder for those who engage in such conduct to benefit from it by, for instance, cracking down on methods for laundering money.

Crucial to the institutional strength of a legal reason is the way in which discretionary actors in the criminal justice system use their discretionary power. A legal reason's strength increases, by the institutional measure, when law enforcement agencies dedicate new resources to combat a certain kind of crime, provided that they do so effectively enough that more state power is being directed against those kinds of crime. A legal reason's strength is also affected by patterns in the exercise of prosecutorial discretion both through formal mechanisms, such as indictments, and less formal mechanisms, such as deals in plea bargaining. If prosecutors are far more likely to indict male-on-female rape than male-on-male, then there is a stronger institutional legal reason for men to refrain from raping women than for them to refrain from raping men. If prosecutors are far more likely to accept plea bargaining deals for three-strike eligible felonies than for those which are not predicates for three-strikes legislation, then there is a stronger institutional reason to refrain from three-strikes felonies than to refrain from those that are not. In addition, procedural burdens imposed on people who commit, or who are suspected of committing crimes, increase the institutional strength of legal reasons to refrain from crime. The observation that sometimes "the punishment is the process," if true, has implications for the institutional strength of legal reasons. When the institution makes it very burdensome to fight a charge of crime, it directs more power against that crime, and thus increases the institutional strength of the legal reasons to refrain.[11]

Money is of significance to the institutional strength of legal reasons in a way that it does not matter to the statutory strength of legal reasons, and to a degree that it does not matter to expressive strength. How much money the state dedicates to fighting a particular type of crime often dictates how much state power is used against that kind of crime. And so the distribution of money is a very good proxy for the institutional strength of legal reasons. It is an imperfect proxy, however, since money is not always used efficiently; if it were, then more money would be more power. But if the state allocates a lot of money to fighting a particular kind of crime, and, despite that, very little power is directed that way, then the institutional strength of the legal reason to refrain from such behavior will remain weak. However, how effectively the state fights a particular kind of crime does not tell us, immediately, how strong the institutional reasons are to refrain from that crime. Drug trafficking, for instance, is ubiquitous, but the legal reasons to refrain from such behavior are very strong by the institutional measure. A large amount of coercive power is exercised against drug trafficking, although it is also true that little of it succeeds in cutting down on the behavior. So, money is an imperfect proxy for power, and crime-reduction is also an imperfect proxy for power.

Since monetary allocations often have no impact on statutes, or, when they do, they have at most a weak impact, money matters far less, if at all, to the statutory strength of legal reasons. Financial allocations, however, bear a closer relation to the degree of community condemnation expressed by legal institutions. Defunding can weaken the expressed condemnation, and funding can strengthen it, even when the money is used very inefficiently. But since so many other factors matter to community condemnation, this is a substantially less important factor in determining the expressive strength of a legal reason than its institutional strength.

So, a very wide range of power-directing behaviors by actors in the criminal justice system matter to the institutional strength of a legal reason. But it is also true that the only behaviors that matter are those that are legally authoritative. If a prosecutor routinely accepts cash payments in exchange for acceptance of lenient plea bargaining deals, this does not institutionally weaken the legal reasons for refraining from any form of crime, assuming that the law does not sanction such deals. This is true despite the fact that this prosecutorial behavior does lessen the overall amount of punishment that defendants suffer, and lessens the expected punishment for engaging in crime. But since the prosecutor's behavior is not a legally authoritative exercise of his power, in such a case, it does not bear on the institutional strength of the legal reasons of relevance.

---

[11] See Malcolm Feeley (1972) *The Process is the Punishment*, New York: Russell Sage Foundation; Issa Kohler-Hausmann (2014) "Managerial Justice and Mass Misdemeanors" in *Stanford Law Review*, 66: 611–94.

The definition of the institutional strength of a legal reason has the implication that the conjunction of all of the features of C1 provides an institutionally stronger legal reason than the conjunction of all of the features of C2 just in case more legally authoritative power is directed against C1 than C2. Determining the strength of individual features of given prohibited acts requires determining what portion of the power exercised against the relevant types of acts is pointed in that direction thanks to the act's possession of that feature. In this way, the institutional measure has something in common with the statutory measure. Both require an interpretation of the rationale for, on the one hand, statutorily specified punishment and, on the other, legally authoritative coercive pressure. Under both measures, the strength of a legal reason, that is, is a function not just of the behavior we find (statutory, coercive power) but also of why we find the behavior we find.

Just as the statutory and expressive strengths of legal reasons are often linked, but not linked with necessity, the institutional strength of a legal reason is often linked to its strength measured in the other two ways, but not with necessity. If legal actors choose to direct their power against acts in proportion to the statutory strength of the legal reasons for refraining from those acts, then the institutional and statutory strengths will align. And the same kind of thing will be true about the linkage between institutional and expressive strength if legal actors take their cue in their exercises of power from the expressive strength of the relevant legal reasons. In addition, the expressive strength of a legal reason is defeasibly matched by its institutional strength, since one of the ways in which the law expresses community disapproval is through the direction of legally authoritative power against an act. We exhibit our disapproval of a type of act by, for instance, arresting those we suspect of engaging in it. But the connection is defeasible since there are often alternative explanations for our allocations of power that undercut the degree to which they display community disapproval. For instance, sometimes very little power is directed against a type of act because it is very expensive to do so and the money can be used more efficiently elsewhere. Imagine that the IRS, for instance, chooses to investigate and prosecute high income tax evasion much more frequently than just as egregious tax evasion by those with low incomes. If the IRS does this because more revenue is generated that way than would be generated if state power was directed against tax evasion independently of the income of the evaders, then no greater disapproval of high income tax evasion than low is expressed by this allocation of power. In such a case, the institutional strength of the legal reason for a high-income person to refrain from tax evasion is greater than that of the institutional strength of the legal reason for a low-income person to refrain. But the statutory and expressive strengths of the reason to refrain are the same for the two groups of people.

There may be legal institutions devised so as to assure that legally authoritative power is directed only in accord with the statutory or expressive strength of legal reasons. If so, then under such institutions the institutional strength of a legal reason will mirror its strength measured in the other two ways. It might be possible, for instance, to construct our *legal standards* for authoritative exercises of power in such a way that any exercise of power out of proportion with the strength of reasons measured in one of the other two ways would, thereby, be non-authoritative. Imagine a system, for instance, in which a prosecutorial indictment is invalid just in case it would involve a direction of power against the relevant crime that was out of proportion with the statutory strength of the legal reason to refrain from that crime. Perhaps such a system would invalidate indictments for crimes that were charged too frequently, relative to the amount of punishment allocated to them by statute. In such a system, the institutional and statutory strengths of legal reason to refrain would mirror one another. But even in this case, the link would not be *necessary*. It is perfectly possible, at least in our system, for legal actors to direct the power given to them under the law in ways that fail to align with statutorily specified punishments or with degrees of legally expressed community condemnation. When they do, the institutional strength of the relevant legal reasons will diverge from their statutory and social condemnatory strength.

5.2.2 *The weight of D's legal reason*

It is an interesting fact that most of the legal reasons that there are are not reasons *for* me, nor are they reasons *for* you, nor for any other particular person. The reason is obvious: there are many more legal systems that make no claim over me, or you, than there are legal systems that do. This fact is explained in large part by citizenship. Legal reasons deriving from facts about American law are legal reasons *for me*, since I am an American citizen, in a way that legal reasons deriving from facts about any other legal system are not. Citizenship is not the only relevant factor, however, since when I am visiting Japan, legal reasons having their source in Japanese law are then legal reasons *for me*, despite the fact that I am not a citizen of Japan. Japanese law is a source of legal reasons, however, regardless of where I happen to be, and regardless of my citizenship. But when I return home to the United States legal reasons having their source in Japanese law are no longer legal reasons *for me*. Legal reasons are out there, as it were, provided that the social facts constitutive of legality are present. But they apply to a particular person, they are legal reasons *for* him or her, only given further facts about that person, such as his or her citizenship and where, if anywhere, he or she is visiting.

It is important to see that a parallel point can be made about moral reasons. There is a moral reason not to kill a human being. But a tiger has no moral reason not to kill a human being; there is no such moral reason *for the tiger*. We can ask, and should, why the difference between people and tigers makes for this important difference in moral reasons. But for now we do not need an answer to that difficult question. The important point for now is only that what reasons there are, on the one hand, and *for whom* they are reasons, on the other, are separable issues. More needs to be said in explanation for why a reason that there is might not be a reason for a particular agent. In the case of legal reasons, citizenship has something to do with it. In the case of moral reasons, personhood does.

The same basic point applies to the *strength* of a legal reason (and, perhaps, to the strength of a *moral* reason), in all of the senses of "strength" identified in the previous subsection. A weighty legal reason might be no legal reason *for me*. But it also might be a legal reason *for me*, while being less weighty *for me*, than it is in general. The goal of this subsection is to say a word about what exactly this means. Or, rather, to elucidate one of the things it means, leaving open the possibility that there is more than one meaningful sense in which a legal reason of a particular strength can be *my* legal reason with a particular strength *for me*.

Given any legal system, grounded in a set of social facts, there are features of acts that provide legal reasons for refraining from those acts. There are also criteria that determine which people are such that the relevant legal reasons are legal reasons *for them* to refrain from those acts. As already indicated, these criteria include, but are not exhausted by, the criteria for citizenship of the country whose legal system it is. Many visitors are also included. Let's call the people who meet these criteria, whatever, exactly, they are, "the insiders" to the legal system. These are the people who have a legal reason to refrain from an act if there is a legal reason to refrain from it grounded in the legal facts generated by the relevant legal system, including facts about which statutes are valid, what legal facts bear on the social condemnation expressed by the law, and what exercises of power are legally authoritative. I assume that the criteria for being an insider can be appealed to to explain why insiders have legal reasons that outsiders lack. They can be used to explain why I lack legal reasons that Japanese citizens have.

It is a fascinating and puzzling fact that the law typically specifies the criteria for being an insider—under American law, for instance, anyone born on American soil is an insider—but may not do so effectively. Were American law amended, for instance, to classify those born in Syria as insiders, it would not suddenly be true that the legal reasons having their source in American law were legal reasons *for* each and every person born in Syria. Lawmakers have some power to draw the line between the insiders and the outsiders, but the power is limited; some efforts to include or exclude people are doomed to failure. This observation is accommodated by legal positivists in the same way that they accommodate the fact that some criteria for legality are in legal actors' control and some are not. Some of the facts that are constitutive of legality are so thanks to the fact that legal actors made them so, others are not. And, similarly, some of the facts about people that make them insiders or outsiders are so thanks to the fact that legal actors made them so, others are not. But in the same way that I assume that there are positivist-friendly criteria for legality, without saying what they are, I assume that there are positivist-friendly criteria for being an insider, without saying what they are. Our purposes here will require that there are insiders, but it will not require a full account of what makes someone one of them. (More will be said about insider status in chapter 7.)

What is of particular importance to our aims here is not the difference between insiders and outsiders, but the differences *among insiders*. Insiders have legal reasons that outsiders lack. But it would be misleading to put this as a point about differences in the *strengths* of the reasons that insiders and outsiders have. Outsiders do not have legal reasons of strength zero, while insiders have legal reasons of greater strengths. Rather, outsiders simply do not have legal reasons, that insiders have, *of any strength*. So, if there is sense, and I believe there is, to the idea that a single feature of an action could provide a stronger legal reason for me than for you, there must be a sense in which the strengths of the legal reasons for insiders can vary. I will explain how this is possible. And it is not merely that I think that it is *possible*. I think it is actually what we find with kids and adults in our, and in many mature legal systems. The legal reasons for kids to refrain from crimes are weaker than the legal reasons for adults to refrain. The legal reasons for you to refrain from crime become stronger the moment you turn 18.

Why think that it is possible for the legal reasons to refrain from crime to be stronger for one insider than another? The reason, I suggest, is that insiders can vary in the amount of say they have over the law. More carefully: For each of the three types of strength of a legal reason, there is, respectively, a body of facts on which the relevant degree of strength supervenes—facts about statutes, facts about legally authoritative expression, facts about the allocation of legally authorized power, etc. Insiders vary in how much say they have over those facts. My suggestions is this: *The strength of a given legal reason for an insider can be (although is not always) a function of the degree to which he has a say over the facts in virtue of which that reason has the strength it has.*

Removing the obscurity attached to this statement will require drawing on a particular schematic account of the source of political authority. And so a disclaimer is owed: Less political philosophy than is fully needed is going to be undertaken in what remains of this section, or even in what remains of this book. Some steps will be taken to fill in the blanks in chapter 6 and 7, but a full defense of the account to be sketched here of the nature of political authority cannot be provided in this book. Still, disclosure, even if not defense, of the guiding account of the nature of political authority is essential.

Ultimately, to fully defend the argument to be sketched here for the claim that the strength of a legal reason for a person sometimes varies with how much say the person has over the law, we would need to fully defend a limited Republican theory of political authority, as contrasted with an exclusively Liberal theory. The distinction should be familiar.[12] According to Republicans, in the tradition of Rousseau, the state acts authoritatively with respect to a given person thanks to the fact that that person has a say over the law permitting the state's action with respect to him. According to Liberals, in the tradition of, for instance, Hobbes, Locke, and Mill, the state's authority over an individual derives from its protection of that individual's liberty from interference by other individuals. As will become clear soon, I am operating here with a *limited*

---

[12] While there is something silly about offering a citation for this distinction, given its centrality to so much political philosophy, a useful discussion, and references to additional sources, can be found in Dominique Leydet (2014) "Citizenship" in *The Stanford Encyclopedia of Philosophy*, Edward N. Zalta (ed.), http://plato.stanford.edu/archives/spr2014/entries/citizenship/ (accessed February 25, 2016).

Republican position.[13] That is, I am operating with the view that *some states* have authority to do *some things* to citizens thanks to the fact that citizens have a say over the law authorizing those state behaviors. Further, the criminal punishment of citizens in the United States today, and many other countries, is an example. What I require, that is, are two claims: First, there exist states and behaviors such that states have political authority to engage in those behaviors only if those affected by them have a say over the law permitting those behaviors. And, second, modern states, like the United States, and the ubiquitous state behavior of criminally punishing, are an example; modern states are justified in punishing their citizens thanks to the fact that their citizens have a say over the laws they violate, laws which also authorize the state to punish violation. But my goal here is less to provide a watertight argument for these claims—that would require a deeper trip into current political philosophy than it is possible to take here—than it is to make them plausible. A bit more will be said in their defense in chapters 6 and 7.

To see the basic idea behind the claim that the strength of a legal reason for a person can be a function of how much say he has over the law, consider a toy example. A group of people decide to start a tiddlywinks club. The plan is for members of the club to meet regularly to play the game. They decide to let anyone who opts in to be in the club; membership provides the opportunity to participate in weekly tiddlywinks tournaments. Those who opt in choose to pay dues between $0 and $100. The amount they choose to pay determines their degree of say in club policy. (I intentionally leave unspecified what exactly it is to "have a say." Chapter 6 offers an account of this notion.) Perhaps this is implemented by number of votes; perhaps by allocated speaking time at club meetings in which policy is set; perhaps by opportunities to introduce policies for consideration; who knows. What we do know is that things are set up so that the greater the dues, the more the say. When the club must decide whether to have a dress code, for instance, members get a say in the question in proportion to the amount of their dues. People who pay $1 in dues have 1/100th as much say as people who pay $100, and people who pay $0 have no say. Imagine that following their procedures, the club sets the rule that members have to wear bow ties to club meetings.

How strong a "club"-reason (as it were) is there to wear bow ties to meetings? There will be analogues to all three of the measures of strength discussed in subsection 5.2.1. The strength of the reason can be measured by what the club bylaws say about the sanction for violation (statutory strength). Or it can be measured by how much the club's official activities express condemnation of those who do not wear bow ties (expressive). Or it can be measured by the amount of officially sanctioned

---

[13] Perhaps the most sophisticated case for the claim that the authority of the United States' government is fundamentally Republican is offered by Bruce Ackerman. See Bruce Ackerman (1991) *We the People, Volume 1: Foundations*, Cambridge: Harvard University Press, esp. chs 9 & 10. However, my purposes here will require only the more modest claim, included in Ackerman's, that the authority of the American government to punish its citizens for violations of statutes derives, in paradigm cases, from the say over the law of those who we punish. As we will see in chapter 7, there are also important non-paradigm cases.

coercive power the club actually directs against non-bow-tie-wearing behavior (institutional). There is also a question of how strong a club reason there is *for any given member* to wear a bow tie to a meeting. Perhaps that's the same as the club-reason's strength by statutory, expressive, and institutional measures. But given the way the club's political structure is organized—where the amount of say that members have over club policy, including the bow tie policy, is a matter of degree and varies from member to member—we can ask the following question: Is the strength of the club-reason to wear a bow tie *for a given member* a function of how much say the member has over club policy?

Imagine that X shows up to a tiddlywinks tournament without a bow tie and he is charged with this grievous offense by the club's officials. Their indictment presupposes that he had a club-reason to wear a bow tie. When X asks why they believe that to be true, they point to the bylaws. And when he asks why they think the bylaws have any authority over *him*, they answer that the bylaws have authority over him because he had a say in their creation. This reply is forceful. It silences a particular objection that X might be raising, an objection that might be voiced by saying "That's not *my* rule!" When X has a say over the bylaws, this is simply not true; it is, to some degree, *his* rule. But notice that X should then reply that the strength of the club reason to wear a bow tie was in part a function of his degree of say over club policy, which might be a lot, or might be a little, depending on the amount of dues he pays. If X pays low dues, he can, at this point, cite that fact in his defense and so show that his offense in failing to regard the club-reason to wear a bow tie was a less onerous offense than it would have been had he paid greater dues, and so had greater say over club policy. This is the central idea motivating my view that the strength of a legal reason for a person is a function, in part, of the degree of say he has over the law.

Return to the moment in the conversation between X and the club authorities at which he asked why they believe that the club's bylaws apply to him. What if the authorities of the club do not answer this query by noting that he has a say over the bylaws. Imagine, instead, that they answer that the bylaws have authority over him because he has elected to be a member of the club; he has opted in. If this is true, then in this case, the strength of the club-reason is not a function of X's degree of say, for the club bylaws do not have authority over him because he had a say, but simply because he opted in to the club, something that he did no more or less than any other member. There are also cases in which the bylaws have authority for yet other reasons, besides X's having a say, and besides X's opting in. Perhaps the club's authorities insist that X had a reason to wear a bow tie because that's just what it is to play tiddlywinks; without a bow tie, you're doing something else entirely. Perhaps this is false, but if it's true then, again, the strength of X's club-reason to wear a bow tie is not a function of how much say X has over that. The result: The strength of an agent's reason to refrain from a particular type of prohibited conduct is a function of how much say he has over the relevant facts *only if* those facts generate a reason for him thanks to the fact that he has a say over them.

If it seems unlikely that a given club-reason's strength *for* a particular member of the club varies with that member's say over the club's policies, it is because, I believe, it is implausible to think that the club's policies have authority over members thanks to the fact that members had a say over them. Rather, in the case of clubs like our imagined tiddlywinks club, the rules typically have authority merely because members have opted in, or because they could opt out, or both. That is, in the case of clubs it is typical that subjection to the club's rules is the price of admission, as it were. That is, the authority of the rules has its source in the voluntary choice to have access to the benefits of membership. But is political authority like that? Sometimes, but often not. There are, to be sure, some citizen-affecting actions by some states that are exercises of authority thanks to the fact that the affected citizens have voluntarily opted in to receive the state's services. But it is also often the case that when the state acts in a way that affects its citizens, the action is legitimate thanks to the fact that the citizens have some kind of say over how they are treated. In such cases, state behavior is the collective behavior of citizens, each of whom has some say over how the collective behaves. And this is not merely a fact about how some governments are set up, but a fact, also, thanks to which states have the authority to engage in some citizen-affecting acts. That is, in such cases, states have authority *thanks to the fact* that citizens have a say over how they will behave.

There are multiple sources of political authority. In different cases, in other words, there are different reasons why the state is acting with political authority when it behaves in a way that affects a citizen. My point is only that in many cases, the answer to the question of why a particular fact provides a legal reason for a particular person is that that person had some say over the setup thanks to which such facts generate legal reasons. This is most obvious in direct democracies. In a direct democracy, the reason that a bit of legislation generates legal reasons for a particular citizen is because it is, to some degree, *his legislation*; he had a say over what that legislation would be. But this is true, also, in representative democracies in which individual citizens have a say over what their governments do by having a say over the behavior of their representatives. Laws against, for instance, defrauding a pawnbroker provide legal reasons for citizens of California, but not for citizens of states that have not passed such statutes, thanks to the fact that citizens of California have a say over who writes their laws and thereby have a say over what those laws say. Even if the legislation was passed a hundred years ago, current Californians have a say over it, for they have a say over the behavior of representatives who are currently refraining from repealing it, an omission that is essential for the present legal-reason-generating power of facts like the fact that a particular person is a pawnbroker.

We have provided a rough groundwork, then, for the central claim of this section. Here D1 and D2 are two insiders and, as before, Q1 is a feature of act C1:

> *Ceteris paribus,* Q1 provides a (statutorily/expressively/institutionally) stronger legal reason for D1 to refrain from C1 than Q1 provides for D2 to refrain from C1 *if*

(1) Q1 provides a legal reason for D1 and for D2 thanks to the fact that D1 and D2 have a say over the facts thanks to which the reason provided by Q1 has the (statutory/expressive/institutional) strength it has, and (2) D1 has greater say over this than D2 has.

In short, in systems in which the law has authority over people thanks to the fact that they have a say in the writing of it, the strength of their legal reason to refrain from prohibited behavior is a function of the amount of say they have. They have a say over what's written in the legal books, and it is thanks, in part, to what's written there that facts about actions—that they involve deception, or that they will cause harm, or that they would be performed without consent—generate legal reasons to refrain from those actions. If we were to model the amount of say that a person has over a set of legal facts as a number between 0 and 1, then we would say that the strength of a legal reason for a person is its statutory, expressive, or institutional strength multiplied by this number.

Given that there is imperfect overlap between the three different bodies of legal facts constitutive of the strength of legal reasons, in the three described senses, it is possible, in theory, for a given citizen to have greater say over the facts constitutive of one kind of strength than another. There is, therefore, the conceptual possibility that the relevant multiplier is different depending on which type of strength is at issue. How strong, then, is the legal reason for me, under the federal law of the United States, to refrain from simple possession of marijuana? The answer is a function of the relevant type of strength, and the degree to which I have a say over the legal facts that are constitutive of that degree of strength. Consider, for instance, the statutory strength, for me, of the legal reason to refrain from simple marijuana possession. The relevant body of facts, that constitute the statutory strength of the legal reason, include: the fact that there is a statute prohibiting this behavior and specifying a certain penalty for it; the facts thanks to which that statute is valid, including that it was passed by the legislature and signed by the president, and has not been repealed; the facts thanks to which *these* facts give legal authority to the statute, such as the fact that there are laws that specify that such procedures result in valid statutes. *Ceteris paribus*, my statutory legal reason to refrain from simple possession is weaker than that of people who have more say over these facts than I have, and it is stronger than those who have less. Similar remarks apply to the cases of expressive and institutional strength. *Ceteris paribus*, the legal reason for one citizen is institutionally weaker than the legal reason for another if the one has greater say than the other over allocations of legally authoritative power, or over the laws that allocate that power in the first place. My legal reasons to refrain from simple marijuana possession are institutionally weaker than that of the attorney general since I have far less say than she over how much legally authorized force is directed against simple possession.

It is very difficult, perhaps impossible, to put actual numbers to these quantities. Is my say over statutes banning simple marijuana possession best modeled as 0.2? 0.4?

0.6? How does that compare to my say over the degree to which state power is directed against simple possession? Is that number higher? Lower? By how much? There is no reason to think that answers to questions of these kinds can be given. But for our purposes they do not need answers. What will matter for our purposes are comparative judgments. In particular, what we will need is to be able to judge how much say kids have over the relevant bodies of facts *in comparison to adults*. And the answer, as we will see developed in chapter 6, is "far less." What this implies, if the picture sketched here is accurate, is that kids' legal reasons are weaker than adults'. And it is that claim that is essential to the argument developed here for leniency towards kids.

The picture just sketched presupposes that there is a difference, in fact, between the case in which the authority of a legal reason derives from the fact that a citizen had some say over it and the case in which this is not so. I hereby acknowledge a commitment to whatever form of moral or normative realism is required to support this claim. However, what will really be required for our purposes is only the weak claim that *it is possible* for a set of legal facts to provide an authoritative legal reason for a person thanks to the fact that the person had some say over those facts. And it seems to me that this claim really requires very little argument, if any. Someone who asserts that a statute is a source of legal reasons for a person improves his argumentative position by showing that the person had some say over the statute. By noting that fact he shows that the pressure placed on the person to act in the way dictated by the statute has its source, in part, in the person himself; he is, in a sense, exerting pressure *on himself* to act when the statute exerts pressure on him. In fact, having a say over a set of facts that constitute legal reasons seems so naturally to positively contribute to the case for the authority of those reasons over a person that one might wonder if it is possible for legal authority to be generated in the absence of it. While it seems to me that benign dictatorships can have legal authority (and maybe even not very benign ones), and so it seems to me that it is possible for a set of facts to generate legal reasons for a person even though he had no say over them, I do not insist on this point. Rather, what is important is that *when legal authority derives from having a say, the more say a person has, the greater the strength of the relevant legal reasons*. If legal authority *always* derives from having a say, then this will always be true.

What has been offered in this section is not merely a picture—a picture in which the strength of a legal reason for a particular person is, often, a function of the degree to which that person had a say over the legality of the facts constitutive of the legal reason's strength—but also an argument for it. The first step of the argument is the observation that the legal reasons having their source in a particular body of facts are not legal reasons for outsiders, such as citizens of other countries living in those countries. Our legal system does not reach them. In cases in which the facts that provide the relevant legal reasons do so because citizens have a say over what is and is not legal, the best explanation for the fact that the relevant facts provide no legal reasons for outsiders is that outsiders do not have a say. Add the further observation that insiders can vary in how much say they have, and the conclusion we seek follows:

When legal reasons are reasons for me thanks to the fact that I have a say, then their strength is a function of how much say I have.

5.2.3 The legal reasons to abide by criminal prohibitions

The previous subsection envisions, broadly speaking, two different kinds of cases in which a given fact provides a legal reason for a given person. In the first, the fact provides a legal reason for the person because he had a say over the laws in virtue of which that fact provides a legal reason. In the second, the fact provides a legal reason for the person for some other reason, such as, for instance, that he opted in, or that he benefits from the state behaviors that are authorized by the law thanks to which the fact generates a legal reason. Essential to the view being developed here—the view of the grounds for giving kids a break when it comes to criminal liability—is that the legal reasons for citizens to refrain from crime are of the first sort. Put more carefully, the features of actions *thanks to which they fall under criminal prohibitions* generate legal reasons for citizens to refrain from such acts because citizens have a say over those criminal prohibitions (and other laws thanks to which those prohibitions have legal force). I have a legal reason to refrain from taking my neighbor's car without his permission thanks to the fact that I have a say over laws against theft, laws that say that those who take other people's things without permission are subject to criminal punishment (and because I have a say over laws that say that prohibitions passed by the legislature and signed by the president have legal force). So, what needs to be shown is that criminal law applies to citizens thanks to the fact that they are *Republican* citizens, enjoying a say over criminal laws. It is not enough to assert that this is possible of some laws in some states. We need to know that *our* criminal law provides legal reasons *for us* thanks to the fact that we have a say over it. It is the aim of this subsection to make an argument for this claim. Criminal law, I suggest, bears a particularly close relationship to the say that citizens have over the law, in contrast to other forms of law the authority of which might or might not have this source.

To see this, start with an observation. When a person has a say over a norm that an agent violated, he is complicit in the judgment that the agent did wrong. This is different from being complicit in the response to the agent's wrongdoing. One could be complicit in the response without being complicit in the judgment that the agent did wrong. For instance, say that a family has a rule: anyone who curses has to put a quarter in the family piggy bank. A curses and B says, "You have to put a quarter in the piggy bank!" When A refuses, C pries the quarter from A's hand and puts it in the piggy bank. So, B judges A's act to be wrongful, and C responds to A's conduct in the way that B takes to be fitting. But we haven't said anything about C's attitude towards A's conduct. Perhaps C does not judge the conduct to be wrong; maybe he's just a hired hand, as it were, tasked with the job of enforcing B's laws. C, in that case, is not complicit in the judgment that A did wrong, although he is more than complicit in the mandated response to A's wrongdoing. By contrast, if C had a say over the rule requiring cursers to feed the piggy bank, then he is complicit, also, in the judgment that A did wrong. He might not *share* that judgment—having a say need not mean getting your way, as we will see in chapter 6—but, still, he is complicit in the judgment. But if he has a say over the norm A violated, then it is, in a sense, *his* norm. Thanks to that fact the judgment that A did wrong is attributable to C in the way in which, in general, the actions and judgments with which we are complicit can be attributed to us even if we did not perform or make them.

Now, the difference between criminal law, and all other branches of law, is that criminal law authorizes the state to *punish*. And punishment is distinctively different from other forms of hardship, such as damages in tort or contract, in well-known, albeit hard-to-articulate, ways. Among them, punishment necessarily represents the act for which it is issued as wrongful. To be sure, damages in tort and contract are often imposed for acts that are, in fact, wrongful. But the imposition of damages does not necessarily represent the action as possessing that quality. This is in part why there is nothing distorting, sometimes, about thinking of damages as a price that one might elect to pay for the right to breach a contract; sometimes, at least, the package of breach and damages is not wrongful, even if breach would be wrongful in the absence of damages. By contrast, this is always a distorted way to think about punishment. The act plus the punishment is never permissible, if the act was wrongful considered in itself. The wrongfulness of the act remains even when coupled with the punishment.

Put together these two ideas, namely, first, that having a say over a norm supplies complicity with judgments of the wrongfulness of acts that violate the norm, and, second, that punishment necessarily represents the act for which it is issued as wrongful. What we get is the further idea that those who have a say over a norm are complicit in at least one significant aspect of the punishment for its violation, namely the punishment's representation of the act as wrongful. They might be complicit in more than that about the punishment, but they are at least complicit in that. Further, those who do not share the judgment of wrongfulness—they do not endorse, or side with the norm violated—and have no say over the norm are not, at least not ordinarily, complicit in this aspect of the punishment. There is no ground for attributing them with the judgment that the act is wrongful. So, having a say over the relevant norm is sufficient for complicity with this important aspect of the punishment, and is necessary in the absence of a judgment that the norm is valid.

If we add the further idea that citizen-affecting government action is justified in part, at least, by the fact that those affected are complicit in that action—that is the sense in which what the government does to them, they do to themselves—we reach the conclusion sought in this section. That those who are affected by criminal laws, particularly those who are punished under them, have a say over those laws is an important part of the justification of state action mandated by criminal law. And, further, having a say plays a more crucial role here than it does in other areas of law, for punishment, which is always in the purview of criminal law, necessarily represents those on whom it is inflicted as wrongdoers. By having a say, citizens come also to be complicit in that representation of their action, and not just in their suffering at the government's hand. The result is that those who have a say over the criminal law are complicit with the punishments inflicted in accordance with it in a deeper way than anyone who does not.

The point of the last few paragraphs can be put a different way. Say that A does X and B intends to punish him for it. A objects: "X-ing isn't wrongful," he insists. Now, because punishment necessarily represents the act for which it is issued as wrongful, this would be a decisive objection to the punishment, if indeed A is correct in his claim. B can respond to the claim by citing the norm that A violates. By citing the norm, B exhibits that in virtue of which X-ing is wrongful: it is in violation of the norm. But this will not silence A if he is in a position to insist on the invalidity of the norm. He might be unable to occupy such a position thanks to the fact that he himself accepts the norm's validity. But he also might be unable to occupy such a position *because he had a say over the norm*. Thanks to the fact that he had a say over the norm, that is, he is estopped, as it were, from insisting on the norm's invalidity. When A has a say over the norm prohibiting X-ing, his objection to the effect that X-ing is not wrongful is therefore severely weakened. Provided that B can indeed cite a norm that X-ing violates, and it is a norm the validity of which A cannot impeach, A cannot complain about the punishment on the grounds that the act for which it is issued is not wrongful.

The result of this line of thought is that in administering criminal laws the state stands on far better justificatory ground if those who are punished in accordance with them have a say over the norms that their conduct violates. This is less important in other areas of law where the state response to citizen conduct need not involve representing that conduct as wrongful. The further implication is that the strength of the legal reasons for a given agent to comply with the demands of criminal laws is *almost* always (although, as we will see in chapter 7, not *always*) a function, in part, of how much say over the criminal law that agent has.

5.2.4 Returning to culpability and desert

We inquired about the nature of legal reasons, and, in particular, about what it is for a legal reason to have a degree of strength because the idea of the strength or weight of a legal reason is crucial to the account of criminal culpability and desert for wrongdoing offered in chapters 3 and 4, respectively. To be criminally culpable is for one's wrongful act to manifest modes of recognition, weighing, or response to legal reasons that are discordant with the facts about the legal reasons one has. To deserve a particular form of suffering for one's wrongdoing is for that suffering to be such as to place the wrongful act, given the modes of transactions with reasons which it manifests, into a place in the space of legal reasons isomorphic to the place that the act occupies for the person who recognizes, weighs, and responds to legal reasons as he ought. Appreciating these formulae requires understanding the nature of legal reasons, and their weight. And, particularly, it requires appreciating the idea that a legal reason can have a certain degree of weight *for a particular person*.

But as we have seen, for any given legal reason, and any given person, there are six distinct senses of weight, or strength. First, there are three different non-agent-relative measures of strength, each drawing on a distinct set of legal facts as constituting the relevant degree of strength. Second, there are, correspondingly, three different senses in which the legal reason has a strength *for* the particular person in question, affected by the degree to which the person has a say over the respective relevant body of legal facts. The legal reason has a statutory strength, and a statutory strength *for* the person; an expressive strength, and an expressive strength *for* the person; and similarly for the institutional measure of strength. And so this raises a question: Which sense of strength is of relevance to the assessment of the agent's criminal culpability? Which sense is relevant to his desert for criminal behavior?

These questions can be pressing; they can make a difference to the question of how culpable a person is for his wrongdoing, and how much suffering he deserves. Consider the example, introduced earlier, of Attorney General Eric Holder's instruction to federal prosecutors to stop prosecuting simple possession of marijuana. I suggested above that following this presumption there remained a statutorily strong reason to refrain from possession, but a very weak legal reason by the expressive measure of a legal reason's strength. Now imagine that while most prosecutors follow Holder's directive, some do not: some instances of simple possession are prosecuted, although far fewer than before the pronouncement. Recognizing the possibility of oversimplification, let s, e, and i be the strengths of the legal reason to refrain from simple possession measured statutorily, expressively, and institutionally, respectively. So far, then, we have three different possible answers to the question of how strong the legal reason is to refrain from simple possession: s, e, and i. And let's assume that $s > i > e$—that is, the statutory strength is greater than the institutional, and the expressive is weakest of the three. Now imagine that a defendant, D, is prosecuted for simple possession and assume that he was, indeed, in possession of a prohibited amount of marijuana. There is some degree to which he has a say over the statutes constitutive of s, some degree to which he has a say over the legal facts expressive of social condemnation of simple possession, and some degree to which he has a say over the amount of legally authorized power directed against simple possession by the institution. Again, recognizing the possibility of oversimplification, let's model these three degrees of "having a say" as h_s, h_e, and h_i, where these are values between 0 and 1. So there are three possible answers to the question of how strong the legal reason to refrain is *for* D: sh_s, eh_e, and ih_i. Which of these six values (s, e, i, sh_s, eh_e, or ih_i) sets the standard for culpability? Which for desert? If e is what matters, or eh_e, then D will be very little, if at all, criminally culpable; while his possession manifested modes of transaction with reasons that involved disregard for the reasons to refrain from such possession, those reasons were very weak, and so it was a small failure to disregard them, or grant them less weight than they actually had. By contrast, if the degree to which our laws express social condemnation of simple possession is not what matters but, instead, the severity of the punishments mandated by statute, whether or not tempered by the consideration of the degree to which D has a say over those statutes, then D will be far more criminally culpable, and deserving of far more severe sanction. What sense of strength is relevant?

I believe that the answers to these questions are constrained by the Principle of Lenity, according to which a criminal defendant is to be painted in the best possible light consistent with the evidence of facts bearing on his criminality. Lenity dictates that the relevant measure of the strength of the legal reason is the measure under which the reason is weakest, since, *ceteris paribus*, the weaker the relevant legal reason, the less criminally culpable is the defendant, and the less suffering is deserved. So, I suggest, any of the six measures of strength might, on a particular occasion, be the relevant one, since any one of the six might be the weakest.

The point here can be put another way: what measure of the strength of a legal reason matters to the question of culpability and desert is not dictated by the very ideas of culpability or desert. Rather, it is dictated, to the extent that it is, by our *reasons for inquiring* about culpability and desert. When we are inquiring for the purpose of determining how the state should respond to the defendant, when we are trying to figure out how miserable the state should make the defendant given his past crimes, then we are constrained by the Principle of Lenity. The state should make the defendant the least miserable that it can consistent with its principled commitment to responding in accordance with culpability and desert. That guiding purpose of inquiry, then, dictates what measure of the strength of a legal reason is relevant to the question.

But what is the status of the Principle of Lenity? It provides an answer to the question of relevance—which measure of strength is relevant to culpability and desert?—but why should we think that the answer dictated by Lenity is the right answer? The claim that Lenity determines the answer presupposes that Lenity has legal authority. But why does it have such authority?

I believe that the Principle of Lenity has legal authority for the same reasons that anything else has legal authority (under the legal positivist position presupposed here): in virtue of the configuration of contingent social facts that are constitutive of legality. Roughly, Lenity has legal authority—and so dictates the relevant measure of a legal reason's strength—only thanks to the fact that it has been granted such legal authority in our system. But what this implies is that it could very well have been otherwise. We can imagine a legal system in which what is valid is not the Principle of Lenity, but the Draconian Principle, according to which a defendant is to be painted in the worst possible light, consistent with the evidence. If that's an animating principle in a given legal system then the relevant measure of a legal reason's strength will not be the weakest, as under our system, but the strongest. In short, the question of which measure of a legal reason's strength is the relevant measure is a *legal* question and so can be answered only in the way that all legal questions are answered: through research aimed at uncovering the facts that are constitutive of the legality of principles, like the Principle of Lenity or the Draconian Principle, that, in turn, supply an answer to the question of relevance. However, it is also the case that the legal system on which we are here focusing, namely the American legal system, is committed to Lenity, and so the measure of a legal reason's strength, relevant to culpability and desert, is the measure under which it is weakest.

Finally, it is important to note that we are now in position to conclude a line of thought begun in chapter 3 concerned with the categories of excuse. There I noted that philosophers have sometimes identified "exemptions" or "status excuses" as forms of excuse that do not belong in either of the classical categories of ignorance or compulsion. To excuse an agent on such grounds is to identify a status that he lacks and which is necessary to be justifiably held to the stringent standards appropriate to those who possess it. My suggestion in chapter 3 was twofold: First, status excuses work because, in light of the missing or diminished status, the relevant set of reasons are either not reasons *for* the agent or are weaker *for him* than they are for those possessing undiminished status. Second, it is not the case that the only relevant status is personhood. Personhood is the status of relevance when what is at issue is moral culpability, and so the strength of moral reasons. But when criminal culpability and the strength of legal reasons is at issue, a status of importance is that of *citizen*. Making good on this pair of ideas required, as indicated in chapter 3, an account of the strength of legal reasons for a particular agent under which the strength of a person's legal reason is, in part, a function of his status as a citizen. Diminished status as a citizen, diminished strength of legal reason. Such an account has been provided in this chapter. Diminished citizenship provides a partial or full status excuse from criminal culpability precisely because those who are diminished in citizenship have diminished say over the facts that constitute the strength of legal reasons. This, in turn, diminishes their culpability in comparison to those who manifest precisely the same modes of transactions with reasons in their conduct, but enjoy full citizenship. The discussion of this chapter, that is, completes the argument for thinking that there is a special and previously overlooked category of excuses: the citizenship-based status excuses.

5.3 Conclusion

As I said in the introduction to this chapter, the goal of this chapter was less to present and argue for a jurisprudential theory supplying the groundwork for the conceptions of culpability and desert offered in chapters 3 and 4 (and, in turn, the argument for giving kids a break to be offered in chapter 6), but, rather, to say enough to convince the reader that there is a jurisprudential theory that can provide the needed support, and which is not clearly indefensible.

Are the positivist position presented here, or the accompanying complex account of the strength of a legal reason, both full stop and for a particular person, *essential* to the views of culpability and desert I have offered? I am uncertain. The argument to be offered for the claim that kids deserve a break depends crucially on the idea that the degree to which a person has a say over the legal import of bodies of facts that are constitutive of the strength of legal reasons bears on the strength of those reasons for him. If an alternative jurisprudence from the one sketched here can be coupled with my accounts of culpability and desert to yield this result, then my central purposes here would not lead me to quarrel with it. But for my purposes it suffices that there *is* a jurisprudence that has the implications the argument requires. I have tried to sketch such a jurisprudence here, although I acknowledge that what I have said in its defense is insufficient to establish it over competitors. And I further acknowledge that if a superior jurisprudence is inconsistent with this claim—if it implies that a person's degree of say over the body of facts constitutive of the strength of his legal reasons is of no relevance to the strength of those reasons for him—then my argument for giving kids a break would fail. But I see no reason to think that jurisprudential views that have this implication (if there are any) are superior; and so I remain optimistic.

6

Giving Kids a Break

6.0 Introduction

Kids who commit crimes are less culpable than adults. Kids who commit crimes are deserving of lesser sanctions than adults. And it is because of these facts that we are warranted in adopting policies under which kids who commit crimes are treated more leniently than adults who commit crimes. The argument for these claims is completed in this chapter.

The argument is supplied, almost in its entirety, by the views presented in chapters 3, 4, and 5. In chapter 3, it was argued that to be criminally culpable for a wrongful act is for that act to manifest a mode of recognition, weighing, or response to reasons different from the one the agent ought to have had. In chapter 4, it was argued that one harm is more deserved than another for a given wrongful act provided that the act conjoined with the one is treated by the agent in deliberation, given his modes of transaction with reasons, in a way that is closer to the way it ought to be treated by him than is the act conjoined with the other. And in chapter 5, it was argued, first, that the strength of a legal reason for a particular person to refrain from criminal conduct is in part a function of the degree to which he has a say over the legal facts that are constitutive of that legal reason's weight. This claim was then used to support the claim that given our legal system's commitment to the Principle of Lenity, according to which criminal defendants are to be treated as though they are as good as they can be reasonably thought to be consistent with the evidence, a criminal defendant's degree of culpability and of desert for wrongdoing is, in part, a function of how much say he has over a certain body of legal facts, namely those that are constitutive of the strength of his legal reasons to refrain from crime. If one criminal has less say over the law than another, then, *ceteris paribus*, he is reduced in criminal culpability and deserving of lesser criminal sanction than the other. This is true even if the two performed precisely the same criminal act, while in precisely the same mental state, and while possessing precisely the same psychological and behavioral capacities. Duplicates in all of these respects can differ in criminal culpability, and be deserving of different sanctions, solely because the one has more say over the law than the other.

If we add the further claim that kids have less say over the law than adults do, then we reach the conclusions we seek: Kids are reduced in criminal culpability and deserving of lesser criminal sanctions, *ceteris paribus*. That is what justifies our policy of giving kids a break. Put simply, kids are to be held to lower standards when it comes to the modes of transactions with reasons they ought to have. Such standards are dictated by the strength of the legal reasons a person has to refrain from norm-violating behavior. The stronger the reasons, the more stringent the demand. Since kids have less say over the law than adults do, and since the authority of the law, especially the criminal law, derives from the fact that those subject to it have a say over it, the legal reasons for kids to refrain from crime are weaker than the legal reasons for adults to refrain. And so the standards of culpability are lower. The result is that less bad things need to be attached to crimes for them to be treated by kids in deliberation in the way they ought to be. Kids are not required to be as averse to crime as adults are required to be, because kids have less say over the law than adults do. This argument provides a principled grounding for a policy to which we are all deeply attached: the policy of giving kids a break.

It is because this argument does not draw on any psychological or behavioral differences between kids and adults in order to justify our leniency towards kids that it evades the criticisms, offered in chapters 1 and 2, of the Proxy for Culpability, Kids Will Be Kids, and They'll Grow Out of It arguments. Under the argument just described, kids ought to be given a break thanks to the nature of their limited political rights. Age has a political meaning: it marks the attainment and the absence of the right to have a say; it marks the moment at which one's say over the law matters to the authority of the law over one. It is because of the political meaning of age, it is suggested here, that we ought to give kids a break.

As is perhaps obvious from this description of the account offered here of the grounds for our policy of leniency towards kids, there is one central piece of the puzzle about which far less has been said so far than needs to be said: the idea of *having a say*. Section 6.1 offers an account of the conditions under which one person has more of a say over the law, in the relevant sense, than another. Section 6.2 substantiates the claim that, in that sense of "having a say," adults have more of a say than kids. The section also explains the sense in which kids have *any* say, which they do, primarily because they are granted some speech protections. Section 6.3 offers a rationale for constructing political institutions to deny kids as much say as we grant to adults. The central claim there is that this is justified to the extent that it is a way of ensuring that we who have a say over today's law, will also have a say over tomorrow's by having a reasonable opportunity today to influence the values of those who will vote tomorrow in a way that is guided by the values we inculcate today. This, it is suggested, is essential for any state that draws its authority from the fact that citizens have a say over the law.

A question that immediately arises concerns the degree to which the same line of thought offered to support giving kids a break supports, or fails to support, giving a break to other groups of people who have less of a say than do fully enfranchised adults such as, for instance, visitors, both legal and illegal, and members of traditionally oppressed groups. I set this issue aside here, and address it at length in chapter 7.

6.1 Having a Say

The view of "having a say" with which I am operating here is as follows: *To have a say over something is to be entitled to exert influence over it, and to be free of those obstacles to the exertion of that influence that one is entitled to be free of.* There are three conditions here, which are necessary and sufficient for having a say, two concerned with entitlements and a third concerned with the facts on the ground, as it were:

> D has a say over L *if and only if* (1) D is entitled to exert influence over L, and (2) D is entitled to be free of a certain class of obstacles, O, to the exertion of influence over L, and (3) D is in fact free of O.

We might summarize this by saying that to have a say one must have a real and meaningful opportunity to exert the influence one is entitled to exert. Without an entitlement to be free of many obstacles to the exertion of the influence one is entitled to exert, one's opportunity is not meaningful; and without the absence of those obstacles, one's opportunity is not real.

Several observations are in order. First, having a say involves an entitlement *to exert* influence, not *to have* influence. One who has a say is not entitled to actually make a difference to the outcome. Many who exert influence have no influence; their exertions are for naught. But they still might have a say. Voters have a say over things on the ballot even when they are outvoted, and so have no influence on the outcome. By voting, they exert their influence, despite having none in the end. Second, having a say is a normative notion. It consists, in part, of a pair of *entitlements*. Many who have powerful influence have no say, for the influence that they have is not an influence to which they are entitled. The ruling party in China, for instance, has no say over American fiscal policy, but it has an enormous influence over it. Many who exert influence, but have none, also have no say. Ineffectual, disenfranchised protesters, living in a regime in which their speech is not protected, have no say. That might, in fact, be the primary thing they are protesting about. Further, many who exert no influence still have a say for they are *entitled* to exert their influence and are not prevented from doing so by anything that they are entitled to be free of. If A votes and B does not only because B was delayed by a flat tire on the way to the polls, then although A exerted his influence over the policies the election concerned, and B did not, A and B equally had a say over those policies for they were equally entitled to exert their influence through the vote and the obstacles to doing so that B faced (the flat tire) were not obstacles he was *entitled* to be free of.

In addition, the obstacles to exerting influence that one is entitled to be free of might be present, and yet overcome. In such a case, one has less of a say than one would have had had one faced no obstacles. Say that A and B are equally entitled to vote, and equally entitled to be free of many work obligations that would impose significant costs on voting. Employers, let's imagine, are required by law to take reasonable steps to allow their employees to vote, and the government is required, by law, to make it reasonably possible for employees whose employers take those steps to vote without incurring significant costs. So, for instance, employers are required to provide at least an hour when the polls are open during which employees are not required to be at work, and the government is required to staff polling places sufficiently as to make it possible for people to vote in less than an hour. Say that the lines at B's polling place are so long that he can vote only if he misses more than an hour of work, and so loses wages, or risks being fired, while the lines at A's are short. But imagine that B braves the lines, votes, and convinces his boss not to dock his pay or lay him off. So B does not suffer the burdens that he has a right to avoid in exerting his influence. His employer makes accommodations beyond those to which B is entitled. Still, B has less of a say than A does, for B *faced* obstacles to exerting his influence that he was entitled not to face, namely lines so long as to make it impossible to vote in an hour. That he overcame the obstacles does not erase the fact that he faced them. So, we cannot conclude from the fact that two people, who are equally entitled to exert influence, and who do equally exert influence, have equal say. The reason is that one or the other (or both) might face obstacles to exerting their influence which they were entitled to be free of, but overcame nonetheless. How much say you have, we might say, is not a function of how loud your voice is. If you are entitled to speak in a quiet room, but the room is noisy, then you have less of a say than others even if you make yourself heard over the din.

While the notion of entitlement of interest to us is *legal* entitlement, this is not built into the concept of having a say. One can have a say in virtue of a moral entitlement to exert influence, and a moral entitlement to be free of certain obstacles to exerting it. We each have a say, in this sense, over who we spend our leisure time with (within limits), for instance, or what we eat (within limits). There also appear to be entitlements that have their source in other things besides law or morality. Membership in the tiddlywinks club might entitle you to attend tournaments. But this isn't a legal entitlement, and it isn't a moral entitlement. But, as appealing as this last thought is, I do not want to insist on it. Even those who think that the entitlements generated by club membership are moral, or legal, should grant the point of primary importance for my purposes. That point is that there are as many different kinds of "having a say" as there are kinds of entitlement. What matters for us is legal entitlement, but if it turns out, contrary to what I believe, that that's a species of moral, or even prudential (if there is such a thing as prudential entitlement), then so be it.

The reason that what concerns us is having a say in the sense which is grounded in legal entitlement, is that it is in that sense of having a say that the strength of a person's legal reasons vary with the amount of say that he has (when the authority of the law over him derives from the fact that he has a say over it). Morality does not have authority over us thanks to the fact that we have a say over its content, and so it is no surprise that the strength of our moral reasons does not vary with the amount of say we have over morality (which is probably none). There are probably non-legal bodies of rules and norms that have authority over people thanks to the fact that they have a say over them. That appears to be the case in certain clubs and related organizations. In such cases, the relevant reasons—"club-reasons," to use the term of art offered in chapter 5—vary in strength for people depending on how much say they have over them. But it is certainly the case that legal authority often derives from the fact that people have a say over the law, and, when it does, the strength of legal reasons varies with the amount of say they have. Since it is the strength of legal reasons that concerns us here—thanks to that strength's import to criminal culpability and desert of criminal sanction—it is the sense of having a say derived from legal entitlements that is of interest to us here.

One can have *more or less* say in three different ways that matter for our purposes, corresponding to the three different conditions involved in having a say.[1] First, one can be entitled to exert more or less influence. The more influence you are entitled to exert, the more of a say you have in this first sense. In this sense, members of Congress have more of a say over the law than do their constituents, since members of Congress are entitled to author legislation. Second, one can be entitled to be free of more or fewer obstacles to the exertion of one's influence. Say that A's entitlement to exert influence is sensitive to the costs of removing obstacles to his exertion of influence. He's entitled to have the state spend up to $100 to remove obstacles, but not more. He would then have more of a say if the state was required to spend more than that to remove relevant obstacles. Similarly, if the law says that every voter is to have a polling place within a reasonable distance of his home, then voters have less of a say than they would under a system that granted a right to a polling place as close as the voter demands, even if the demand is unreasonable. Third, one can actually face more or fewer obstacles than one is entitled to be free of. If we are both entitled to have a polling place close by, but you do not get what you are entitled to in this respect, since your polling place is far, while I do get what I am entitled to since mine is close, then I have more of a say than you have.

Which of these three senses in which a person can have more or less of a say is relevant to the question of how much say kids have over criminal laws prohibiting behavior? The answer is "all three." Recall, again, the point that the strength of the legal reason for a person to refrain from crime varies with her amount of say over the law prohibiting the relevant behavior *only if* the law has authority over the person in virtue of the fact that she has a say over it. If the law draws its authority from a different source—if it has authority over the person in virtue of her enjoyment of state-produced benefits, for instance, or in virtue merely of her having opted in—then her degree of say over the law is not relevant to the question of how strong the legal reasons are

---

[1] There are other senses also. For instance, one can have a stronger or weaker entitlement. Say that both A and B are entitled to be free of obstacle O to the exertion of influence, but when circumstances conspire such that if A is free of it B will labor under it, and vice versa, A takes precedence; A's entitlement, let's imagine, trumps B's. In that case, A has more of a say than B does because his entitlement is stronger. Put another way, one's entitlement can vary in the degree to which it is subject to conditions. The less stringent the conditions, the greater the entitlement, and the greater the sense in which one has a say. But I set aside this way in which having a say can vary by degree.

for her to refrain. This point helps us to think through the issue of which sense of more-and-less say is relevant to our policy of giving kids a break.

Start with an observation, already introduced in chapter 5: states that draw their authority from the fact that the governed have a say over what state actions are authoritative ground their authority in citizen autonomy. Or, put another way, they justify what they do to citizens on the grounds that citizens are, in a meaningful sense, *doing it to themselves* when the state acts. Of course, this is not *literally* true. It is a rare prisoner who imprisoned himself. But if it is not literally true, in what sense is it true? I suggest that the sense in which it is true is this: if the state's authority derives from the fact that citizens have a say, then citizens are complicit in state actions. Their agency is implicated in what the state does, provided that the state acts in a way that is legally authorized. In general, one's complaint about another's behavior is weakened if one is complicit in that behavior. States that draw their authority from citizens' say over the law exploit this fact: citizens' complaints about state actions are weakened in such cases because the citizens themselves are implicated in that behavior; they are complicit in it.

This points us towards the following question: Under what conditions is a person complicit when a government acts? Under what conditions, for instance, are people complicit in the United States' government's actions against detainees at Guantanamo Bay? There are many different routes to complicity. One can give information that the government uses to capture and detain people, for instance. Or one can omit to interfere with the aim of furthering the government's actions. These are forms of complicity that are grounded in the intentional or knowing provision of aid. They have to do with one's causal contribution to what the state does. But a significant part of what the state does is the *legality*, or *authority*, of its conduct. The state doesn't just lock people up; sometimes it *exercises its authority* in locking people up. Those who contribute to this *normative fact* are also complicit.

This last point is very important and so deserves emphasis. It is well known that people's actions can make a difference to the normative facts.[2] If you promise to X, then you make it the case that you ought to X; prior to your promise this was not true. If you cause it to be the case that X-ing is legally prohibited, then you cause it to be the case that there is a legal, and so in that sense normative reason for people not to X. And, similarly, if you are complicit in the fact that the prohibition on X-ing is legal, and so generates a normative reason for people not to X, then you are also complicit in the things that are done with color of law in response to violations of this prohibition. So one form of complicity, the crucial form for our purposes, derives from one's real and meaningful opportunity to exert influence over the law, where it is in virtue of

---

[2] I intend the remarks to follow to be consistent with, although different from, the view of normative facts, and the significance of conduct that alters them, offered in David Owens (2012) *Shaping the Normative Landscape*, Oxford: Oxford University Press.

that real and meaningful opportunity on one's part that the government's actions are authorized.

If we assume that the government is *allowed* to do what it does, we can then ask why it is so allowed. Where did this normative fact come from? The answer points to a body of legal facts in virtue of which the government's behavior is legally authorized. In virtue of what do those facts have legal authority? Often the answer will appeal to the fact that a group of people subject to them also had a say over them. If you are a member of that group, then you are complicit, in a meaningful sense, even if different from other forms of complicity, in the government's behavior. You either exerted influence over the law, or forewent a real and meaningful opportunity to do so. And so the government's behavior is, in a sense, *your* behavior, for you had a say over it. The more influence you were entitled to exert, the more complicit you are. And the more real and meaningful the opportunity to exert your influence, the more complicit you are.

So, how much say you have *in all three senses in which having a say varies by degree* the more complicit you are in authorized government behavior, the authority of which derives from the fact that people have a say over the law. Further, when the person against whom the government acts *is you*, then you are complicit in your *own* suffering at the government's hand. And the more say you had, the more complicit you are. To say to a fully enfranchised adult who is punished for a crime, "It's your own damn fault!" is to speak the literal truth. He is complicit in the force used against him and so his punishment is, in a meaningful sense, self-inflicted.

The account of having a say, and having more-or-less say, offered here can feel stipulative, or merely verbal. Perhaps there are other ways to use the term. But although I am stipulating how the term is to be used, I choose *for a reason* this particular way of stipulating the use of the term. The reason is that it is in this sense of having a say that citizens can be complicit in legally authoritative government actions thanks to their entitlements and their opportunities to exercise their entitlements. And so it is in this sense of having a say that the force that the state applies to a person who violates a criminal prohibition can be meaningfully thought of as force that he applies to himself, despite this not being true in a causal sense. When states draw their authority from this fact—when part of what justifies what they do to citizens is that citizens are thereby doing it to themselves—then the agent's degree of complicity in state actions, under the law, bears directly on the appropriate standards with respect to which his modes of transactions with reasons are to be judged. The more complicit he is, the stronger are his legal reasons to refrain from crime because the more complicit he is the more the standards with respect to which he is judged are *his* standards. And so the more say he has, in the sense of "having a say" offered here, the stronger are his legal reasons to refrain from crime. To act autonomously is to act on one's own reasons. The more those reasons are one's own, the more one's act is autonomous. Similarly, for the state's act to be the autonomous act of citizens is for the state to be acting on reasons that are the citizens' own. The more they are their own, the more the state's act is the autonomous act of citizens'. And so the more say one has over the law, the more legal reasons are *one's own* legal reasons, and the stronger are the legal reasons for one to refrain from violating criminal laws.

In short, to have a say over the law is to have a real and meaningful opportunity to exert influence over it. To either take advantage of or forego such an opportunity is to be complicit in government action that is authoritative thanks to being legal. The more one is complicit, the more the legal reasons provided by facts are one's own legal reasons. And the more they are one's own legal reasons, the stronger they are for one, in a system that grounds its authority in the autonomous agency of citizens.

6.2 How Much Say Do Kids Have?

Before we can answer the question of how much say kids have over the law, we have to have some sense of how much say *anyone* has over the law. Under the account of having a say offered here, the degree of say that full participants in the legal system have will vary from legal system to legal system. This is so since the relevant entitlements are legal, and so to know what a person's legal entitlements are, such as a legal entitlement to exert influence over the law or to be free of certain obstacles to the exertion of that influence, one has to examine the law governing that person. Further, we are likely to find differences in how much say people have even under two legal systems that are constructed in exactly the same way, for people with the same legal entitlements might differ in their social conditions, and so might differ in their freedom from obstacles to the exertion of influence that they are entitled to be free of. So everything that follows in this section comes with a caveat, for general assertions in this domain are perilous.

However, some things can be said. Generally speaking, if a person is entitled to do more, it is that much harder to make it possible for him to do it; more doors have to be unlocked. The success of a government authorized to act thanks to citizens having a say over its behavior depends upon citizens actually having the opportunity to exert their influence over the law. So a state that entitles its citizens to *too much* say will find it virtually impossible to empower them to exert their say, and so will fail. If every citizen had a say over every word of every law, or if the government could never take a step without the authorization of every citizen, the government would never do anything, or, worse, would act tyrannically. Further, and importantly, big entitlements are highly sensitive to vicissitudes. The more you are allowed to do, the more things can interfere with your ability to do it. Since the government cannot control very much, by granting too much say to too many people, the government guarantees inequality. The government will not be able to remove all the obstacles to exerting influence that people are entitled to be free of, and so there will be inequality in the say of those who are unlucky enough to encounter such obstacles and those who are lucky enough not to. A workable legal system has to strike a balance. It must give people enough say to warrant the claim that they are complicit in the government's actions; but, if it is committed to equality, it must not grant them so much say that it cannot provide people with the freedom to exert the influence to which they are entitled.

The use of voting as the primary instrument for the exertion of influence to which people are entitled is a first step towards striking the needed balance. In a system in which *the only* form of influence people are entitled to exert is the vote, giving people an equal say is, if not easy, at least practicable: the government needs only to make it possible for people to vote and for their votes to count; or, rather, the government must remove various obstacles to voting by, for instance, making polling places available, providing a means for communicating one's vote that is relatively easy to master, and ensuring that reasonable steps are taken to count all the votes registered. Imagine, for comparison, a consensus-based system in which citizens join each other in a room and speak with the aim of influencing the crowd's opinion. Such a system is almost never one in which each person has an equal say, for there are many obstacles to the exertion of one's influence that people should be entitled to avoid and which are very hard, if not impossible, to equally distribute in such a system. If the system is designed so that, for instance, each is entitled not just to speaking time, but to be listened to during that time, then it is inevitable that some people will have far more say than others in this system. There is no chance that the government will succeed in leveling the playing field in this respect since factors such as charisma, or a talent for public speaking, inevitably make an enormous difference to the degree to which a person is listened to by a crowd. The government would have to take drastic measures to correct for such factors, and it would almost certainly fall short. So: in a system in which the only entitlement to exert one's influence is the entitlement to vote, where decisions are made on the basis of a count of those votes (no matter what count decides the question—majority, supermajority, unanimity), a person has a full say just in case he has a real and meaningful opportunity to cast a full vote.

But this is not our system. While it is true that having a say, in our system, is in large part constituted by the entitlement to vote, the entitlement to be free of many obstacles to voting, and the actual existence of mechanisms through which votes can be registered, such as the provision of polling places, laws barring various forms of interference with voters, and so on, it is also true that we are entitled to exert our influence over the law in other ways too. And, in our system, those other ways are far more important and prevalent. First, our system is a representative democracy, and, as such, representatives, and other legal officials, such as judges and actors in administrative agencies, are entitled to exert much more influence than are individual voters. For the rest of us, our votes exert influence by proxy, by exerting influence over our representatives and those whose employment in the government depends upon those we elect by vote. Since the most important votes we cast are not for legislation, but, instead, for our representatives, our primary means of exerting influence over the law is by proxy rather than directly. We exert our influence over the law by casting, omitting to cast, and threatening to cast our votes for those who are entitled to exert their influence over the law directly. In fact, often our entitlement to vote is not even an entitlement to influence the law by proxy, but, instead, to exert influence over those who will exert influence by proxy. Our representatives, that is, are often entitled to exert influence only by installing judges, or others with legally authorized discretion to exert direct influence over the law.

Further, and importantly, it is not the case that the only entitlement to exert influence we enjoy is by vote. Our system protects, and so entitles us, to exert our influence over the law through verbal and other expressive acts aimed at influencing other voters, as well as our representatives. Of course, no formal consequences are predicated on the outcome of speech, in the way that formal consequences are predicated on the outcome of elections, and so it is hard to tell how much of a say people have over the law thanks to speech protections. Suffice it to say, our entitlement to exert our influence through speech is, like most of the votes we are entitled to cast, an entitlement to exert influence over the law by proxy. Some forms of speech that lawmakers are entitled to make serve to exert influence over the law directly, such as, for instance, speech written into bills they propose. But these cases are rare. Speech of that kind is not of the sort that the rest of us are entitled to. To the extent that our speech protections are entitlements to exert influence over the law, they are entitlements to persuade and cajole those who are entitled to exert such influence directly.

The entitlement to exert influence through political speech, as important as it is, has introduced enormous inequality in the degree to which individuals have an actual influence over the law in the United States. Since the more money one has, the more it is possible to say, and the more people it is possible to say it to, our system's protection of the right to spend as much as one likes to speak guarantees that the rich will have louder voices than the poor. Does it follow that the poor have less say over the law than the rich? People are not *entitled* to have as much money as they would like to spend on political speech—although they might be entitled not to be *prevented* from accumulating that much money—so if there is a difference in the degree to which the rich and the poor have a say it is, oddly enough, not because the poor do not have enough money to exert much influence through political speech. Further, some inequities in speech are inevitable and so it cannot be that people are entitled to have *just as much* power to exert influence through speech as *everyone else*. A government that adopted such a position would be either paralyzed or tyrannical since it would never succeed in establishing laws over which citizens had a say. But, arguably, in a democracy like ours people *are* entitled to *relatively small* differences in the degree to which they, in comparison to others, others equally unentitled to formal legal powers to exert influence over the law, can exert influence over the law through speech. Extreme inequities, that is, are, in fact, obstacles to the exertion of influence which we are all entitled to be free of. At least, arguably. Of course, this immediately raises the question of how much inequality in this respect we are entitled to be free of. I have no answer to this question. But for our purposes, the most important point is that the contrast between adults and kids, when it comes to having a say, survives the observation that there are also differences among adults. Each American adult has as much say as a real and meaningful opportunity to vote, and a real and meaningful opportunity to speak, can give him or her. We could have more say, of course. And it is likely that we could have more say consistent with the capacity of the government to remove those obstacles to the exertion of our influence that we are entitled to be free of. And, of course, there are subgroups of adults who are burdened by many obstacles, both to voting and to speech, that they *are* entitled to be free of. But adults *as a class* do not labor under such obstacles.

It is for this reason that the thesis of this book can be summarized with the following slogan: Kids ought to be given a break because they are disenfranchised. Kids are not entitled to vote. So, in that extremely important sense, they lack a say over the law that adults enjoy. This is a very striking fact, and hard to rationalize. (A rationale is proposed in section 6.3.) But it is important to see that kids do have *some* say over the law, albeit less than adults. As we will see, what say they have derives from their speech rights. They *do not* have a say over the law thanks to the fact that kids are entitled to have their parents and guardians act in their interests. To be sure, there is such an entitlement. It is rooted in legally authorized force against parents who fail egregiously in this respect, through neglect and abuse, but also through gentler, albeit firm pressures applied on parents, such as pressures to provide adequate education for children, and through parental liability in tort and contract for the behaviors of children. Further, it is often the case that parents do exert what influence they have over the law, taking into consideration their children's interests. This might lead one to think that kids exert influence over the law through proxy; their parents exert influence for them. But this is a mistake. The reason is that kids have no entitlement that their parents *exert influence over the law* in a way that furthers their best interests. The fact that one has a child imposes no constraints whatsoever on one when it comes to one's entitlements to exert influence over the law. In so far as having a say is a normative notion—it consists in a real and meaningful entitlement to exert influence over the law—children's entitlement that their custodians should act in their interests is not an entitlement of the sort that suffices for having a say over the law. Children do not exert influence over the law by proxy when their parents do so. Put another way, a child is not complicit in the legally authoritative exercises of power against him thanks to the fact that the state will punish his parents for neglect or abuse. The protections of him that the state thereby provides do not give him a say in its legally authoritative conduct.

However, kids are entitled to speak, and in so far as speech is a mechanism of exerting influence over the law, whether the speaker is an adult or a child, kids do have some say over the law thanks to their speech-based legal rights. It is widely recognized that speech protection in the United States, for adults, is far from unlimited. The aphorism that "You can't scream 'Fire!' in a crowded theater," summarizes the idea: protected speech can be harmful, on balance, but if it is *too* harmful, it is not protected. Of course, whether a form of treatment, speech, or something other than speech, will harm someone depends on that person's vulnerabilities. And age is an excellent marker of both vulnerability and invulnerability to certain kinds of harm. The elderly are at risk of harms that the middle-aged are not, for instance. Many movie theaters offer screenings of films in which parents are invited to bring their infants. These films often have violence and sex in them, but it would be ridiculous to fear the harm to infants from such exposure, despite the fact that four- or five-year-olds could suffer some harm from viewing such material.

A very large percentage of the Supreme Court cases involving children and First Amendment speech protection—whether protection of rights to speak, or rights to hear speech—turn, essentially, on the way in which the harm calculation is affected by the child's position as a speaker or hearer. Sometimes children's special vulnerability to harm is a function of their developmental stage. Cases involving children and obscene material, for instance, are premised on the idea that kids are more likely to be harmed by such material than adults, and so obscene speech by or for children is less strongly protected than similar speech by or for adults.[3] But sometimes the special vulnerability of children derives, not from their "natural" qualities, but from the risk of interfering with their legally guaranteed entitlements. Having been granted certain benefits under the law, children are vulnerable to the harm of loss of those benefits thanks to speech by or for them; this is a vulnerability which adults do not share, since they are not granted the same benefits. All of the Supreme Court cases involving speech at state-funded schools, for instance, turn on this. Consider, for instance, *Hazelwood School District v. Kuhlmeier* (484 U.S. 260 (1988)). Student-written articles on teen pregnancy and divorce were excluded from the school newspaper by school officials, and the students challenged the constitutionality of the exclusion on First Amendment grounds. The courts, eventually, sided with the school, ruling that speech by children in schools does not enjoy the same protections as speech outside of the school setting. The central driving idea is the simple one that anything that serves as a setback to the school's educational mission is harmful to the children being educated there. Further, it was up to the school to decide what was, and was not, a setback, on balance, to its mission of educating children. Since children have a protected right to a state-funded education, anything that interferes with their exercise of that right is harmful to them; this is a harm to which adults are not vulnerable since they do not have the same legally mandated right to an education.

Limits on speech deriving from the prospect of harm differentially affect adults and children because, in general, they are vulnerable to different harms. But that is not a difference of interest to us here since it makes no difference to the degree to which adults and children have a say over the law thanks to an entitlement to exert influence through speech. We are all, regardless of age, potentially barred from speech that could badly hurt other people. So far, then, to the degree to which we have a say over the law thanks to speech protection, adults and kids are the same. However, there is a very important asymmetry between adults and children: many aspects of child speech are subject to parental consent. The Supreme Court has granted, for instance, many limitations on the access of children to obscene material. Even cases in which

---

[3] See, for instance, *Ginsberg v. New York* (390 U.S. 629 (1968)).

the court seems to weaken limitations on access to objectionable material by children support this contention. For instance, in *Brown v. Entertainment Merchants Association* (131 S.Ct. 2729 (2011)), the majority of the court struck down a law that, among other limits, attached criminal penalties to the sale of certain violent video games to children, but allowed such games to be purchased or rented for children by parents and guardians. The majority of the court's reasoning, however, was that many horrific violent depictions fall short of "obscenity," which the court took to be an essentially sexual category. The implication of the court's reasoning is that there would be no First Amendment problem with requiring parental consent for minors to access sexually obscene video games, or criminalizing those who sell to children without parental consent; the problem was the limits the statute imposed on access to *violent* video games. Justice Thomas, in his dissent in that case, asserts that the First Amendment does not grant unconditional rights to children to hear *any* kind of speech; all such rights, he thinks, are conditional on parental consent. But even assuming that Thomas is wrong about the scope of the conditionality of kids' First Amendment rights on parental consent, the fact that at least some of the rights granted to children under the First Amendment are conditional in this way is not contested.

But for our purposes here, a more important, although related, way in which child speech is subject to parental consent derives from consideration of the way in which the law allows parents to restrict the movements of their children, and their children's access to other people, in ways that adults cannot be legally restricted. The First Amendment, of course, protects not just a right to speech, but also a right to "assembly." The right to assembly is ordinarily taken to be implicit in the right to speech: part of what it is to have a meaningful right to speak is to have reasonable access to hearers of one's words. Put in the language of the present context, the First Amendment grants a right to *having a say*. This means that it grants both an entitlement to exert one's influence through speech, but also an entitlement to be free of various obstacles to gathering with other people in order to speak and be heard. We give meaning to this second entitlement in part, albeit only in part, through the criminalization of kidnapping, an offense which includes many acts of restraining another's movements without his or her consent. But many restraints which would certainly constitute kidnapping, if applied to an adult, are perfectly legal if applied to a child *provided the child's parent consents to the child being restrained in that way*. The result is that a parent can legally lock up a child in order to prevent the child from attending a political rally, or to prevent the child from filing a petition at City Hall. And, in general, there would be no objection, on First Amendment grounds, to legislation which granted children access to means of communication only with parental consent. The point might be put this way: while children are entitled to exert their influence over the law through speech (subject to the same restrictions as adults, most of which are harm based), they are only *conditionally* entitled to be free of the obstacles to the exertion of their influence that adults are entitled to be free of; the relevant condition is parental consent. The result is that children have less of a say over the law thanks to speech protections than adults have, for children can be barred from exerting influence over the law through speech if their parents do not consent to the removal of certain obstacles that prevent them from doing so. Kids' speech-based say over the law is parentally gated.

That kids' say over the law, grounded in speech rights, is *parentally* gated is important. When an adult is subjected to legally authoritative force, in a system like ours, he is complicit in the state's behavior in part thanks to the fact that he had a speech-based say over the law; this is part of what makes it true that what he suffers is, in a meaningful sense, self-inflicted. When a kid is subjected to legally authoritative force, he too is complicit in the state's behavior in part thanks to the fact that he had a speech-based say over the law. But his complicity in the act is mediated by his parents' role. The thought that I am to blame for what is done to me with the color of the law is diluted when had by a kid. It is, instead, the thought that I-*and-my-parents* are to blame for what is done to me with the color of the law, since what say the child has over the law through speech is subject to parental consent. So, kids do have a speech-based say over the law, but it is weaker than that of adults.

For our purposes here, what is of principal importance are two claims: first, that kids do have some say over the law, and, second, that they have less say than adults. Adults are entitled to exert influence over the law through votes and speech. Kids are entitled to exert influence only through speech, and even then they are entitled to be free only of those obstacles to speech that their parents are willing to allow to be removed. The result is that when a kid is subjected to harm at the hands of the state, acting with legal authority, it is true both that he is complicit in what is happening to him, since he had some say over the law, and also that he is substantially less complicit, *ceteris paribus*, than an adult in his shoes would be. Add the further claim, offered in chapter 5, that the strength of the legal reasons for a person to refrain from crime is modulated by the amount of say that she had in the law prohibiting her behavior, and we reach the further result that the legal reasons for kids to refrain are weaker than the legal reason for adults to refrain. Add the views of culpability and desert developed in chapters 3 and 4 and we reach the conclusion that kids are diminished in culpability for their crimes, in comparison to adults, and are deserving of lesser sanctions.

Still, this does not quite complete the argument in favor of leniency towards kids who commit crimes. If our legal institutions ought to be set up in such a way that kids are given as much say over the law as adults, then our legal institutions ought to be set up in such a way that leniency would be inappropriate. So, at this stage what can be said is that *given* that kids are disenfranchised, and enjoy weaker speech protections than adults, they also ought to be given a break when it comes to criminal liability. But a complete argument for giving kids a break would also show that the way things are in this respect is the way they ought to be; it would involve showing that kids ought to be given the lesser say over the law that we actually give them. This is the task of section 6.3.

6.3 *Should* Kids Have Less Say Than Adults?

Say I described a political system in which legal authority is derived from the fact that citizens have a say over the law. Further, it's a vote-based system; the primary mechanism through which citizens are entitled to exert influence over the law is by vote. But about 25 percent of citizens lack the vote and so are significantly diminished, in comparison to the rest, in the degree of say they have over the law. I further add that the criterion of exclusion is based entirely on a physical characteristic over which no individual has control, and which is not in itself morally significant; the characteristic that suffices for exclusion is as morally irrelevant as having a long nose, or a particular skin color. Based on this description alone, you might think that the system being described differs very little, if at all, from South African apartheid. But, of course, this is *our* system, albeit that the quality sufficient for denial of the vote is age, rather than race. This difference, however, makes all the difference. Our system is on a completely different moral footing from apartheid. But the question is why. The question is why age is a legitimate ground, maybe even a morally obligatory ground, on which to deny people the vote.

It is obvious that the ground for denying kids the vote cannot be that they, all of them, are lacking the psychological capacities to wield it well. For one thing, many kids would be great voters, if given a chance. And many adults, perhaps even most adults, are not. It cannot be that the issue is factual knowledge, for there are many kids who know plenty about government, about public policy, about politics, and many adults who know almost nothing of relevance. And, were the vote given to kids, then many kids would attain the knowledge they need since we would want them to have it, and they would have a use for it and so would seek it.

There is no property of interest lacked by *everyone* under 18, so perhaps age is of significance to the vote because it is a proxy for something else. As discussed in chapter 1, any policy that sorts particulars on the basis of their possession, or lack of possession, of a proxy property, rather than the property of real interest, must be supported by a showing to the effect that preferential rates of false and true positives and negatives are achieved by sorting on that basis, rather than through use of a different, equally implementable sorting method. But before we can engage with the question of the false and true positive and negative rates of a sorting method, we need to know what the property of real interest is. When will we have gotten it right in granting or denying the vote to a particular person on the basis of age? It seems to me that there can be no adequate answer to this question, and so it seems to me that age is not relevant because it is a proxy for some other property that warrants enfranchisement.

To see this, start with the obvious observation that, if there were some property for which age was a proxy, then it is a property that newborns lack and many adults possess. So it's a property acquired along the way. Still, many properties that meet this very weak requirement, including many that are necessary for a claim to a voting right, cannot be the property for which age is a proxy. For instance, it cannot be that age is a proxy for the absence of the base level psychological capacities needed to register a vote and know what one is doing in doing so. We can see this by reflecting on laws that deny the franchise to adults on grounds of incompetence. Many, although not all, states in the United States have such laws.[4] However, an adult cannot be denied the vote without a specific finding to the effect that he or she is not competent. This requires a hearing in which experts testify about the person's capacities, and the person has an opportunity to plead his case to remain enfranchised. Children, by contrast, are disenfranchised in the absence of any finding of incompetence, much less are children entitled to hearings in which such findings are made. Further, the competency bar for the adult vote is very low. The state of Hawaii, to give just one typical example, bars the vote to "incapacitated persons" and defines that term by statute like so:

[A]n individual who, for reasons other than being a minor, is unable to receive and evaluate information or make or communicate decisions to such an extent that the individual lacks the ability to meet essential requirements for physical health, safety, or self-care, even with appropriate and reasonably available technological assistance. (HAW. REV. STAT. § 560:5–102)

Since many healthy 8-year-olds, and virtually any healthy 12-year-old, would count as sufficiently competent to vote by this standard, it is no surprise that, in this statute, Hawaii specifically bars minors from being adjudged competent or incompetent using this definition. The state of California goes so far as to exclude from the vote only adults who cannot fill out an "affidavit of voter registration" (CAL. ELEC. CODE § 2208(a)), which is a very simple form requiring only information, like name and address, that most school children can easily provide, much less young teenagers who regularly fill out job and school applications. There is an irony to the fact that an adult would be judged incompetent by this standard if he required his 10-year-old granddaughter's assistance to fill out the voter registration forms.

If absence of those qualities necessary for an adult to retain the vote were what age is a proxy for—if a 17-year-old possessing such psychological capacities counts as a false positive in a system, like ours, that denies that vote to those under 18—then it is just obvious that an age threshold of 18 for the vote is far too high. If in setting an age threshold for the vote we are really trying to sort those who are capable of filling out an "affidavit of voter registration" (CAL. ELEC. CODE § 2208(a)), from those who are not, then an 18-year-old threshold has an enormously high false positive rate which could be reduced without almost any significant loss in the true positive rate, by dropping the voting age to 12, or perhaps even lower. Almost anyone who can fill out such a form at the age of 18 can also do it at a much younger age.

Those who think that age thresholds for the vote make sense because age is a proxy for something else need an account of the relevant property under which there is a good reason not to exclude those who are of age from the vote on the grounds that they

---

[4] A fifty-state survey of such laws can be found here: http://www.bazelon.org/wp-content/uploads/2017/01/voting-rights-guide-2016.pdf 2016.pdf (accessed October 2, 2017).

lack that property. At least, that is what is required if they are to accept our policy of denying the vote only to adults who are severely incapacitated. This is a tall order. One way to meet this requirement would be to show that age is a proxy for a property that once possessed is never lost. But given how little psychological commonality there is between, for instance, 19-year-olds and 80-year-olds, it is hard to believe that there is any such property. Alternatively, our practice of denying the vote only to those adults lacking capacities possessed by quite young children would make sense if there is a difference between the properties that warrant retaining the vote, if you had it already, and the properties that warrant being given the vote, if you did not. But this cannot be right. If a person is entitled to something because of the way he is, then when he stops being that way, he loses the entitlement. This is no less true of the vote than anything else. Put another way, a child who differs not at all in any significant way from many adults who have the vote has a valid complaint about his disenfranchisement and this complaint is not dispelled by noting that the adults in question *used to* have properties that qualified them for the vote.

We need a completely different kind of story if we are to justify disenfranchisement on the basis of age, a story that does not pretend that age is a proxy for a property that warrants enfranchisement. I want to suggest that the policy of denying the vote to kids, and granting it to them when they cross into adulthood, is a good way to serve two distinct values to which we are committed and ought to be: equality and self-government. As I will now argue, a commitment to equality, given some empirical assumptions, places us under pressure to deny the vote to kids. By contrast, a commitment to self-government, given those same empirical assumptions, places us under pressure to grant the vote to kids. The age threshold is an extremely good way to serve both values, to the extent that that is possible. I explain.

A first observation is that parents enjoy two relevant entitlements with respect to their children. First, parents have a say over what their children do. Parents are entitled to make demands of their children and, within fairly strict limits, to exact compliance from them through coercive pressures, and other forms. They are entitled to exert influence over their children's behavior, and entitled to be free of various obstacles to the exertion of that influence. The point is not that parents in fact have the power to make their children do what they demand; some have such power, some don't, and there is much variation. The point is, rather, that they have *a legal entitlement* to exert a certain amount of pressure on their children to do as they say, and a legal entitlement to be free of various obstacles to the use of such pressures. Compare what the law allows you to do to cause your own children to be quiet late at night compared to what it allows you to do to cause your neighbor's children to do so. Second, parents have a say over their children's values. Parents are entitled to control their children's educations, associations with peers, reading materials, and so on. Parents enjoy legal entitlements the function of which is to entitle them to exert influence over who their children are and will become, in the deepest sense. Parents *have a say* over their kids' values. Here, again, it's important to emphasize the difference between power and entitlement.

Parents vary greatly in how much power they have over their kids' values—some have a lot, some very little. They also vary in how much effort they exert to influence their kids' values. It is also common for parents to have less power over their kids' values than do other people—peers, teachers, etc. But parents enjoy an *entitlement* in this respect that others do not enjoy, and to have a say is to have a set of entitlements. So even if others happen to have greater influence over a child's values than her parents do, her parents *have a say* over her values where others do not.

If kids had the vote, then these two parental entitlements—say over kids' behavior, and say over their values—would both be mechanisms through which parents with kids would have a say over the law. Parents would be entitled to exert influence over their kids in ways that would in turn influence their voting behavior. And, the more kids a parent had, the more say he or she would have over the law. Given that there is inequality in the distribution of children—some people have none, some have lots—to give kids the vote would be to introduce significant inequality in the amount of say adults have over the law, given parental entitlements to exert influence over kids' behavior and values. Therefore, our commitment to equality in this respect—we aim to have those who have an equal entitlement to exert influence over the law to have equal say over it—places us under pressure to deny the vote to kids. Note, however, that this pressure expires with the expiration of the parental entitlements to have a say over their children's behavior and values. When parents stop being entitled to a say over their children's behavior and values, they also stop having a say over the law through the exercise of such entitlements. This is not to say that parents stop *actually* influencing the law through their children once these entitlements expire; they might or might not. Their children might or might not vote the way they tell them, or vote from values that they inculcate. The point is, rather, that since having a say is a matter of entitlement, with the expiration of these entitlements comes the expiration of the possibility of parents having a say over the law through these mechanisms. So, we can reach the following conclusion: Our commitment to equality places us under pressure to deny the vote to children while their parents have a say over their behavior and their values.

We can imagine three different systems that would serve the value of equality. The first is a system in which parents *never* have a say over their children's behavior and values, and their children have the vote. We can dismiss this kind of system immediately. It's just obvious, given some basic facts about the dependency of children on their parents, that we ought to have a system in which parents have a say for at least some period of time over their children's behavior and values. The second is a system in which parents *always and forever* have a say over their children's behavior and values, and their children never have a say over the law. The third is our system: a system in which parents have a say over their children's behavior and values *while they are kids*, and when they stop being kids they come to have a say over the law. Our commitment to equality in the degree to which each of us from whom the government draws its authority have equal say (to the degree to which we have an equal entitlement to exert influence over the law) does not help us to choose between the second and third kind of system. But our commitment to self-government, I suggest, strongly favors the latter kind of system in which there is an age threshold at which parents lose a say over their children's behavior and values, and children gain a say over the law.

States, like ours, that draw (at least some of) their legal authority from the fact that citizens have a say over the law are dedicated to the idea that authoritative behavior on the part of the government is behavior in which citizens are complicit, thanks to having a say over the law, and so over what forms of behavior are and are not authorized. Call this a dedication to "self-government," recognizing that the term is sometimes used to refer to other kinds of government; for us, this will be a term of art. A dedication to this kind of self-government also requires an account of who is, and is not included among "the people," and how much say subgroups of "the people" have.

Can a dedicated commitment to self-government allow us to adjudicate between competing criteria for determining who has and lacks a say over the law? Or, can two states that are equally dedicated to this form of government adopt radically different criteria for having a say over the law, and for determining how much say people have, without constraint, consistent with this shared commitment? I believe that a dedication to self-government places a significant constraint on the criteria that allocate having-a-say, and, further, this constraint is met by an age threshold system like ours. A dedication to self-government places us under pressure to arrange things so that we have a say over not just today's law, but also tomorrow's. If our government is to persist, it must continue to be government *by us*. It must be true, for instance, that our government today in the United States is also the government of George Washington. But if this is to be true then it must also be true that George Washington had a say over the law in the United States today. Did he? He did, provided that he had a real and meaningful opportunity to exert influence over it. But if that is to be true there must be some mechanism that he was entitled to use in the eighteenth century that would involve the exertion of influence over law in the twenty first. Similarly, our commitment to self-government requires that we today have a say over the law tomorrow. This places us under pressure to adopt some mechanism through which today's citizens can have a say now over the law in place after they are dead. This is made possible, I suggest, by giving today's citizens a say over something that *will persist* after they are dead, and which will in turn structure the way in which influence is exerted over the law: their children's values.

The way in which people who have a say exert influence over the law is, to the extent that they are rational, guided by their values, by what they care about and take to be important and worth promoting. The result is that one way in which a person can exert influence over the law is by exerting influence *over the values of another person* who, in turn, exerts influence over the law. A lobbyist can exert influence over the law, for instance, by causing legislators *to care* about things that will lead them to exert influence over the law in a way that the lobbyist seeks. It is, in fact, in part because of this mechanism for exerting influence over the law that it would introduce inequality to give the vote to kids: since parents have a say over their kids' values, if kids had the vote, parents would thereby have more than an equal share of say over today's law.

The mere fact that a person exerts an influence over another's values, however, does not imply that he has a say over the law, in the sense of "having a say" of interest to us here. The reason is that it does not follow from the fact that a person exerts influence over another's values that *he is entitled* to exert such influence, much less that he is and *is entitled* to be free of certain obstacles to the exertion of such influence. A might have an influence over the law because he has an influence over B's values. But he only *has a say* over the law, through this means, if he is *entitled* to exert influence over B's values. Imagine that A influences B's values, and B has a say over the law, and the state acts in a way that is authorized by the law over which B has a say. A is complicit in the state's actions, thanks to being complicit in the authority of those actions, *only if A was entitled to exert influence over B's values*. So, an important mechanism through which people can have a say over the law is through entitlements to exert influence over the values of those who have a say over the law, entitlements that they have a real and meaningful opportunity to exercise.

Now, imagine that at t1 a certain group of people have a full say over the law and anticipate that at t2 their membership will be different: some who have a say at t1 will no longer at t2, perhaps because they will be dead, and others will have joined. The group can adopt legal criteria for determining which new people, not in the group at t1, will be included within it at t2. *Dedication to self-government places pressure on the t1 group to adopt criteria that will allow in people whose values the t1 members have a say over.* Such dedication does not place pressure on the t1 group to adopt criteria that allow in people with *shared* values, values like those of the t1 group. The t1 group might like that, but their dedication to *self-government* does not place pressure on them to adopt such criteria. The reason is that self-government permits exercising one's power to inculcate very different values in others than those one holds. Nor does dedication to self-government place the t1 group under pressure to adopt criteria that will allow in people whose values *they in fact influenced*. The reason is that they may have influenced the values of others *without legal authorization* and so were they to have an influence over the values of the t2 group thanks to such efforts, their influence would not contribute to their *having a say* over the law produced, and upheld, by the t2 group.

To elaborate on the point, if the t1 group is really dedicated to self-government, then they must adopt criteria allocating having-a-say thanks to which the t1 group has a say over the t2 law. That is a substantive constraint appropriate to a group dedicated to self-government. If there are people lacking a full say at t1 whose values members of the t1 group have a say over, then that is an excellent group of people to recruit into the t2 group. By granting them a say at t2, the t1 group has a say over t2 law, since they have a say over the values of the new t2 members, values that will inform the way in which those new members exert influence over the law. Provided that t1 members of the group lack a say, at t2, over the values and behavior of the new members, inequality will not be introduced by this system. But, of course, there is one particular group of people whose values adults have a say over *now*, and whose values they will not have a say over in the future: their children. These are, therefore, the perfect people to add to the voting rosters at t2.

So, children are given a vote once they come of age, I suggest, so as to give parents a means to exert influence over future law by exerting the influence which they are entitled to exert over their children's values. Self-government places us under pressure, that is, to give children, who will outlive us, a say over future law by giving them the vote. On the other side, our dedication to equality places us under pressure to deny children the vote while parents' retain their say over their kids behavior and values. These two pressures together favor a system in which kids are denied the vote, and come to have it when they come of age. It is no coincidence, then, that parents lose their say over their kids' values and behavior at the same moment that their kids gain the vote.

Of course, some children will never accept their parents' values; others will accept them far earlier than 18. Some parents will never even try to inculcate values in their children; others will try hard but fail. Some children will come to share their parents' values, but never exert influence over the law once they come of age because they never vote. Others will vote often but never do so guided by the values that their parents' aimed to inculcate. All of the combinations are possible. But, recall, again, that having a say over the law is not a matter of actually influencing it. It is a matter of having a real and meaningful opportunity to exercise one's entitlement to exert influence over the law. The way in which age thresholds give parents a say over future law is far from guaranteeing that they will succeed in making any kind of difference to future law. It is, rather, that they have a real and meaningful opportunity to try, by having a real and meaningful opportunity to affect their children's values.

Much besides parents influences a child's values. In fact, parental efficacy in this respect is probably easily overestimated (by parents, anyway). Children are probably more influenced by their peers, their teachers, the media, and so on, than they are by their parents. But none of these other people who influence a child's values are *entitled* to that influence. And so none of them have a say over the law through the child's later votes guided by the values they affected. Parents are special in this regard.

Many time limits in the law are there to provide reasonable opportunities to take advantage of one's entitlements. If, for instance, one is required to file a grievance within a certain amount of time following an allegedly harmful incident it is because one is entitled to complain, and entitled to be free of certain obstacles to exercising that entitlement; but neither of these entitlements is unlimited. The thought is that one is not entitled to be free of *all* temporal obstacles to complaining; one is entitled to a reasonably large window of time in which to complain. I suggest that age limits on voting are exactly like this. Parents are entitled to exert influence over future law by exerting influence over their children's values. But they are not entitled to more say over the law than other adults. So, they need to have a reasonable period of time in which to exert influence over their child's values, while their children do not enjoy the vote. The age threshold is a way of identifying that reasonable amount of time. If you haven't managed to exert influence over your kids' values in eighteen years, well, then, you're out of luck. You've had a reasonable opportunity to influence future law through this mechanism and can't expect more of an opportunity than you have had. Age thresholds for voting are, fundamentally, about providing real and meaningful opportunities for parents to exercise their entitlement to exert influence over future law, an entitlement that is an essential part of self-government, but it is not an unlimited entitlement. Were it unlimited it would fail to serve its end, in fact.

It is because our policy of denying kids the vote, and granting it to them when they turn 18, is primarily about giving parents' real and meaningful opportunities to exert influence over tomorrow's law, that there is nothing wrong with denying the vote to those kids who are equipped to wield it well, and granting it to many adults who are not. Voting age thresholds are *not* efforts to sort people in ways that roughly approximate their possession of a hard-to-observe quality, like competence to vote well. We should not assess a system with a voting age threshold by examining its rates of false and true positives and negatives. We get it right, when we deny a 17-year-old the vote, if the values of equality and self-government are best served by the policy that denies it to her. The question is not whether she *deserves the vote*. That is never the right question to ask when we look at the criteria that the system employs for allocating the vote. *Any* such system will inevitably deny the vote to many who deserve it as much as those to whom it is granted. Rather, the right question to ask is whether the relevant criteria serve the values to which we are, and ought to be, committed, namely the values of equality and self-government. If the arguments of the previous paragraphs succeed, then an age threshold system does indeed serve these values, and so we are justified in denying the vote to many a responsible adolescent and granting it to many an irresponsible adult.

An influence over one's children's values is not, of course, the only mechanism through which those who today have a full say over the law have a say over future law. *Stare decisis*, for instance, serves as a mechanism through which *anyone* who has a say over today's law also has a say over tomorrow's. But, still, age thresholds for enfranchisement are one important mechanism. Further, they serve to give legal color to a method of influence over future law that is all but inevitable. It is inevitable that parents will exert influence over their children's values. This is not to say that parental influence is the only thing that matters. Political ideology has been shown to be strongly influenced by genes and discoverable from entrenched patterns of primitive response to stimuli. It can be decoded, for instance, from the brain activity found when a person views disgusting images.[5] Early childhood influences that do not appear at all political

---

[5] W.Y. Ahn, K. T. Kishida, X. Gu, T. Lohrenz, A. H. Harvey, J.R. Alford, K.B. Smith, G. Yaffe, J. R. Hibbing, P. Dayan, and P. R. Montague (2014) "Non-Political Images Evoke Neural Predictors of Political Ideology" in *Current Biology*, 24(22): 2693–9.

almost certainly have powerful effects on later political decision-making of all sorts. But still, parental influence is part of the story. What age thresholds for enfranchisement do, together with laws entitling parents to exert influence over their children's value, is to harness these inevitable mechanisms for influencing future law to the end of promoting the value of self-government; they use the natural facts as a way of giving people say over future law and so make it the case that the future authority of law is derived in part from the fact that today's parents have a say over it.

What should we say about the childless? Do they have less of a say over future law than parents do? The answer depends on why they are childless. People have some legal entitlements to have children. The law grants them some opportunity to do so, and to be free of some obstacles to doing so. This is far from unlimited. Nobody has a legal right to fertility or to a willing partner. Nor does anybody have the right to a fully informed desire to have children. Those who are childless by choice are not encumbered by obstacles to parenthood that they have a right to be free of. But we have legal rights with respect to our consensual sexual partners; the law can bar adults from consensual sexual relationships only in very limited circumstances, such as incest. And we do have some rights to be free of certain causes of infertility, such as involuntary sterilization. And we have legal rights to pursue parenthood through adoption, and other related means. Of course, it would be silly to suggest that all of these entitlements that support the possibility of parenthood are in the law in order to make it possible for us to have a say over future law. There is much more than this that those who want to be parents are seeking. But, still, these entitlements do serve as an entitlement to take advantage of a particular mechanism for exerting influence over future law, and so in so far as the childless have real and meaningful opportunities to have children, opportunities that they may have forgone, they have a say over future law.

It is important to contrast the proposed rationale for the disenfranchisement of kids with the rationale according to which being a kid is a proxy for the absence of a quality in light of which enfranchisement is warranted. One is not warranted to vote thanks to the fact that one shares one's parents' values, or even that one's parents had a real and meaningful opportunity to mold them. These facts are irrelevant to one's *right* to enfranchisement. The world is full of people who would be fitting voters in the United States. Many, many people are deeply affected by American law, and the authoritative actions of the United States government. So, if these effects bestow a moral entitlement to have a say over American law through the vote, then there are many, many people who have such a moral entitlement. Of course, American kids are among the disenfranchised who are deeply affected by American law, but they are hardly the only ones. Think of the citizens of our trading partners, or our military enemies and allies. Think of the citizens of Iraq or Mexico. The rationale for the disenfranchisement of kids, and their enfranchisement once they come of age, brackets the question of who has a moral entitlement to have a say over the law through the vote. If we assume that we can be justified in denying the vote to many who have such a moral entitlement, then the mere fact of moral entitlement does not settle the question of who to enfranchise, who not to, and on what basis. Rather, we decide that question through consideration of that which we must care about if we are to bother inquiring in the first place about who to give the vote to: equality and self-government. We can then ask how to use enfranchisement as a means of maintaining self-government consistent with equality's constraints. What I've suggested in this section is that when we ask that question we find that an excellent way to further these values is to enfranchise kids only after parents have had a reasonable opportunity to take advantage of their entitlement to exert influence over their children's values. By doing so we give us today a say over our law tomorrow, whether or not we, or our children, are morally entitled to it, and we do so in a way that is consistent with our commitment to giving equal say to those who have an equal entitlement to exert influence over the law.

My proposed account of the grounds on which kids are excluded from the vote, and granted it when they reach an age threshold, intersects with the legal question of whether kids are a "discrete and insular minority." The term was coined in the famous footnote 4 in the Supreme Court's opinion in *United States v. Carolene Products* (58 S.Ct. 778) which supplies the authority for the claim that legislation aimed at a certain set of minorities—the "discrete and insular minorities"—is to be given strict scrutiny by the court. Racial minorities are of the "discrete and insular" variety, and other minorities also fall under that banner. The question then arises whether kids are a discrete and insular minority. In a 1973 publication, Hillary Clinton (then Rodham) suggests that they should be. She writes,

> [A]ge categories should be open to scrutiny for some of the same reasons well established suspect classifications are. The assumption that age qualifications are generally rational is not borne out by much of the evidence about the abilities of children at various ages and developmental stages before twenty-one. Thus, a group discriminated against on the basis of age could constitute a discrete and insular minority if their access to the political system were limited solely because they were young. They might possess the requisite rationality to participate, but be forbidden to do so. If this were the case, then they would be a suspect minority and state action affecting their interests should be required to demonstrate a compelling governmental interest in maintaining legal disabilities.[6]

I believe that Clinton is exactly right. However, when we turn to our denial of the vote to kids, we find, I think, a compelling governmental interest that is thereby furthered: an interest in giving current adults a say over future law, by providing them with a real and meaningful opportunity to inculcate values in their children that will guide voting decisions, while at the same time complying with the demands of equality. I believe, that is, that strict scrutiny of legislation denying the vote to kids is appropriate, and also that such legislation ought to survive it.

Finally, it is important to call attention to the fact that my proposed rationale for age thresholds for enfranchisement appeals to empirical claims about the rough age at

---

[6] Hillary Rodham (1973) "Children Under the Law" in *Harvard Educational Review* 43(4): 512.

which children are likely to vote in lock-step with their parents, and the age at which they are likely to vote in a way that is informed by values which their parents influenced. Eighteen is an appealing age threshold, I suggest, precisely because people of that age tend to be free enough from their parents to make their own decisions, albeit guided by values their parents might have inculcated, and, further, if they have not come to be guided by the values their parents' inculcated, they are not likely to do so ever. These empirical claims concern the plasticity of childrens' values, especially in relation to their parents. If developmental psychology has an important role to play in helping us to understand the grounds for leniency towards kids who commit crimes, I suggest, it is because it might provide some insight as to the accuracy of empirical claims that inform our choice of 18 as a voting age threshold. The psychology of kids, then, is not totally irrelevant to our topic; but it matters for different reasons, and so different discoveries about kids' psychology matter, than we might have thought. If we want to understand whether our social policy of giving kids a break accords with the discoveries of developmental psychology, we should be looking at what developmental psychology tells us about the ways in which children learn the values their parents' aim to inculcate in them.

6.4 Conclusion

The promise of this chapter was to complete the rationale for giving kids a break. Chapter 5 was intended to establish the claim that the strength of a person's legal reason to refrain from a crime is a function, in part, of the degree of say that the person has over the law prohibiting the behavior, the law thanks to which the behavior in question is criminal. This in turn implies, given the views of culpability and desert presented in chapters 3 and 4, respectively—views under which culpability and desert are in part matters of the standards with respect to which one's modes of transactions with reasons are appropriately judged—that psychological and behavioral twins can differ in culpability, and be deserving of different sanctions, thanks to the fact that they have different degrees of say over the law. Add that kids have less of a say over the law than adults, and we reach the conclusions that they are reduced in culpability, in comparison to adults, and deserving of lesser sanctions, regardless of their degree of psychological and behavioral similarity to adults. The essential missing piece in this argument, not developed in previous chapters, was the idea of having a say. This chapter's goal has been to explain what it is to have a say over the law; explain the sense in which kids do and do not have a say over the law in the United States; and to offer a justifying rationale for the primary mechanism through which they are diminished in their say over the law, namely through disenfranchisement, the denial of the right to vote.

Deference to recent developments in psychology and neuroscience, when it comes to discussion of kids and criminal justice—"Their brains are different!," it is often piously asserted, as though it were obvious why that matters—has become a way of signaling one's sympathy with the view that our system is insufficiently lenient towards child criminals. But to advocate for leniency on these grounds is to commit oneself to two positions, neither of which is attractive, and one of which is intolerable. The first, and the less problematic of the two, is the view that immature adults—adults, that is, who are like kids in their psychology, their behavior, or their brain development— ought to be treated more leniently than other adults who commit crimes. Some who ground their belief that kids deserve a break in the claims of developmental psychology and neuroscience are willing to accept this result. This seems palatable only because it is assumed that immature adults are reduced in culpability thanks to the psychological differences between them and mature adults. If they are psychologically different in relevant respects, however, then there is room in our current system to give them a break just as there is room to be lenient towards children who are reduced in culpability thanks to their psychological differences from adults. The law is replete with grounds of excuse available, in principle, to anyone accused of a crime, whether adult or child. The appeal to immaturity is an idle wheel in an argument for leniency, so understood. What matters is whether, for instance, they act from less objectionable mental states than the mature, or find themselves in a condition like that of duress, or trigger some other relevant excusing condition. If, by contrast, the immature adults do not differ psychologically from mature adults in a way that triggers an excuse, then it is hard to see why they should be treated leniently. It would be like treating more leniently those who are no better at math than second graders when they commit crimes of violence; their immaturity, while real, bears not at all on their culpability and so cannot ground leniency of treatment. The grain of truth in the thought that immature adults are owed leniency, that is, is just the thought that we should look closely for excuses when a criminal defendant is immature. Fair enough. But we should not favor leniency towards immature adults simply because they are immature.

But the second commitment of those who hope to ground leniency towards kids in the facts about developmental psychology and neuroscience is not just flawed, but morally intolerable. They are committed to the view that *precocious* kids, ahead of the curve in maturity, are not owed a break. But that just can't be right. Precocious kids are kids; and kids are owed a break, period. The view presented here provides us with what we need, for precocious kids are equally denied the vote, and so have as little say over the law as kids who are developmentally normal. They are reduced in culpability even in comparison to the adults whose maturity they match. They are properly held to a lower standard—a standard set by the strength of the legal reasons for them to refrain from crime. Those who are committed to leniency should be committed to leniency towards *all* kids, including the precocious. And so they should accept that the ground of leniency is political, not psychological or neural. Kids are to be given a break because they have less say over the law than the adults for whom our procedures and punishments are in the first instance devised.

It has been the goal of this chapter to make good on this idea. Kids enjoy significantly weaker entitlements to exert influence over the law than do adults. Thanks to this arrangement of our political institutions, adults who enjoy the entitlement to influence the values of children, such as parents and guardians, are able to have a say over future law. This makes future law *our* law, and so contributes to self-governance. After all, future law, like much law in a system like ours, has authority only if we have a say over it. Thanks to the disenfranchisement of kids, and our entitlement to exert influence over their values, we do.

7

Who Else Is Owed a Break?

7.0 Introduction

The rationale offered in chapter 6, building on the work of chapters 3–5, for the policy of giving kids a break would seem to extend to any group of people who are diminished in their say over the law in comparison to fully enfranchised adult citizens. It would seem that, if the argument succeeds, then anyone diminished in this respect ought to be given a break when it comes to criminal liability. And this is not a mere conceptual possibility, for there are several categories of people who we hold to account for violating our criminal laws who are not entitled to vote, and so who do not have a say over the law in that distinctive and important way. If members of these groups are owed a break, then our practices are in need of very significant reform. Visitors and immigrants, both legal and illegal, whether adults or children, fall into this category. Virtually every state in the United States denies the vote to prisoners. Many deny it also to those on probation or parole. And a significant number deny it to felons even after they have served their sentences and are no longer under government supervision.[1] Are visitors, immigrants, and those who are disenfranchised thanks to prior crimes all owed a break?

There are also categories of people who *are* entitled to vote but still lack a say over the law, under the account of "having a say" offered in chapter 6. Although they are entitled to vote, and entitled to be free of various obstacles to voting, they are not free of all the obstacles they are entitled to be free of. The indigent, for instance, often find it much harder to register and be assigned a polling place than do the rest of us. Lingering racism, whether explicit or implicit, sometimes drives policies and practices that make it far harder for members of traditionally oppressed racial groups to exert their influence over the law through the vote, an influence to which they are entitled.

---

[1] The American Civil Liberties Union offers a useful summary of the state-by-state differences, in all of the different respects just referred to, here: https://www.aclu.org/map/state-criminal-re-enfranchisement-laws-map (accessed March 1, 2016). If the data contained there is correct, then only two states, Vermont and Maine, allow prisoners to vote. It is very common for other democracies to provide no restriction on the voting rights of felons and prisoners. A picture of the range of positions adopted internationally can be found here: http://felonvoting.procon.org/view.resource.php?resourceID=000289 (accessed March 11, 2016). For a helpful account of the sordid history leading to America's disenfranchisement of those who have committed crimes in the past, see Jeff Manza and Christopher Uggen (2008) *Locked Out: Felon Disenfranchisement and American Democracy*, New York: Oxford University Press. See, also, Gideon Yaffe (2016b) "Give Felons and Prisoners the Right to Vote" in *The Washington Post*, July 26, 2016.

They encounter obstacles that they are entitled to be free of. Anyone entitled to a wide and empty road to the vote who enjoys at best a narrow, cluttered one falls into this category, as is true of many traditionally oppressed minorities today. Should we say that these groups too are deserving of a break when it comes to criminal liability? These are the questions that this chapter aims to address.

The answers, as we will see, vary. Different groups are different from each other, and from kids, in ways that matter to the applicability of the argument for giving a break. This chapter argues in section 7.1 that visitors and immigrants, whether legal or illegal, are not owed a break; the argument of chapter 6 does not extend to them. But, as argued in section 7.2, the argument does extend to those who have committed crimes in the past whether they are under state supervision, and denied the vote for that reason, or denied it even after they have been released having served their sentences. By denying them the vote, we also make it the case that they are owed a break. And, finally, section 7.3 shows that the argument extends to some, but not all, of the poor, for people are entitled to be free of obstacles to the exertion of influence over the law through the vote that poverty, especially extreme poverty, produces, often by having a corrosive effect on psychology that undermines motivation necessary to exercise one's legal entitlement to exert influence over the law. In short, other disenfranchised groups are both alike and different from kids in ways that matter to efforts to extend the argument of chapter 6 in support of giving them a break.

The issue under discussion in this chapter—the issue of which categories of people deserve a break for the same reason that kids do—can be framed as an objection to the account I have offered of why kids are to be given a break. After all, if the argument I have offered supports also giving a break to, for instance, illegal immigrants who commit crimes on our soil, and if that group of people are not in fact owed a break, then it follows that there must be something wrong with the argument offered for giving kids a break. The account would be thereby shown to be overinclusive.

In part, the answer to this objection just involves noting the inevitable role of reflective equilibrium in moral-philosophical argument. If there are intuitions in support of the claim that, for instance, illegal immigrants who commit crimes are owed no leniency, in comparison to fully enfranchised adult citizens, and those intuitions clash with principles that support even more firmly entrenched intuitions, such as the intuition that kids are to be given a break, then we have a choice between jettisoning the principles and jettisoning the intuitions with which they clash. To jettison the intuition that illegal immigrants are owed no breaks when they commit crimes is not to stop feeling its pull; it is, rather, to stop making inferences about, for instance, how we or our government should respond to crimes by illegal immigrants through appeal to this stubborn intuition. So, we should not conclude from the fact that the argument for giving kids a break extends to other groups that there is something wrong with the argument, even if intuition supports denying a break to members of those other groups. Perhaps reflective equilibrium needs to be created by jettisoning the conflicting intuition.

To some degree, as we will see, I rest on this line of thought in this chapter, albeit not with respect to the example just given: I believe that there are principled reasons for thinking that adult visitors and immigrants are *not* to be given a break for the reasons that kids are. The argument concerning kids does not extend to them, for reasons to be explained. But not all of the examples under discussion here are like this. I believe, for instance, that disenfranchised prisoners who commit crimes while in prison, or under other forms of state supervision, such as probation, are owed a break that it would be inappropriate to give to fully enfranchised citizens who are identical in their psychology and their behavior. (For this reason, among others, it is wrong to deny the vote to felons and at the same time fail to give them a break when it comes to criminal liability.) If there are intuitions opposing this conclusion—and many people have strong ones—I think they are to be jettisoned.

But appeal to reflective equilibrium's mandate to jettison some cherished intuitions is not the only line of response to be developed here to the charge of overinclusivity. In some cases, as we will see, the argument for giving kids a break does not extend to a particular group of people *even though members of that group are disenfranchised.* The basic reason for this is that it is not always the case that the state's authority to try and punish a person, as dictated by criminal law, is grounded in the say over the law of that person. There are other sources of that authority. And when such sources are present, the person's legal reasons for refraining from crime might be no weaker than that of a fully enfranchised citizen. The darkness surrounding this remark will be removed, I hope, in section 7.1.

As already indicated, the vote is not the only mechanism through which people exert influence over the law. Recall that in chapter 6 it was suggested that a crucial source of say over the law is speech protection. An entitlement to exert influence on others through speech, together with an entitlement to be free of obstacles to such exertions, such as obstacles to assembly with those who might want to listen to one's speech, constitute what it is to have a say over the law without a right to vote. Speech protections provide an indirect route to the exertion of influence over the law. To protect speech is to provide an entitlement to exert influence on those who have a say over the law (or those who have influence over those who have a say, etc.), rather than a direct entitlement to exert influence over the law itself. But in this, speech protections are similar to entitlements to vote for representatives; such votes give us an entitlement to exert influence over the law only by proxy, much as speech protections do.

The fact that speech by kids is protected is quite important to the argument of chapter 6. As was noted there, kids enjoy weaker speech protection than adults since their speech is parentally gated. Kids do not enjoy the same entitlements of access to mediums through which speech can be made, much less access to hearers of their speech, that adults enjoy; their access is limited by parental consent. But, still, it is thanks to the fact that kids enjoy speech protections at all that they can be said to have some say over the law. And so it is thanks to the entitlement to exert influence over the law, should their parents consent to their exertion of such influence, that kids are complicit, to the degree to which they are, in the validity of criminal prohibitions that they sometimes violate. Since they have some say over the law, the legal reasons to refrain from acts prohibited by criminal law have some strength for them, albeit less strength than they have for fully enfranchised adults whose speech protections are not subject to the consent of anyone else, and who enjoy the vote.

So, if we are to make progress on the question of the degree of say that other disenfranchised groups have over the law—visitors, prisoners, etc.—we need a clearer picture of what kinds of speech by them is and is not protected and what kinds of protections they enjoy. So, some discussion of speech protections will be given in what follows. Still, since the fundamental challenge to the argument of chapter 6—namely, that if it succeeds it rationalizes giving a break to many disenfranchised people who are not owed one—derives more from consideration of disenfranchised groups, than from the relatively weak speech protections of some groups, speech will be mentioned, but will not be my central focus in this chapter.

To appreciate the set of arguments to be offered in sections 7.1–7.3, recall the distinction between Republican and Liberal citizenship. For the Republican citizen, citizenship is constituted, at least in part, by having a say over the law. The Liberal citizen, by contrast, is subject to the law in virtue of the law's role in safeguarding freedom, including his own. I believe that citizens are often citizens in both senses: they are subject to the law both because they have a say over it and because it serves to safeguard their freedom. But it's clear that it is both conceptually possible and actually the case that many people enjoy the distinctive features of one of these two forms of citizenship and not the other.

In chapter 5 it was suggested that criminal laws, in contrast to other forms of law, bear a particularly important relationship to Republican citizenship. The government behavior dictated by criminal law—most notably, trying and punishing offenders—involves representing the acts of individuals as wrongful. To punish is, in part, to represent the act for which punishment is issued as violating some norm. Rebutting a charge of wrongfulness, while admitting that one's conduct violated a norm, requires denying the applicability of the norm to one's conduct; it requires denying that one's conduct is wrongful, not because it fails to meet the description of conduct pertinent to a prohibitory norm, but because the relevant norm is not applicable to one. If you are to be punished for spitting on the sidewalk, and you admit that you did indeed spit on the sidewalk without justification or excuse, and you admit that the norm against spitting on the sidewalk is law, the only shield available to you is rejection of the claim that the norm applies to you, that you are appropriately judged with respect to it. Such a rebuttal is available to, for instance, a citizen of the United States who spits on a New York sidewalk and who, per impossibile, the Singaporean government tries to punish. Such a person can admit that there is a law (of Singapore, but still) prohibiting conduct of the kind in which he engaged. But he objects to the punishment, and legitimately so, on the grounds that the law in question is not applicable to him since he is neither a citizen of Singapore, nor a visitor there, nor in any other way linked to the relevant legal norm.[2] But such a rebuttal is closed to Republican citizens of the state whose laws are in question. Republican citizens are complicit in the validity of the legal norms—prohibitions of certain forms of behavior—and so are barred from disavowing their applicability to their own behavior. They are, as I put the point in chapter 5, complicit in the judgment of the wrongfulness of their conduct essential to punishment, even if they do not share that judgment. By contrast, those who have no say over the law are not barred *for this reason* from offering this kind of complaint. There remains an open question whether they are barred from making it for some other reason. To respond to an offender who insists his conduct was not wrongful by saying, "It was in violation of a norm, and you cannot disavow the application of that norm to you," there needs to be some obstacle to the disavowal of that norm. Complicity with the norm's validity is one such obstacle; and we find such complicity on the part of those who have a say over the law. But perhaps there are other obstacles.

Given this way of conceptualizing the territory, we can ask about any group of people who lack a say over the law whether there is some other obstacle, in their case, to the disavowal of the law's applicability to them. As we will see, sometimes there is, and sometimes there isn't. When there is, the line of thought leading to the conclusion that kids should be given a break does not apply to the relevant group; when there is not, it does.

7.1 Visitors and Immigrants, Legal and Illegal

Visitors to the United States do not enjoy the same speech protections that citizens enjoy. This is clear from the relatively recent case of *Bluman v. FEC* (800 F.Supp.2d 281 (D.D.C. 2011)). The plaintiffs were foreign nationals living in the United States who were barred by law from making campaign and other political contributions, where it was granted on all sides that a similar ban on citizen contributions would be in conflict with the First Amendment. They challenged the law on the grounds that it curtailed their First Amendment rights. But they lost; the First Amendment, the court affectively ruled, does not grant the same entitlement to exert influence over the law to visitors as it does to citizens. But this is not to say that visitors do not enjoy *some* speech protections in the United States. A visitor could not be barred from participation in a political rally, for instance, consistent with the First Amendment. Further, to the degree to which speech protections do give a visitor say over the law, they provide the same say to visiting adults as to citizen adults, and the same say to visiting children as to citizen children. A visiting child's access to a political rally would be subject, like a citizen child's access, to parental consent.

---

[2] If you are tempted by the idea that what Singapore law bans is not spitting on the sidewalk, per se, but, instead, spitting on *Singaporean* sidewalks, which the person in our example did not do, then imagine, instead, that he pays someone to spit on a sidewalk and the person who accepts the payment chooses a Singaporean sidewalk as his target. When Singapore tries to prosecute this person as an accomplice, he can object that Singapore law does not apply to him.

So far, then, one might reach the conclusion that visitors are in a position similar to that of citizen kids: they have no say over the law through the vote, and although they have some say over the law through speech protections, they have less than do adult citizens. If we were to end here, we could follow the reasoning of the argument offered in chapter 6 for giving kids a break to the conclusion that visitors, too, are owed a break when they commit crimes. But this would be a mistake. The reason is, I suggest, that the status of visitor places one in a very similar position with respect to state power as the position occupied by fully enfranchised adult citizens. Say over the law is not the crucial source of the strength of the legal reasons that visitors have to refrain from crime; there is an alternative source relevant in the case of visitors. The alternative source is a commitment, essential to being a visitor, not to disavow the applicability of the law to oneself. Elaborating this point is the central task of this section.

An important first observation concerns the role that principles of equality play in any argument to the conclusion that a visitor enjoys this or that right, just as a citizen does. In cases in which the Supreme Court has concluded that visitors to the United States enjoy the same right as a citizen, whether some First Amendment right, or a right to procedural protections in criminal trials, such as the right to confront witnesses, which is granted to visitors, the court always draws on Fifth and Fourteenth Amendment requirements of equal protection.[3] The claim is that those amendments apply to everyone—the government is committed to the equality of *everyone* and not just its citizens—and so, setting aside the limitations of the sort that arise in cases like *Bluman*, we adopt a legal fiction of citizenship with respect to visitors when assessing what the government can and cannot do to them. If the government would be punishing without due process were it do such-and-such to a citizen, then it cannot do that to a visitor. The result is that even though visitors lack the vote, they are to be treated, sometimes, in the same way as those who have it. Those who have the vote are justifiably treated in certain ways by the government thanks to the fact that they have a vote-based say over the law. But visitors, even in some of those cases, are justifiably treated as citizens thanks instead to the fact that the government is required to treat them in the same way it treats citizens. Commitment to equal treatment provides a bridge from the permissibility of a form of treatment of citizens, justified by their say over the law, to the permissibility of that same form of treatment of visitors.

A pressing question is why the exceptions are exceptions. Why does our commitment to equal treatment require us, when it comes to visitors, to abide by due process, but not to abide by some of the First Amendment's speech protections, such as protections of campaign contributions? There is much that is arbitrary and undertheorized in the jurisprudence on these issues. Even if we focus exclusively on the domain in which visitors enjoy the same rights as citizens, thanks to our commitment to equal treatment, things are very hazy. In particular, we lack an explanation for why protections

---

[3] See, for instance, *Wong Wing v. United States* (163 U.S. 228 (1896)), *Almeida-Sanchez v. United States* (413 U.S. 266 (1973)).

given to visitors do not apply to *everyone in the world*, including those who are not citizens and are not visiting. The *Bluman* case would have been even easier for the courts if the plaintiffs had not been visiting the United States but were simply trying to make payments to political candidates and causes from afar. There would have been no equal protection argument to be offered in favor of extending First Amendment protections to them in that case. "Equal protection" would not apply because, the thought is, our commitment to equality is a commitment only to treat visitors, sometimes, as we treat citizens; non-visitors who are also not citizens do not fall under equality's umbrella. Fair enough. But why not?

We can put this question in the other direction: Why do visitors have *any* legal reason to comply with our laws? Non-visitors have no such legal reasons, and also enjoy none of our law's most basic protections. So, what is it about visiting that changes the facts about legal reasons? The answer, I propose, is this: *visiting is in part constituted by waiver of a right to complain about the inapplicability to oneself of the norms that are authoritative for citizens.* Just as a visitor to a home would be violating rules of etiquette if he objected to the house rules on the grounds that this isn't *his* house, it is impermissible for a visitor to a country to complain that the norms to which the government there wishes him to comply are not *his*. By visiting one incurs one of the same obligations incurred when one is complicit in the authority of law thanks to having a say over it: an obligation not to disavow the law, or insist that its norm are not one's own. (What is it about visiting that causes this normative change? More about that central issue shortly.)

The only answer to the question of why a commitment to equality on the part of our government does not extend to everyone, including those who are not even visiting, is that non-visitors who have no say over the law here have a decisive complaint against anything that our government might do to them as dictated by our law: the law is not theirs, it is not applicable to them. This is also true of visitors; our law is not theirs either. But they are not allowed to offer this complaint to shield themselves from our government's actions affecting them.

To use this point, as I aim to, in support of the claim that visitors are owed no leniency when it comes to criminal liability can seem odd, or even incoherent. Consider the following dilemma. Does the fact that the law does not apply to one undermine the authority of the government to act against one in accordance with it, or not? If it does, then it would seem to be tyranny to, for instance, punish an immigrant for a crime committed on American soil. But if it does not, then it would seem perfectly possible for someone not visiting, and not a citizen, to be subject to the state's authority. We need to be able to say both that the government of Singapore is authorized to punish a visitor to Singapore, who is not a citizen of Singapore, and who spits on the sidewalk, but also that that same government is not authorized to punish that same person when he spits on a sidewalk while he is not visiting Singapore. The explanation for the latter fact is that, in that case, Singapore law is not applicable to him; it is not his law. But since it is not his law in the former case either, and yet he is justifiably punished, there is a dilemma here.

To appeal to norms against offering a complaint is to insist that this is a false dilemma. The fact that the law is not one's own undermines the authority of the government to act against one *provided that one can permissibly offer this complaint*. The proposal is that visiting undercuts the permission to offer this complaint, even though it is true that the law is not the visitors' own. The sidewalk-spitter whom Singapore wishes to punish *has* the same complaint, as it were, before his visit and during; but he can only permissibly *offer, or voice* that complaint when he is not visiting.

The reason that this is important is that this is precisely the complaint, it was suggested in chapter 5 and again in chapter 6, that is unavailable to those who have a say over the law. They cannot object when held to legal standards that those standards are not applicable to them; they are complicit in their legality and this places them under normative pressure not to offer this complaint. The result is that visitors are in precisely the same position in the dialogue—they are precluded from making precisely the same complaint when the law is enforced against them—as those who have a say over the law. This is true *even though visitors have no vote-based say over the law and are not on those grounds complicit in its authority.* The source of the normative pressure not to complain is different in the two cases, but it points in the same direction and has the same effect.

The point here is important and so worth repeating. Imagine that the law prohibits X-ing. Fully enfranchised Citizen and unenfranchised Visitor both X and the state takes steps to punish them. Citizen cannot complain that he does not think X-ing wrongful for him; he cannot complain that the law against X-ing does not apply to him. The reason is that he had a say over the law prohibiting X-ing, and so he is complicit in the validity of that law. But neither can Visitor complain that X-ing is not wrongful for him; he and Citizen are barred from making the same complaint. The reason, however, is different for Visitor. The reason Visitor cannot complain *is that he's a visitor* and so is subject to a norm barring complaint, on these grounds, about the applicability to him of the norms of the place he is visiting. By contrast, a kid, who is a citizen, *could* complain by questioning the applicability of the law barring X-ing to him. There is something to be said for his complaint for he lacks a full say over the law, and, at the same time, he is not precluded by his status, as Visitor is, from offering this complaint. Since he is less complicit in the law than Citizen, and permitted to complain about the law's validity, his legal reasons to comply with the law are weaker than either Citizen's or Visitor's. The result: the citizen kid is owed a break, but neither Citizen nor Visitor are.

What about kids who are visiting? They, I believe, are owed the same breaks that citizen kids are owed. The reason is that thanks to being visitors they are barred from complaining that the law is not applicable to them. But this complaint only allows the treatment of them by the government that would be appropriate for a citizen who was otherwise the same as the visitor. Since kids who are citizens are owed a break, that same break is owed to kids who are visitors.

Let's circle back to the claim, essential to this line of thought, that visitors are under the same normative pressure not to complain that the laws are inapplicable to them that fully enfranchised citizens, with a say over the law, are under. In a sense, they are under normative pressure to act *as if* they are complicit in the law, even though they are not in fact. Why should we think that this is true? One might think that the relevant norms here are moral norms. Visitors, the thought is, are under moral pressure to behave as though the norms of the places they visit are their norms, or, at least, not to object that they are not when their hosts aim to punish them for violation. This might be a truth of morality, but even if it is, the moral validity of the relevant norms cannot be what is relevant here. The reason is that, as discussed in chapter 5, the moral significance of a fact, given our presumption of legal positivism, has at most indirect bearing on the question of whether it provides a legal reason for an agent. To provide a legal reason, the fact must be linked to social facts thanks to which norms appealing to it are legally valid; moral validity is insufficient in itself.

Instead, I suggest, norms barring visitors from complaining that the laws are not theirs are *legal norms*. Visitors, I suggest, are under legal pressure not to complain that laws prohibiting behavior are inapplicable to them. But this raises a worry about regress. Under the proposed view, visitors are under the same normative pressure to comply with the law as citizens thanks to the normative pressure not to complain that the law is not theirs. But if that normative pressure derives from a law *that is not theirs*, then it would seem to be normative pressure under which they labor only if they are precluded from complaining that the relevant law is not theirs. But why are they precluded from making that complaint? The answer seems to push us yet another step down a regressive line of reasoning. The following conversation, in other words, seems to end in the wrong place:

> STATE: You X'd and so are to be punished under the law prohibiting X-ing.
> VISITOR: That law doesn't apply to me.
> STATE: Under the law, visitors cannot permissibly offer that objection.
> VISITOR: *That* law doesn't apply to me either.

Unless the state gets the last word here, there is a problem.

But the problem is solvable. The solution, I suggest, is that a condition of entry—a condition, that is, *of being a visitor*—is acceptance of the legality of the norm barring the objection that the visitor offers in this dialogue. That is, the state *does* get the last word:

> STATE: That law *does* apply to you, for part of what it is to be a visitor is to accept the legality of the norm barring the complaint that you offered in this dialogue.

This reply places the visitor in the position of either withdrawing his objection to being punished for X-ing, or else disavowing his visitor status. I believe this is a genuine choice; disavowing one's status as a visitor is a real option. But it is not one that many visitors would wish to take, for it amounts to also disavowing treatment by the state equivalent to the treatment reserved for citizens. Given that one is present in a place in which the state that one is disavowing has control, this would amount to placing oneself entirely at the mercy of that government. One could be subject then to much greater unpleasantness thanks to this disavowal than one would have been had one accepted one's visitor status. The state would be under no obligation to constrain its power in the ways that it constrains it when directed at citizens. There are, to be sure, governments so tyrannical that they treat their own citizens much less well than they treat those who are not their citizens. In such cases, it might be most prudent for the visitor to disavow his visitor status and take his chances. But in states in which this is not the case, the visitor is best off accepting that he is a visitor and so cannot complain that the norms with respect to which his conduct is being measured are not applicable to him.

What are the implications of this discussion for illegal visitors, those who are barred by the law of the visiting country from visiting but are there nonetheless? The answer, I believe, is that there are no special implications for that group; they are in the very same position as legal visitors. The reason is that the status of visitor is possessed by those non-citizens on our soil unless disavowed by them. The status, that is, is in part constituted by an omission to disavow the status.[4] The status, that is, is not conveyed upon visitors thanks to their legal entry. It is, instead, possessed by them thanks to their presence on our soil and their omission to disavow their status. Illegal visitors, that is, are visitors still and so cannot object that the laws they violate do not apply to them, unless they wish to disavow their visitor status, and take their chances.

A thought experiment might help to quiet residual doubts about the argument just offered. Imagine a country with a law that empowers anyone who wishes to be treated, for a given calendar year, just as a citizen is treated, under the country's criminal laws. All that such a person is required to do is to pay a fee on January 1. Under this law, someone who pays the fee will be held to the same standards of criminal conduct as citizens, subject to the same criminal procedures as citizens, and be subject to the same penalties as citizens for violation. V1 pays the fee on January 1 and violates the country's law against X-ing on January 2. When, on January 3, the state seeks to punish V1 in precisely the same way as a citizen who had done what V1 did would have been punished, V1 objects that none of the laws involved here—neither the law against X-ing, nor the law granting to those who pay the fee the right to be treated as citizens are treated—are *his* laws. This objection is clearly out of place. V1 has committed to a legal status under which he is barred from offering this objection and so the state is justified in treating him the same way it would treat any citizen who, for the reason that they have a say over the law, is barred from making this very objection.

---

[4] In this way, visitor status is like the status of the possessor. For discussion see Gideon Yaffe (2014b) "In Defense of Criminal Possession" in *Criminal Law & Philosophy*, 10(3): 441–71.

Anyone who accepts the conclusions just reached about this hypothetical ought to accept the argument that I have offered for the claim that *legal* visitors cannot avail themselves of the argument I have offered for leniency towards kids. To enter the country legally is, I suggest, analogous to paying the fee in the hypothetical. It is a way of undercutting the complaint—perfectly legitimately in the absence of legal entry—that the laws do not apply to one. But what about illegal visitors? Continuing the hypothetical, consider V2 who *declines* to pay the fee on January 1, X's on January 2, and offers the objection that the law is not his in response to the state's efforts on January 3 to punish him as a citizen would be punished. Is this hypothetical state justified in punishing V2 as if he were in the same position as a citizen? The answer, it seems to me, is no. The legal status that provides the state with grounds for ignoring the relevant complaint ("not *my* law") is possessed, in this hypothetical, only by those who pay the fee. But is V2 analogous to an illegal visitor in our system? No. V2 is analogous, instead, to someone who is a non-citizen *and does not even visit*. In our system, that is, we predicate the relevant legal status not on the paying of a fee, *but on presence on our soil*. To see the point, consider V3 who, on January 1, perpetrates a fraud to make it appear that he's paid the fee, X's on January 2, and objects that the law is not his when, on January 3, the state attempts to punish him as a citizen would be punished. V3 is analogous to an illegal visitor. But should the state credit V3's complaint that the law does not apply to him? I think not. His fraudulent efforts undercut his standing to offer that complaint.

I take myself to have shown, then, that visitors are in precisely the same position as citizens when it comes to criminal liability. The strength of a citizens' legal reasons to comply with the law are a function of how much say over the law he has, for how much say he has is a measure of how complicit he is in the authority of the law, and so it is a measure of the degree to which he is blocked from objecting that the law does not apply to him. The strength of a visitor's legal reasons, however, is equivalent to the strength that they would have for him were he a citizen. The reason is that part of what it is to be a visitor is to trigger a bar that we impose on those on our soil from complaining that the law is not applicable to them. Given our commitment to equality, visitors are thus to be treated as though they had whatever say over the law is reserved for citizens who are otherwise like them. They are to be treated as though they are to some degree complicit in the authority of the law, even though they are not in fact. Thus, visiting adults are owed no breaks, whether they are legal or illegal visitors, and visiting kids are owed the same breaks as citizen kids. Just as kids are owed a break not because of anything distinctive about their behavior or their psychology, but, instead, because of the political meaning of age, visitors are owed no break thanks not to their psychological and behavioral similarity to citizens, but, instead, because of the political meaning of visiting, a meaning constituted in part by the nature of the legal status of visitor and in part by our commitment to equal treatment not just of citizens, but of everyone.

7.2 Prisoners and Felons

While there is active debate in the United States, and differences across states, in the degree to which felons who have served their complete sentences are to be denied the vote—some states allow it, some states do not, and states vary in what conditions, if any, felons can meet to restore their voting rights[5]—there is hardly any debate at all as to whether those serving sentences in prisons should have the vote. They virtually never do, and those advocating against this policy are few. It is true that two states, Vermont and Maine, allow inmates to vote. There are also some opportunities for inmates serving sentences for misdemeanors to vote. And states vary in their willingness to allow those under state supervision through probation or parole to vote. It is not the case that the fact that one is currently undergoing a punishment for a past crime is an *absolute* bar, in *every* jurisdiction, to voting in the United States. But the vast majority of inmates serving sentences for felonies in the United States have no say over the law through the vote. Given the enormity of the prison population in the United States, not to mention those under state supervision through probation and parole, this implies that a surprisingly large percentage of the adult population is denied the vote. By some estimates, it is as much as 2.5 percent—a large enough number to make the difference between victory and defeat in many elections. Had Wisconsin inmates been allowed to vote, Hillary Clinton might have beaten Donald Trump in the 2016 presidential election. Had Florida inmates been allowed to vote, Al Gore might have beaten George Bush in 2000. The United States might not have gone to war in Iraq.

A rationale for the practice of denying inmates the vote is rarely offered. The temptation is to assert that somehow inmates do not *deserve* the vote, as though the vote were a benefit and part of the deserved punishment is denial of it. The rhetoric of desert also plays an important role in the rationale sometimes voiced for denying the vote to felons who have served their sentences. Sometimes, implicitly or explicitly, it is suggested that criminals are not worthy of a kind of respect that goes along with the vote. Sometimes, instead, things are muttered about how if you break "the social contract," then you are not to be trusted with the vote, or need to jump through extra hoops to enjoy full participation again. This kind of thinking is motivated by a quid-pro-quo picture of the relationship between citizens and their government—as though the government gets law-abiding behavior and, in exchange, gives citizens a say over how it behaves. In this way of thinking, inmates do not deserve the vote because they haven't held up their end of "the bargain."

But none of this sort of talk makes any sense. Governments do not get a benefit out of law-abiding behavior. And even if we conceive of things that way, perhaps by imagining that social goods, like security or crime reduction, are benefits to the government, it's simple-minded to imagine that the vote is provided in exchange for that.

---

[5] See the ACLU's summary of the differences across states referred to in footnote 1.

After all, we do not and should not deny the vote to tortfeasors, or contract-breakers, or any of the many others who interfere with the achievement of social goods of a sort that we create law to protect and realize. In general, desert, whether of the quid-pro-quo variety or of some deeper sort, has nothing whatsoever to do with the distribution of the vote.

Imagine that there were criteria that a person has to meet to deserve the vote. Any plausible account of such criteria would be both massively under- and overinclusive. There will be many law-abiding adult citizens who fail to meet those criteria, many children who do, and many citizens of other nations who do. For instance, it seems plausible that one deserves the vote in part at least because one's interests are strongly affected by the government's behavior. But the actual criteria that we use to determine who has and lacks the vote, have nothing to do with the degree to which interests are affected. After all, whose interests are more affected by government behavior than inmates? It is plausible to imagine that only those worthy of respect as autonomous, functioning members of our joint community deserve the vote. But plenty of children meet this criterion, as do plenty of citizens of other nations, and plenty of adult citizens do not.

As I see it, the question of whether inmates, and others who have committed crimes in the past, are to have the vote is to be answered largely through consideration of two things: (1) whether we achieve anything, especially something of importance to self-governance, by denying the vote, and, perhaps more importantly, (2) coherence with our other legal practices. In the case of kids, if the argument of chapter 6 succeeds, we accomplish something through denial of the vote—we enhance self-government by providing a mechanism through which today's adults can have a say over future law—and are thereby required, by considerations of coherence, to give kids a break when it comes to criminal liability. Coherence, given what culpability, desert, and legal reasons are (as detailed in chapters 3–5, respectively), requires us to give kids a break if we are to deny them the vote, which we have good reason to do. Similarly, if we have good reasons to deny the vote to inmates, then coherence requires us, also, to give them a break when it comes to criminal liability. This would mean, for instance, that an inmate who commits a crime while in prison would have to be treated more leniently than someone who commits precisely the same crime outside of prison. This, I suspect, will strike most people as quite unacceptable. But let's not let conflict with intuition settle the matter. If there is some good reason to deny the vote to inmates and others who have committed crimes in the past, then it is a result we should embrace.

But what could be said in favor of the practice? If we agree that the question of desert of the vote is not relevant, then there is little left to say in its favor. One might, I suppose, insist that those who have committed crimes, serious ones, anyway, have shown themselves to have poor judgment. And, you might think, we get a better government when people with poor judgment do not have a say over the law. But this can't be a sufficient reason to deny the vote to inmates. The world is full of people with poor judgment, who have proved themselves quite publicly to have poor judgment, who retain the vote. Further, there is far too much variation among those who have committed crimes to think that they have all shown themselves to have poor judgment of a sort that should make us doubt their ability to wield the vote well. There is really no reason whatsoever to think that someone who was in possession of some cocaine, or sold some to a friend, is not capable of making intelligent decisions about, for instance, tax policy, or even health policy. In fact, inmates and former inmates, generally, probably have a perspective on criminal justice that gives them far greater claim to wisdom about policy in that domain than the rest of us. In general, we fear with good reason judgment tests for the franchise. The worry is that they will be wielded by those with power to exclude from the vote those with whom they disagree independently of the merits of their positions on matters of policy. And so we should fear, on these same grounds, any rationale for excluding inmates from the vote through appeal to their putative poor judgment. In short, there appears to me to be nothing of value that can be legitimately pursued through denying the vote to those who have committed crimes in the past.

Notice that the considerations just offered do not establish that inmates should retain the vote. There are plenty of things that our government does simply because something needs to be done and there might be no good reason to do this rather than that. We could, in theory, offer the vote to the citizens of Mexico. We do not currently do that, but I see no *principled* reason why we should not, if we were willing to accept the further implications of such a move. There are surely pros and cons of retaining our policy of Mexican disenfranchisement and of giving it up. The same is true of inmate enfranchisement. We get nothing, that I can see, out of denying inmates the vote, but that does not mean we should grant it to them. But, *if we are to retain our policy of inmate disenfranchisement, then we must also accept the implications of that policy; in particular, we must give inmates a break when it comes to criminal liability.* I object, that is, to the incoherence of our current system, but I have no positive argument favoring the enfranchisement of those who have committed crimes in the past over, instead, leniency towards them when they recidivate. If you are among those who find the prospect of leniency repellant, then you should opt for the former option.[6]

7.3 The Poor

The two examples of disenfranchised people discussed so far—visitors and those who have committed crimes in the past—are both denied an entitlement to vote. Such an entitlement, while necessary for having a vote-based say over the law, is insufficient

---

[6] One might think that coherency could be achieved by removing felons of their citizenship and treating them then in the way we treat visitors. The Supreme Court has ruled it unconstitutional to strip a citizen of citizenship (*Afroyim v. Rusk*, 387 U.S. 253 (1967)). But even setting that aside, to strip a citizen of citizenship is not to place him in the same position as a visitor, since visitors have another political home where the citizen stripped of citizenship is a citizen of nowhere.

for it, under the account of "having a say" offered in chapter 6. In addition, a person must be entitled to be free of certain obstacles to the exercise of her entitlement to vote, and must be actually free of those obstacles. So, it is possible to eliminate or reduce a person's say over the law without taking away her entitlement to vote. To do so, you can either (1) narrow the range of obstacles to voting she is entitled to be free of, or (2) place obstacles in the way of her voting that she is entitled not to face.

The question of whether the poor have less of a say over the law than the rich is only superficially a question of whether poverty actually makes it harder to register one's vote. Since, in general, money makes it easier to do things, it would be quite surprising if the poor didn't find it harder than the rich to register their votes. The more interesting question concerns entitlement. Consider an obstacle to voting that a poor person cannot overcome thanks to his poverty, but a rich person could; it is an obstacle that money can beat. Are we, all of us, entitled to be free of that obstacle? If so, then it would appear that the poor have less say over the law than those who are not. And it would follow, further, from the position given in chapter 6 (in the absence of a story of the sort that we gave for thinking that visitors are not owed a break despite their disenfranchisement), that the poor are owed a break when it comes to criminal liability. Much turns, then, on the question of whether obstacles to voting that can be defeated with money that the poor lack are obstacles we are entitled to be free of.

This issue is at most a hair away from the question of how much money, if any, we are entitled to have, independently of our labors. The moral question, which is the deep one, is not one on which we are going to make progress here. But since our focus for now is on the coherence or incoherence of our legal practices, we can ask the legal question instead. The law entitles us to a certain amount of money through many different mechanisms, most notably through welfare provisions and other related programs for providing money and goods to those who cannot subsist on what they earn. This amount is, in turn, a measure of what monetary obstacles to voting we are legally entitled to be free of. We are legally entitled to be free of any obstacle that could be overcome by anyone, for instance, whose sole source of income is state-provided welfare. This is a low bar. It implies that the price for voting—whether in the form of a price on transportation to the polls, or the price of a stamp for a mailed ballot—must be very low, especially given that no thought is given to that price when welfare amounts are set. It is not as though, for instance, social services branches of the government calculate an allowance for voting when determining how much money people are entitled to.

What this suggests is the following test for determining whether someone entitled to vote lacks a vote-based say over the law thanks to poverty: Would someone in the agent's position who had only the income to which a person with nothing is legally entitled be able to vote? If not, then the agent has less say over the law than those with money; if so, then he is not diminished, on these grounds, in his vote-based say over the law. Those who are diminished in their say over the law under this test are, I believe, owed a break when it comes to criminal liability. They are less complicit in the law's authority than those with more money than themselves, and I can think of nothing that would block their right to offer this objection were the state to deny them leniency for their crimes.

Advocates for the poor are likely to see this reasoning as far too narrow; and it is. Poverty interferes with one's ability to exert influence over the law in ways that are much less obviously tied to money than I seem to be suggesting. Poverty has enormous numbers of effects that manifest as inabilities to take advantage of legal entitlements. The psychological effects of poverty, and the stigma that both precedes and follows such psychological effects, for instance, can severely diminish motivation to exert influence over the law in many ways, not least by instilling a sense of exclusion and powerlessness that undercuts motivation to vote, much less to inform oneself about candidates or issues. Are not those whose poverty has had such an erosive effect on their lives diminished in the say they have over the law through the vote?

I believe that the position that I am pressing can accommodate this point to some degree. If we are entitled to be free of poverty-induced psychological diminishment of the kind that interferes with our capacities to exert influence over the law in the ways we are entitled, then those who have suffered in this respect are indeed diminished in their say over the law. They encounter obstacles to voting—internal obstacles, but still— that they are entitled not to face. What follows is that their legal reasons to refrain from crime are weaker than fully enfranchised adults. And, given the views of culpability and desert that I have been pressing, it further follows that they are diminished in culpability for their crimes, deserving of lesser sanctions, and so owed leniency.

But this group is not in precisely the same position as kids. The argument for giving them a break is far weaker than that for kids. To see this, think about precocious children, fully capable of voting, free of any of the obstacles to doing so, whether internal or external, that plague those who have been damaged and diminished by poverty. That group of children, I hold, are also owed a break when it comes to criminal liability. They are not entitled to vote, and so have less say over the law, and so are diminished in culpability and deserving of lesser sanctions for their wrongful behavior. The parallel group of people, when we turn to the poor, are those who, for whatever reasons, have not suffered the kinds of psychological harm that poverty so frequently produces. Perhaps they won the resilience lottery. They are entitled to vote, entitled to be free of obstacles to voting, *and they are in fact free of such obstacles*, despite the fact that, being poor, they were at risk of facing significant constraint to exerting their influence over the law through the vote. This group of poor people are not, for the reasons described here, owed a break. Their legal reasons to refrain from crime are no weaker than those applicable to the rich.

The result is that where the line of reasoning offered here supports a *blanket* policy of leniency towards kids, it supports *case-by-case* consideration of the poor. Some of the poor are worthy on those grounds of leniency, others are not, depending on the degree to which their poverty has imposed on them constraints in their say over the law, constraints from which they were entitled to be free. Or, put conversely and more provocatively, those who support a blanket policy of leniency towards the poor, when it comes to criminal liability, should also support their disenfranchisement. Rather, it seems to me, what is preferable is a discretionary policy, granting to those legal actors most informed about particular cases, such as judges or attorneys, the power to be lenient in the face of the recognition of the corrosive effect that a criminal defendant's poverty had on his ability to exert influence over the law through the vote. Where a blanket policy of leniency is appropriate for children, leniency should be granted only to those enfranchised poor whose poverty has produced in them obstacles to voting that they were entitled to be free of.[7]

7.4 Conclusion

Under the rationale offered in chapter 6 for giving kids a break, kids' disenfranchisement matters because, in light of it, their say over the law is diminished. And in light of *that*, they are less complicit in the legal authority of criminal prohibitions than are those enjoying the franchise. And in light of *that*, the strength of their legal reasons to refrain from legally prohibited acts is diminished. And in light of *that*, they are both less culpable for their criminal acts than their behavioral and psychological twins enjoying a full say over the law, and deserving of lesser sanction. And in light of *that*, a policy of leniency towards them is justified.

What has emerged from the discussion of this chapter is that this chain of ideas can sometimes be broken. Visitors, lacking the vote, are also less complicit in the authority of criminal prohibitions than those who have the vote. But it is not true, in their case, that in light of that the strength of their legal reasons to refrain from legally prohibited acts is diminished. It is not true because a hidden premise in the argument as applied to kids is that kids *can permissibly note* their diminished complicity with the law's authority in their defense; this premise is not true of visitors. The premise is true of those who are disenfranchised in response to prior criminal behavior, and thus it follows that those subject to state supervision as punishment for crimes, and those who have served their sentences, are diminished in criminal culpability and deserving of lesser sanctions. While the most appealing moral to draw from this result is that we should not disenfranchise anyone in response to prior criminal behavior, including those who are incarcerated for serious, violent felonies, nothing in the arguments offered here forces that conclusion. What is forced, I believe, is coherence: we should either enfranchise those with criminal pasts, or hold them to lower standards; we cannot continue to deny them the vote and treat them as though they have a full say over the law.

The logic of the argument changes significantly when we turn to those who have less say over the law despite the fact that they have both an entitlement to vote, and an

---

[7] The position offered here is importantly different from but not inconsistent with that offered in Tommie Shelby (2016) *Dark Ghettos: Injustice, Dissent and Reform*, Cambridge: Harvard Press, esp. ch. 8.

entitlement to be free of obstacles to voting, but who face some of the obstacles that they are entitled to be free of. I've suggested that this can be true of the poor in two ways at least. Sometimes they simply cannot afford to register a vote, where the price is not low enough to be paid by those who have only what they are entitled to in the way of government assistance. Sometime, more perniciously, crushing poverty has prevented the development in them of the cognitive conception of themselves as potentially meaningful participants in democratic governance necessary to be moved to exercise the entitlement to vote. While I doubt that anyone is entitled to such a conception of themselves, full stop, it seems to me close to certain that we are all entitled not to lack such a conception *thanks to poverty*. And so it seems to me that the poor who fall into this second group are also less complicit in the authority of law than the fully enfranchised, and so they, too, are owed leniency when it comes to criminal liability. Since this is true not of all the poor, but only those whose poverty has had this kind of deleterious effect on their psychology, a weaker ground of leniency has been identified here towards the poor in general than we have found for kids.

This chapter, then, has aimed to answer the worry of overinclusivity, the worry that on the view I advocate, many who should not be given a break are said to be owed one. While the argument for giving kids a break does imply that there are others, too, who are owed a break and for the same reasons, it has also been shown that many of the disenfranchised do not fall into this category. Our practices need revision—we should give the franchise to inmates and we should be more lenient towards some of the poor—but they do not need as much revision, in light of the arguments offered here, as one might have feared.

8

What Breaks Are Owed?

8.0 Introduction

The rationale for lenience towards kids who commit crimes offered in this book can seem quite distant from on-the-ground legal practice. And in many ways it is. The principled account defended here has few implications for those who implement, rather than set the law. Importantly, the account does not have immediate, or anyway obvious implications for the appropriate *form* of our lenience towards kids. It tells us why we should be lenient, but it is not clear what its implications are for *how* we should be lenient. It does not tell us directly in what currency we are to pay our debt of lenience. Nor does it tell us how lenient we should be. It does not tell us *how big* a break a kid is owed, or even how to measure a break's "size." Still, as we will see in this chapter, some things can be said.

Section 8.1 offers some observations about the variety of legal mechanisms through which we might institute leniency towards kids. While in the end a law's degree of leniency towards kids is to be measured with reference to the amount of punishment it allocates to kids, in contrast to otherwise identical adults, we should not focus solely on sentencing mitigation as the mechanism for giving kids a break. Procedures matter too. To take a step towards identifying the kinds of procedural breaks kids are owed, section 8.2 discusses a recent Supreme Court case that centered on a police interrogation of a kid. The section argues that, in at least one important respect, the grounds for giving kids a break offered here can provide legal actors who do not issue sentences, but engage with kids at a different point in the process, with specific and substantive advice. Some police interrogations of kids are simply impermissible, even when comparable interrogations of adults would be acceptable, given the argument offered here for leniency towards child criminals. The principles underlying our impulse to give kids a break, that is, can tell us some things, although not everything, about how the government should behave towards kids with whom the criminal justice system interacts.

8.1 Forms of Lenience

Since, at the end of the day, criminal law is about punishment, the question of whether a policy succeeds in being lenient towards kids, in comparison to adults, turns on the question of how much punishment will be given, *ceteris paribus*, to a kid, thanks to the policy, in comparison to an adult. The *"ceteris paribus"* clause is important. Laws prohibiting those in public office from taking bribes allocate no punishment to kids, and some to adults, for the simple reason that kids are barred by other laws from holding public office. But such prohibitions are not more lenient to kids than adults, because it is not the case that all else is equal between those who do and do not suffer punishment thanks to the policy. Or, put another way, such laws in and of themselves would allocate no less punishment to a kid who, per impossibile, holds public office and takes a bribe than they to do to an identical adult. To test whether a policy is lenient towards kids we have to see how the policy would treat *behavioral and psychological twins* who differ only in age. If such a policy allocates no less punishment to the kid than to the adult, then it is not helping the system of which it is a part to conform to the principles outlined in this book. The rationale offered here for lenience towards kids has the implication that, one way or another, our system should be set up so that, *ceteris paribus*, child criminals end up with less punishment at the state's hand than adult criminals.

It is possible to institute lenience through the definitions of crimes. Some laws prohibiting sexual offenses against children, for instance, require an age gap between the victim and the perpetrator large enough to make them impossible to be committed by a kid. Such a law, for instance, might make it a crime to have sex with someone between 14 and 16 years of age, provided that the perpetrator is at least five years older than the victim.[1] Although this is not the aim of the relevant statutes, such crimes are defined in such a way as to ensure that the perpetrator is old enough to vote. But few statutes defining crimes are like this. Most can be completed, in theory, by anyone of any age. More importantly, the suggestion that in general we should be lenient towards kids by adjusting our definitions of crimes runs counter to the rationale for our lenience offered here. After all, age matters, on the view presented here, to *culpability*, not to wrongdoing—the kid and the adult who both commit robbery commit the same *wrong*. The definitions of crimes set, first and foremost, the boundaries of wrongdoing. So to institute leniency through the definitions of crimes would be to predicate leniency on the wrong thing.

Much more legitimate is for lenience to be instituted through sentencing mitigation. Sentencing mitigation takes place either through granting a sentencing judge the power to issue a lesser sentence to a kid *for the reason that he is a kid*, or by denying the judge the power to sentence kids as harshly as adults. Even if a kid is tried as an adult, judges are often free to give a sentencing discount because the kid's a kid. Laws that grant that power to judges offer sentencing mitigation of the first variety. By contrast, judges in the juvenile delinquency system virtually always lack the legal power to mandate that the state treat a juvenile defendant as harshly as an adult would be treated

---

[1] There are many examples of such statutes. A federal criminal law in the United States, 18 U.S.C. §2241(c), for instance, criminalizes crossing state lines with intent to have sex with a 14-year-old, provided that the defendant is four or more years older than the intended victim.

for the same offense. A judge in the juvenile system cannot send a 14-year-old who commits an offense with a maximum penalty of three years, for instance, to a maximum security prison. Such a judge has a menu of options for state detention and supervision of such a defendant, but the harshest of penalties inflicted on adult offenders are not on the table. Sentencing mitigation takes place, in such cases, through the second mechanism, by tying the judge's hands. Similarly, under the federal sentencing guidelines (particularly §4A1.1.c), a prior sentence is an aggravating factor for sentencing purposes only if the sentence was issued for a crime committed when the defendant was an adult. This provision prevents judges from taking a history of crime as a child as an aggravating factor for crimes committed as an adult. In tying judges' hands in this way, some leniency is given to child criminals, albeit for crimes that they later commit as adults.

Laws that grant judges the power to mitigate sentence of kids, because they are kids, are only lenient to the extent that judges exercise that power. If judges do not, then such laws do not, in the end, allocate less punishment to kids than to adults. To see the point, consider the recent Supreme Court decisions under which juveniles cannot be sentenced to *mandatory* life without parole.[2] Mandatory sentencing regimes are draconian because they deny judges the power to mitigate sentences for certain crimes. Under the recent Supreme Court decisions, therefore, the law is potentially lenient towards kids since they serve to grant judges the power to punish a kid less harshly than an otherwise identical adult who the judge would be required to punish with a life-without-parole sentence. But whether the law is *actually* lenient towards kids, in light of the Supreme Court's decisions, will depend on whether judges actually issue less harsh sentences now that they have the power to do so. If, for instance, those defendants who are re-sentenced in light of the Supreme Court decisions are all, or almost all, given such long sentences that they still spend their entire lives in prison, then the law the Supreme Court announced will not turn out to be a law that gives kids the breaks they are owed. And this is particularly worrisome since the Supreme Court reached the decisions that it did *out of the recognition that kids ought to be given a break*. The court did not decide those cases out of a desire that judges should have a power that laws requiring them to issue life without parole sentences was denying them; the people whose rights the court took itself to be vindicating *were not judges*, but, instead, those whom judges sentence. The court's rationale requires that judges *use the power the court judged them to have in a particular way*, namely to mitigate sentence. So, whether kids are actually given a break by the system that the court says is legally required will depend on what sentencing judges *actually do* with the power that the court says they have. We do not know the answer yet, and so we do not know whether the Supreme Court has successfully taken steps to bring the law in line with the principles supporting giving kids a break.

---

[2] *Miller v. Alabama* (132 S.Ct. 2455 (2012)), *Montgomery v. Louisiana* (136 S.Ct. 718 (2016)).

In addition, and most importantly for the purposes of this chapter, lenience can be instituted through laws that mandate different procedures to be followed in dealing with kids who have committed crimes in contrast to adults. I am not including under the banner of "procedural mechanisms" laws that grant sentencing judges the power to mitigate kids' sentences, or deny them the power to sentence kids as harshly as adults. Those laws, for our purposes, fall under the banner of "sentencing mitigation mechanisms." Rather, procedural mechanisms for instituting lenience are laws setting procedures thanks to which a kid has an opportunity to be found not guilty of an offense, or found guilty of a lesser offense, where an otherwise identical adult would not have such an opportunity. A law, for instance, that forbade the police from interviewing a child suspect without the presence of an advocate would be an example. The presence of the advocate protects the child from forms of self-incrimination from which an adult is not protected. Since self-incrimination increases the likelihood of being found guilty of a particular offense, such a law would be an example of procedural lenience. Overall, thanks to such a law, less punishment would fall to kids than to adults because such a law would alter the distribution of guilty verdicts in a way that favors kids.

Similarly, a law that instituted different rules about the admissibility of evidence for kids in comparison to adults—either by making it harder for the prosecution, or easier on the defense, to introduce a piece of evidence at trial, when the defendant is a kid—would be an example of procedural lenience. In juvenile proceedings, for instance, it is not uncommon for the judge to directly address the defendant's parents or guardians, who are present in the courtroom to lend support, even though they have not been sworn in, have not been warned that they would be asked to speak, and the testimony they give has not been vetted in advance by lawyers for either side. The judge might, for instance, ask whether the defendant obeys curfews, and does her homework— "character" evidence of a kind that would likely be excluded entirely from the trial of an adult, or, if allowed, introduced with much greater restriction. Relatively loose procedures of these kinds might help kids by allowing them to tell a fuller story of the world from which their wrongful conduct sprung. Or they might hurt kids by preventing them from keeping out of the courtroom facts about their past behavior that do not speak to their guilt, innocence, or culpability for the crimes with which they are charged. It is an empirical question. If procedures of this kind help kids to avoid conviction, or to secure conviction for lesser crimes, then they would be an example of procedural lenience.

It can be difficult to tell, in some cases, including the one just described, whether laws mandating special procedures for investigating or trying kids are, or are not, lenient. For instance, in the United States, children tried through the juvenile delinquency system do not have the option of a jury trial. All the trials in the juvenile system are bench trials, while adults have the option of being tried by a jury. Is this procedure lenient to kids? To know the answer, we would have to know whether juvenile judges are more or less likely to convict of a given offense than juries. And there are other factors, too, that would need to be measured. For instance, in jury trials, juries are instructed on the law by the judge so as to direct them to the right factual questions. The process of issuing jury instructions forces the judge to review the law relevant to the case and explain it to laymen. In bench trials, by contrast, there is no comparable mechanism for forcing the judge to remind him or herself of the law of importance. Does this result in more legal mistakes in bench trials than jury trials? If so, do those mistakes tend to favor defendants, or go against them? These are empirical questions to which we would need answers in order to know whether laws mandating bench trials for juveniles are lenient.

At the point that we recognize the possibility of procedural lenience, we open the possibility that two people could receive exactly the same punishment, for the same crime, at the state's hand, and yet the one might have been treated more leniently than the other thanks to the fact that he was subject to procedures that provided him with more opportunities to escape conviction, and so punishment, than the procedures to which the other was subject. A child subjected to lighter police pressures, thanks to laws requiring the police to go relatively easy on children during investigations, might still be convicted of the same crime and given the same sentence as a psychologically and behaviorally identical adult. Such a child, however, is still treated slightly more leniently by the state, for there were opportunities—opportunities forgone, but still— for him to avoid this harsh punishment thanks to less aggressive police treatment. This is not nothing. Who wouldn't prefer a shot at less punishment?

A kid who enjoys *only* procedural lenience is subjected to procedures that allocate less punishment, overall, than those to which adults are subject, but, still, is punished just as harshly as an otherwise identical adult. Has such a kid been treated more leniently *in the way that matters*, in the way that gives him the break he is owed? The question is closely related to the well-known question of whether someone who is subjected to a risk of harm, but not harmed, has suffered a setback to his interests. The question here is whether an unmaterialized chance of a good (or bad) outcome furthers (or is a setback to) one's interests.[3] I will not make progress on this question here. Rather, the point of importance for our purposes is just that where you stand on that issue will affect your attitude towards the adoption of more lenient procedures towards kids.

Those who think that to be subjected to more lenient procedures is, in itself, to be given a break, even if you end up with the same punishment in the end, will see procedural lenience as one way to ensure that the criminal law conforms to the principles supporting lenience towards kids. However, even those on the other side of this issue should not be opposed to more lenient procedures for kids. Those who think that unmaterialized chances do not make a difference to one's interests are going to deny that procedural lenience ever *suffices* to provide the breaks kids are owed. For theorists of this stripe, procedural lenience provides a break only if, thanks to it, less punishment

---

[3] For an important discussion of the issue, see Claire Finkelstein (2003) "Is Risk Harm?" in *University of Pennsylvania Law Review*, 151: 963–1001. Also relevant: John C.P. Goldberg and Benjamin Zipursky (2002) "Unrealized Torts" in *Virginia Law Review*, 88: 1625.

is suffered by the offender who is subjected to the more lenient procedures. But even someone who holds this view should favor subjecting kids to more lenient procedures; that will be an effective way to give some of them the breaks they are owed, even if those whose shot at a lesser punishment is not realized need to be given a break through alternative means in addition, such as mitigation in sentencing.

We can, thus, imagine two different extreme approaches. At one extreme, all the work of giving kids a break is done through mitigation in sentencing. We investigate and try kids using exactly the same procedures we employ with adults, but then mitigate sentences for child criminals in comparison to adults. At the other extreme, all the work is done by subjecting kids to less draconian procedures. Our actual system is somewhere in between: kids are subjected to more lenient procedures, and their sentences are often mitigated, even when there is no procedural bar to sentencing them as harshly as an adult. The empirical problem of measuring the adequacy of either extreme system, or of any of the systems that fall in between, is exceedingly difficult, and made more difficult by the debate highlighted in the previous paragraph. Those who think that unmaterialized chances at outcomes bear not at all on one's interests will judge that some kids have not gotten the breaks they are owed, even while those on the other side of this debate will judge that those very same kids have. Even those who think that risks of harm (benefit) are themselves harmful (beneficial) may think that they are *less* harmful (beneficial) than materialized harms (benefits). But how much less? Even putting such debates aside, we cannot assess the adequacy of any system on the continuum just described without a way of measuring *by how much* one form of treatment by the state is harsher than another. How much less bad is a year in juvenile detention than a year in adult prison? How much less bad is a year of house arrest and probation than a month in jail? This aggregation problem is a seemingly intractable problem in the philosophy of punishment—in fact, in value theory more generally[4]—currently unaddressed.

Unfortunately, I will not be remedying these limitations in this chapter, or in this book. An account of the grounds for lenience leaves important public policy problems unsolved. Their solution requires something that we are sorely lacking in the philosophy of criminal law: a complete theory of sentencing. However, as we will see in section 8.2, the observations made in this section about the variety of forms of lenience can guide us in thinking about the grounds for adopting more lenient procedures towards kids.

8.2 Interrogating Kids

Policies concerning what police interrogations are and are not legally permitted have real and important implications for the allocation of punishment. Roughly speaking,

---

[4] For discussion of the problem in value theory, see the essays in Ruth Chang (ed.) (1998) *Incommensurability, Incomparability and Practical Reasoning*, Cambridge: Harvard University Press.

the less the police are allowed to do, the less punishment there will be. And the more that is allowed with respect to suspects with certain distinctive features, the more punishment there will be of people with those features. The question, for us, is whether there are good reasons to accept criteria that sort legitimate from illegitimate interrogations that are lenient towards kids. Such policies would bar some interrogations of kids that are allowed of psychologically and behaviorally identical adults. Ought the police be required to interrogate child suspects differently from the way they interrogate otherwise identical adults?

I am formulating this question in a way that is intended to bypass the question of the bearing of the psychological differences between adults and kids on how it is fair and smart to interrogate them. Young children are known to be highly susceptible to suggestion, for instance. They will sincerely affirm that they witnessed or even did things that did not happen, if an adult gently, and even unconsciously, nudges them in that direction.[5] It is possible that there are interrogations of the suggestible that are unjustified, even though there would be no parallel objection to the same interrogation of someone less suggestible. But acknowledgment of this possibility does not answer our question, since, again, in such examples all is not equal. What we need to know is whether the police should be barred from some interrogations of a kid that they would be allowed to make of an adult *even when there is no difference in suggestibility, or any other psychological feature known to be more prevalent among kids than adults.*

For the same reason, I aim to bypass the question of the actual knowledge of kids, in contrast to adults, about their rights under the law. Studies have confirmed that kids know less about what forms of interrogation they are protected from by law than do adults.[6] This implies that the risk of violating the rights of a juvenile in an interrogation is much higher than when the suspect is an adult. That fact matters for public policy. Perhaps, for instance, it implies that the police should never interrogate a juvenile without a lawyer present; or perhaps a requirement of parental presence suffices.[7] But, still, policies designed to compensate for differences in the psychology or the state of knowledge of children, in contrast to adults, are not lenient to kids *in the way identified in section 8.1*. Such policies do not allocate less punishment to kids *ceteris paribus*; they do not allocate less punishment to kids than to those adults who have the same level of knowledge. My question, instead, is whether we ought to adopt policies under which police are barred from interrogating kids as aggressively as they are permitted to interrogate *otherwise identical* adults.

---

[5] For an overview, see Maggie Bruck and Stephen J. Ceci (1998) "The Suggestibility of Children's Memory" in *Annual Review of Psychology*, 50: 419–39.

[6] Thomas Grisso (1981) *Juveniles' Waiver of Rights: Legal and Psychological Competence*, New York: Plenum Press.

[7] For discussion, see Bary Feld (2000) "Juveniles' Waiver of Legal Rights: Confession, *Miranda*, and the Right to Counsel" in Thomas Grisso and Robert G. Schwartz (eds.), *Youth on Trial: A Developmental Perspective on Juvenile Justice*, Chicago: University of Chicago Press, pp. 105–38.

The question can also be illuminatingly posed not by emphasizing limitations on the police in their behavior towards kids but, instead, by emphasizing the ground of such limitations: the right to avoid self-incrimination, concretized in the Fifth Amendment to the United States Constitution. The question is whether kids have a stronger right to avoid self-incrimination than adults, *ceteris paribus*. The answer is, as we will see by the end of this section, that they do. The reason is that the strength of the right to avoid self-incrimination is inversely proportional to the strength of one's legal reason to refrain from the behavior that one is protected from incriminating oneself in. Since kids have weaker reasons to refrain from crime than do adults, for the reasons described at length in preceding chapters, they have stronger rights against self-incrimination, *ceteris paribus*. It follows that there ought to be greater restrictions on the police when interrogating kids than when interrogating adults.

To get a grip on the issue, it helps to have an example. Consider the facts of importance in the recent Supreme Court case of *J.D.B. v. North Carolina* (131 S.Ct. 2394 (2011)). J.D.B., who was 13 years old, was called from his junior high classroom to a meeting with several adults, including school officers and two uniformed police. No parent, lawyer, or advocate for him was present. The adults interrogated him about several burglaries in the neighborhood. Eventually, J.D.B. confessed to being involved. However, he was never "Mirandized"; his rights were never explained to him. Under federal law in the United States, the government can use information attained in an interview against a suspect who is never given a Miranda warning, and who never explicitly waives his Miranda rights, only if a reasonable person would recognize that he could terminate the interview at will.[8] So the question of whether J.D.B.'s confession could be used against him turned on whether it was reasonable for J.D.B. to believe that he was not permitted to just walk out of the room, rather than submit to questioning. Eventually the case went to the Supreme Court, which ruled in J.D.B.'s favor. The court ruled that J.D.B.'s confession was inadmissible since it was not unreasonable of him to think that he had no choice but to stay in the room to be interrogated.

Consider three salient facts about J.D.B.: (1) He was not given any indication during the interview that he was suspected of involvement in the burglaries. (2) The interview took place on school grounds, during school hours, and present in the room were school officials vested with authority over J.D.B., the authority, in particular, to control his whereabouts in many respects. And, (3) He was a kid.

In theory, the court could have sided with J.D.B. on the grounds that a reasonable person possessing any one of these features would have believed it impermissible to leave. Had the court chosen the first feature, and sided with J.D.B. on the grounds that a reasonable person who did not know he was suspected would have thought himself barred from just walking out—perhaps reasonable people think that the law requires them to cooperate with police when they are not suspects—then the ruling would have had significant impact on the Mirandizing of anyone, whether adult or child. It would

---

[8] *Miranda v. Arizona* (86 S.Ct. 1602 (1966)).

have made it much more difficult for police, for instance, to interrogate an adult whom they suspect without alerting him to the fact that they suspect him by issuing a Miranda warning up front. A strategy of beginning an interview with a suspect by making it appear as though he were not a suspect would have been much more difficult to employ, had the court flatly ruled that a reasonable person, not alerted to the fact that he was a suspect, would not have known that he could walk away from the interview. Such an approach would have been sweeping, and would not have involved granting any special lenience to J.D.B. in virtue of the fact that he was a kid.

Had the court wanted to avoid this sweeping effect on police interviews, they might have chosen the second feature of J.D.B. as the salient one. They could have ruled that a reasonable person in J.D.B.'s position might have believed that *students are not permitted to walk away from interviews with school officials on school grounds during school hours without permission*. Such a ruling would not have established a policy of leniency towards kids in police interviews, generally, but instead a policy of leniency towards any student, whether adult or child, interviewed on school grounds during school hours with school officials present. Such a ruling would not have barred police, for instance, from using the fruits of an interview with a kid conducted in that kid's front yard without a Miranda warning. But police, under such a ruling, could not use the result of an interview with an 18-year-old suspect, or any other adult student, on school grounds without a Miranda warning. Such a ruling also would have raised questions about other authority relations besides that of school officials over students. Could the police use the results of an interrogation of an employee at work with his boss present and without a Miranda warning? How about parolees with their parole officers present? And so on.

But the court did not rule in J.D.B.'s favor for either of these reasons. Rather, the court took a step in the direction of leniency towards kids *because they are kids*. The court ruled that for purposes of determining whether a juvenile suspect has a right to a Miranda warning, the right standard to employ is that of a "reasonable *child*" (131 S.Ct. 2394 (2011) at 2403). So, in short, even if a reasonable adult would have known that he could leave any time, if a reasonable kid would not have known that, then a Miranda warning must be given to a kid (although not to an adult in similar circumstances). The court ruled, that is, that the reasonable person standard is to be "individualized" with respect to the age of the defendant, when the reasonable person standard is used to assess the acceptability of the government's failure to issue a Miranda warning. This result affects all police interviews of kids, whether on school grounds or elsewhere, but has no impact on adults.

It is important to appreciate just how bizarre the court's reasoning is. The tacit implication of the decision is that it might have gone the other way had J.D.B. been 18 or older. In that case, the validity of the interrogation would have turned on what a reasonable *adult* would have believed. And so the court seems to think that adults and children, provided they are reasonable, might have different beliefs, in circumstances like those that J.D.B. faced, about the permissibility of walking away from the interview.

But is this really true? Let's grant that more adults than children know that it would be permissible for a kid to walk away in such circumstances, especially when thinking clearly and not caught up in the heat of the moment. But even granting this, the issue is actually quite subtle. Ordinarily, a student at school is required to be where school officials tell him to be. So the conclusion that J.D.B. was permitted to walk away from the interview requires the judgment that the ordinary authority of school officials is suspended, or outweighed, by the presence of the police. While it is an empirical question, I suspect that many adults would fail to recognize this. Many adults would think that the school gets to decide where a kid is to be, and so if school officials want a kid to stay put for a police interview, then that is what he is required to do. And so it does not seem that we can rationalize the court's approach to the case by appeal to the plausible factual claim that lots of kids would not know they were allowed to leave. Many adults would not know that also, and yet the court thinks that appeal to the reasonable *kid*, as opposed to the reasonable *adult*, makes a difference to the outcome in the case.

It is more plausible that, instead of taking the court at its word, we should instead see that the court's position manifests an unarticulated normative position. The court thinks that kids are appropriately held to different and lower *standards*, when it comes to their beliefs about what they are free to do, than are adults. The issue is not what adults and kids actually believe, when thinking clearly. The issue is what beliefs they are to be faulted for having. There are beliefs, the thought is, that an adult could be faulted for having, while no kid could be. There is something very intuitive about this idea, to be sure; but it is very easy to be misled about its basis. The thought underlying the intuition might be that a kid in school *shouldn't be expected to know* that under certain circumstances he is allowed to walk away from meetings with school officials without their permission. Kids are often expected to do what principals and teachers say, whether they like it or not. In fact, we work hard to inculcate an attitude of deference towards school officials in our kids. We try to teach them to do what they are told in school, trusting that what they are told to do is for their own good. How can a kid who has internalized the lesson, and come to believe that the school's officials get to decide where he goes and when (on school grounds and during school hours), be faulted for not knowing that he can walk away from a police interview (on school grounds and during school hours) without permission? And we might extend the point to other contexts. We want our kids to be able to trust the police and turn to them for help when something serious is wrong and we are not there to help. A kid who imbibes the lesson might not know that it is permissible to walk away from an interview with police in any context, whether in school or away from it. Perhaps this thought is what motivates the court's appeal to the reasonable juvenile standard?

But as appealing as this line of thought is, and it might be the one the court actually has in mind, it does not provide support for the *J.D.B.* decision. The reason is that the issue in the case is not whether J.D.B. is culpable for his failure to leave the interview. Sometimes, indeed, we inquire about reasonableness in order to assess culpability. This is what we are doing when we try to determine whether it was reasonable of a defendant to be oblivious to the risks to other people that his conduct posed, for instance. A good test for determining whether an inquiry about the reasonableness of a belief concerns culpability is to ask whether actual knowledge on the part of the person undercuts the force of the claim that ignorance would have been reasonable. Someone, for instance, who knew his conduct was risky cannot point, in his defense, to the fact that a reasonable person would not have known that. His actual knowledge establishes his culpability, even if he knows more than the reasonable person would have. But imagine that J.D.B. was more savvy about the law than reasonable kids; imagine that he actually knew that he could leave, but elected not to. Does that imply that his confession can be used against him? No. The reason is that the police are required to treat J.D.B. *as if* he had the knowledge of a reasonable kid *even if he has more (or less) knowledge than that*. Even savvy kids are owed a Miranda warning when they are suspected.

What this shows us is that the inquiry about the reasonableness of the belief that one can walk away from a police interview is not an inquiry about culpability. But that's not the only role that reasonable person standards play in the law. When the reasonable person standard appears in law, and not as it bears on culpability, it frequently serves to direct legal actors towards a weighing of competing interests and values.[9] When in tort, for instance, we ask whether it was reasonable for someone who caused harm to have taken a precaution that would have averted the harm, we weigh the burden on the defendant involved in taking such a precaution against the risks to the plaintiff in the failure to take it. (That is, essentially, what the well-known Hand Formula's test for reasonableness requires us to do.[10]) If the former is weightier than the latter, then the failure was reasonable; if not, then not. This is not an assessment of the defendant's *culpability*. Even if the defendant falsely believed that the burden of the precaution was far outweighed by the risks, but callously omitted the precaution anyway, he would still not be negligent if, in fact, the burden wasn't worth taking. "Reasonableness" in tort negligence directs legal actors to make a normative judgment in situations in which there are legitimate considerations and interests on both sides.

Similarly, when it comes to police interrogations, the reasonableness of the interrogated party's false belief that he could not walk away invites a normative judgment. Here, what is to be compared is the weight of the legal reason for the police to avoid deception (by omission of a warning, in this case), on the one hand, and the weight of the legal reason for the police to gather incriminating information when they can, on the other. The thought is that the latter reason outweighs the former provided that a class of people—namely, the "reasonable" people—would not have been deceived. But why should "reasonableness" of the *interrogated party* matter at all to the question? If, as I suggest, the question is whether the *police* have stronger legal reason to collect

---

[9] The distinction being made here is Peter Westen's distinction, as I understand it, between what he calls "reasonableness 1" and "reasonableness 2." See Peter Westen (2008) "Individualizing the Reasonable Person in Criminal Law" in *Criminal Law and Philosophy*, 2: 137–62, esp. pp. 140–4.

[10] *United States v. Carroll Towing Co.* (159 F.2d 169 (2d. Cir. 1947)).

information than to avoid deception, then why isn't the question just whether the police's omission of the Miranda warning was reasonable? The answer is that the stronger the interrogated party's legal reasons for refraining from the crime being investigated, the stronger are the police's legal reasons to gather incriminating information. The stronger the interrogated party's legal reasons to refrain, that is, the more deception the police are permitted to use. So, to give weight to the legal reasons that the police have to investigate whether a person committed a crime, we need to know how strong that person's legal reasons were to refrain from commission of that crime. When we ask whether an interrogation without a Miranda warning was permissible, we are asking whether the deception was worth it. It's worth it just in case there is very strong legal reason for the police to discover the offender. But the strength of that reason is a function of how strong the interrogated party's legal reasons were to refrain from engaging in the offense. And, as we've seen, *that* is a function, in part, of the degree of say that that person has over the law defining the offense.

It is a very short step from here to the claim that there are interrogations of kids that are impermissible, even when such interrogations of an adult, *ceteris paribus*, would be permissible. The reason is that kids have weaker reasons to refrain from crime than adults, *ceteris paribus*, and so weaker legal reasons to refrain from police deception can outweigh in the case of a kid when they would not in the case of an adult.

Let me repeat the point. Imagine that Adult and Kid are being interrogated separately for exactly the same offense. The probability is 0.2 that Adult falsely believes that he cannot leave the interview and, to keep things the same, let's assume that the probability that Kid has this false belief is also 0.2. So, in omitting to Mirandize, the police are imposing a 0.2 risk of being involved in deception that they have legal reason to avoid. Is this risk worth it? It depends how strong the police's legal reasons are to gather information through the interrogation. That, in turn, is a function of the strength of the legal reasons that the suspected offender had to refrain from engaging in that offense. Since Kid's legal reasons to refrain were weaker than Adult's, the risk of deception is less likely to be worth it in the interrogation of Kid than it is in the interrogation of Adult. Or, we might say, that the thing we need to know in the case of Kid is whether this is a permissible interrogation of a "reasonable *kid*." This, I suggest, is the idea that rationalizes the court's decision in *J.D.B.* (even if the court does not know it).

The underlying point is obscured by the focus on *the belief* as to whether one can walk away from the interview. What's confusing is that the strength of the interrogated party's legal reason to refrain from the crime does not seem to be what is at issue when we ask what a reasonable person would have believed about their right to leave. But the confusion disappears if we remind ourselves that the issue is not the factual one of what kids believe in contrast to adults. The question is the normative one of what kids *can be expected to believe* in contrast to adults. Everyone, of no matter what age, can be expected to believe that the police are authorized to be more intrusive when there is more at stake. But when it is a kid who is suspected, there is less at stake. And so a kid in J.D.B.'s circumstances ought to expect less police pressure, less aggressive tactics, to be permissible. The result is that the police are required to be more careful when interviewing a child suspect than an adult; they must take greater care to avoid deception, including deception by omission of a Miranda warning.

Return to the proposition that links the rationale on offer for giving kids a break to the decision in *J.D.B.*: the idea that how much coercive pressure the police are authorized to use against a suspect is a function of the strength of the legal reasons the suspect had to refrain from what he is suspected of doing. Much was made, in the press and elsewhere, of the fact that Freddie Gray, killed in Baltimore by the reckless driving of a police van in which he was riding, had been arrested for a very minor crime: the crime of carrying a "switchblade," a folding knife that can be opened with one hand. From one point of view, that fact is entirely irrelevant: the police should not risk the lives of those arrested for serious crimes any more than of those arrested for minor crimes. But from another, it makes a great deal of difference; it makes a difference to the degree of wrongfulness of the police behavior. Included in Freddie Gray's treatment by the state in response to his suspected criminal behavior was his treatment by the police during and following his arrest. Since the crime he was suspected of committing was very minor, he did not deserve to be subject to harsh treatment by the police. Had he been suspected of a more serious crime, then the same treatment by the police would have been less bad—very bad, still, bad enough to constitute a crime by police, still, but less bad—for it would have been less distant from that which Gray deserved.

It is this same thought, I suggest, that supports the decision in *J.D.B.* J.D.B. deserved to be free of subjection to coercive police treatment of a sort that a psychologically and behaviorally identical adult would not have deserved to be free of. This was so because what he was suspected of doing was less strongly opposed by his legal reasons than that same act would have been, *ceteris paribus*, for an adult.

It is important to see what has, and what has not, been achieved by the line of reasoning offered in this section. The court in *J.D.B.* did two things: First, the court established that the relevant reasonable person standard in this kind of case is that of the reasonable juvenile; second, they ruled that when that standard is applied, it turns out that the interrogation of J.D.B. was not permissible. The line of thought offered here, deriving from the rationale for giving kids a break developed in this book, supports the first of these two points, but it neither supports nor opposes the second. What we can learn from the reasoning here is that there will be police pressures placed on child suspects that are impermissible, even when the very same pressures placed on an otherwise identical adult suspect would be permissible. But whether the pressures placed on J.D.B. himself were of this class is not forced by the principles described here. The court reaches the conclusion, yes, and it's not a crazy conclusion to reach. But to provide a grounding for it we would need more than what has been offered in this book; we would need a way of measuring how much lenience J.D.B. deserved, and a way of measuring how harsh the interrogation that he suffered was. We do not have this. And so, as a matter of practice, we rely on the perhaps unprincipled guesses of our courts, hoping that intuition does not lead them astray. We have principled reasons for thinking that interrogations like J.D.B.'s need to be examined for permissibility by taking into consideration the fact that he was a kid; but we have only intuition to guide us about the proper outcome of such an examination.

8.3 Conclusion

It is common to find that there are multiple ways to construct a legal system in conformity with principles dictating how the law ought to be. We ought, for instance, to have a legal system that assigns liability to people who use deception to induce others to give them their money. But whether we therefore define theft broadly so as to include deceptive taking, or, instead, define a separate crime of fraud is unclear. Perhaps one choice or the other is better. But we need to appeal to more than just the principled reasons for criminalizing deceptive acquisition of another's property in order to decide in favor of one regime over the other. There are many other examples. What has been suggested here is that while there are surely multiple different ways of constructing a legal system that gives kids a break, and does so in a way that comports with the principled grounds for thinking that we should, we can nonetheless assess given features of our legal system, such as the laws governing police interrogation, by appeal to the principles offered in this book in support of giving kids a break. If, for instance, we had very strong sentencing mitigation mechanisms in place, then there would be no reason to think that the police should be required to go easier in their investigations of kids than adults. The really important question is whether *the system*, assessed holistically, promises less punishment to kids, *ceteris paribus*, than adults. But given the imperfections of our sentencing regimes, and their not infrequent failure, all by themselves, to give breaks to kids in comparison to otherwise identical adults, there is reason to seek and support procedural leniency, as well.

To be procedurally lenient, we need to consider the way in which what procedures it is proper to follow, in bringing offenders to justice, is often a function of the strength of the offender's legal reasons to refrain from the offense. Once we recognize this, we can see that how much questionable police behavior we are willing to tolerate should be, and to some degree *is*, a function in part of both the offenses they are investigating, and who they suspect. Kids are owed less pressure from the police, not because of their fragility, in comparison to adults, but because, again, of the political meaning of age. They have less of a say than adults over how it is permissible for the police to behave, and so they are owed a lighter touch.

Conclusion

The science of child development—especially psychological and neural development—is helping us to see just how different kids are from adults in ways that matter directly to their culpability for crime. Not every difference matters, of course, but many do. For instance: What risks one was aware of when one acted in a way that harmed another matters, directly, to one's culpability. The greater the risks of which one was aware when acting, the greater the culpability. If kids are different from adults in the way they perceive risks, then this matters to their culpability; and, in fact, there is evidence suggesting that they are. Using empirical discoveries in this way is extremely important if we are to give kids their due.

Lines of reasoning which build a bridge from science to law, in this way, start by specifying a class of people, defined independently of age, who are reduced in culpability in comparison to the norm: in the example, those who perceive the risks of harm to be less than what other people perceive them to be. The next step is to cite empirical discoveries showing that kids are much more likely to be in that class than are adults: studies, for instance, showing that kids underestimate risks in comparison to adults. The same form of reasoning can be employed with respect to any distinctive and culpability-relevant feature of kids uncovered by the science of child development. The fact that a defendant is a kid is, therefore, *probative* of culpability, in light of the discoveries about child development.

It is easy, as a conceptual matter, to adopt social policies that acknowledge that a particular fact is probative of criminal culpability. All we need is a criminal law that predicates differences of punishment on culpability and allows introduction of the evidence that is probative of it. And, in fact, we *have* such a criminal law already, designed for adults; we had it before we ever even developed a juvenile delinquency system. Offenses are often graded by culpability and sentences can often be reduced in light of reduced culpability. And criminal defendants have many opportunities to submit evidence of reduced culpability, including scientific evidence that helps juries to see how certain features of them are probative, if it is not obvious. So why do we need a policy of giving kids a break? *If age mattered to criminal liability only because it correlates with membership in groups who are reduced in culpability, then we would not.* What this shows is *not* that we do not need a policy of giving kids a break. Quite the reverse. What it shows is that such a policy is not justified by the facts about kids uncovered by the science of child development. This is, in its essentials, the central argument of the first two chapters of this book.

The reason that more than this needed to be said in those opening chapters is that social policies are designed to be implemented. So, when we want to predicate differential state treatment on a hard-to-observe property, like criminal culpability, we often adopt social policies that predicate such treatment, instead, on more easily observed qualities, like age, that correlate with it. Perhaps that is what we are doing in adopting a policy of leniency towards kids. But this, as we have seen, cannot be right. Such a claim comes with a picture of what *progress* would be in our policies, a picture in which our policies would *improve* were we to find better proxies for the properties of real interest. And so such a claim would commit us to thinking that we ought to deny breaks to kids who we have good reason to think are not reduced in culpability in comparison to the norm. This implies, based on what we know today, that we ought to deny breaks to 16- and 17-year-old girls, who we have every reason to think are more like 19- and 20-year-old boys in the psychological features that matter to culpability. But this is obviously ridiculous. To insist on it would be monstrous. Girls should not be denied breaks that are given to boys. The question is *why not*, given that we could improve our rates of true and false positives and negatives were we to do so. The solution to the puzzle is to recognize that the wrong way to assess our policy of giving kids a break is by conceptualizing age as a proxy for something else. Rather, age must matter *in and of itself*. But how could this be?

The next four chapters of the book were dedicated to providing an answer to this question. In a sense, the answer is simple: age matters because we have given it political meaning; we have set an age threshold for having a say over the law through the vote, and having a say through speech that is not limited by parental consent. This point is simple, but there is an enormous gap. Why does the political meaning of age matter to criminal culpability and desert of punishment?

The answer is supplied by accounts of criminal culpability, desert for wrongdoing, and legal reasons. Under the account of criminal culpability that I propose, to be criminally culpable for illegal conduct is for that conduct to manifest a failure to properly weigh and respond to the legal reasons to refrain from that conduct provided by the conduct's legally salient features, the features in virtue of which it is prohibited by law. To give someone what he deserves for wrongdoing is to attach to the act a consequence such that, had the agent deliberated about the act with that consequence attached, he would have treated it in his practical reasoning in something like the way in which good citizens treat the act without consideration of that consequence. The result is that both the degree to which a person is culpable for his wrongful conduct, and how much suffering he deserves for it, vary with the strength of the legal reasons that he had to refrain from that conduct. The stronger those reasons, the worse it is for him to have weighed them as he did. The stronger those reasons, the more suffering needs to be attached to the act for him to be as rationally averse to it as he ought to have been.

But there is still a gap. We need to know why it is that the strength of a person's legal reasons to refrain from crime is a function of his age. The answer offered in chapters 5 and 6 is this: The strength of a person's legal reasons to refrain from a crime is in part a function of the degree to which he is complicit in government action against people who commit that crime, including government action against himself. Complicity of this kind silences a complaint—the complaint that the law violated was not *my* law, or was inapplicable to me; if you're complicit in the law, then it *is* your law. Or, rather, it is your law to the extent that you are complicit in it. The more you are complicit, the weaker the entitlement to disavow the legal norms that one's conduct violates.

But what is the mechanism through which people become complicit in the law? The answer is that they become complicit in the law by having a say over it. They become complicit thanks to their real and meaningful opportunity to exert influence over the law, an opportunity provided by the real and meaningful opportunity to vote and to exert influence through speech over those who create the law. Since age has a political meaning—kids have less say over the law than adults—it also marks a difference in complicity with legal norms. Kids are less complicit than adults. The result is that kids are in a better position than adults to complain that the law is not theirs. And so they have weaker legal reasons to refrain from crime and so are reduced in culpability in comparison to otherwise identical adults. They are also deserving of less suffering for their illegal conduct since less suffering need be attached to such conduct for them to be averse to it in a way that aligns with the strength of their legal reasons to refrain. It is a short and clear step to the conclusion we sought: kids are owed a break when it comes to criminal liability, whether they are psychologically, behaviorally, and neurally normal or whether, instead, they are precocious in these respects. Even kids who are little adults—and don't all of us know some?—are owed a break when they commit crimes.

Say that the reason that we deny the vote to kids is because they are immature, not psychologically ready for the burden. If that were the case, then it would turn out that, in the end, even if my proposed rationale for giving kids a break were correct, it would still be the case that, ultimately, we give kids a break because of their distinctive psychological features, the features that undermine their entitlement for the franchise. It is worth noting that even if kids are denied the vote because of their immaturity, the argument I am offering would still have important implications. Some psychological features of kids that are thought by my opponents to support leniency towards kids would actually not provide any such support. Consider, for instance, empirical discoveries indicating that kids are less good than adults at making decisions in heightened emotional states. This fact about kids does not justify denying them the vote, since people rarely vote while in heightened emotional states; and so even if kids are denied the vote because of their immaturity, *this* fact about their immaturity would not support the policy of leniency towards child criminals.

But, more importantly, it is not true that kids are denied the vote thanks to their psychological immaturity. Many kids are far more psychologically mature than they need to be to vote well. More importantly, a showing that an adult was no less psychologically mature than an average 12-year-old would be insufficient ground to deny the vote to that adult. Who we give the vote, and who we do not, has next to nothing to do with possession of the capacity to understand what one is doing in voting, or to do it well.

Nor does it have much to do with who is affected by the policies that are affected by the vote; many who are deeply affected, such as citizens of neighboring countries, have no say over our law. But, still, there are substantive constraints on the distribution of the vote dictated by our dedication to self-government. A dedication to self-government places us under pressure to institute mechanisms through which we who are the authors of today's law can be the authors, also, of tomorrow's. At least, we are under such pressure to the extent to which it is important to us that tomorrow's legal system be the same legal system under which we now live, a legal system that persists until tomorrow and continues to draw its authority from the say that we have over it. By denying the vote to kids, and granting it to them when they come of age, we produce a mechanism through which we can have a say over tomorrow's law. We can have such a say thanks to our entitlement to exert influence over our children's values, an influence that we can expect to extend to their future voting behavior. To the extent that we care about self-government, we *should* deny the vote to kids. And so we *should* assign age a political meaning under which those below an age threshold are denied as much say over the law as adults. And so we *should* have a system where kids are owed a break when it comes to criminal liability, and are, on those grounds, given one.

At its heart, the argument of this book is a coherence argument. Coherence arguments have implications for reform, but their implications are sometimes equivocal. The observation that a system that includes X is coherent only if it also includes Y provides no reason yet to prefer a system that contains both X and Y to a system that includes neither. Still, when there is a reason to prefer a system that includes X to one that does not, then coherence gives us a ground to prefer systems that include Y. Coherence requires us to be lenient towards kids, provided that we are dedicated to self-government and provided that we give ourselves a say over future law by denying kids a say over today's law. Since we should adopt systems with these features, we have a reason also to adopt systems that institute leniency towards kids. Coherence, then, requires us to institute lenience somehow, certainly through sentencing mitigation for kids, but also, perhaps, through more lenient procedures, including the procedures followed by police and others tasked with enforcing the criminal law. But coherence, it has been argued, does not require us to give a break to visitors and immigrants, despite denying them a say over our law. We can consistently deny them a say over the law and treat them just as we treat fully enfranchised adult citizens. Nor does coherence require us to give a break to prisoners and others to whom we deny the franchise in light of past criminal activity. We could, instead, maintain coherence by giving them the franchise; in fact, in contrast to the case of kids, there is no good reason to deny it to those who have committed crimes in the past, even when they are serving sentences for those crimes.

While considerations of coherence, then, give us some substantive advice about *what we should actually do*, how we should actually construct our institutions, it is important not to overstate what has been shown in this book in that respect. The book is, after all, a work of philosophy, not a work of policy analysis. Important open questions remain about whether the institutions we have conform to the principled reasons to be lenient towards kids and how they can be improved. Still, I believe that all such work should be structured and led by an appreciation of the grounds for leniency towards child criminals, grounds that I take myself to have articulated here. Age matters to our say over the law, to our complicity in the laws with respect to which our conduct is measured, and so to our criminal culpability and to what we deserve for criminal conduct. It is because they have less say over the law than adults that kids are owed a break, and this fact should guide us in our thinking both about how to construct our institutions to respond to criminal behavior by kids, and about the bearing of scientific discoveries on our efforts to institute justice in this important domain.

Bibliography

Ackerman, Bruce (1991) *We the People, Volume 1: Foundations*, Cambridge: Harvard University Press.

Ahn, W. Y., K. T. Kishida, X. Gu, T. Lohrenz, A. H. Harvey, J. R. Alford, K. B. Smith, G. Yaffe, J. R. Hibbing, P. Dayan, and P. R. Montague (2014) "Non-Political Images Evoke Neural Predictors of Political Ideology" in *Current Biology*, 24(22): 2693–9.

Albert, Dustin, Jason Chein, and Laurence Steinberg (2013) "The Teenage Brain: Peer Influences on Adolescent Decisionmaking" in *Current Directions in Psychological Science*, 22(2): 114–20.

Aristotle (2012) *Nicomachean Ethics*, Robert C. Bartlett and Susan D. Collins, trans. Chicago: University of Chicago Press.

Aronson, Jay D. (2009) "Neuroscience and Juvenile Justice" in *Akron Law Review* 42(3): 917–30.

Arpaly, Nomy and Timothy Schroeder (2014) *In Praise of Desire*, Oxford: Oxford University Press.

Austin, John (1832) *The Province of Jurisprudence Determined*, London: Weidenfeld & Nicolson.

Baird, Abigail A., Christy L. Barrow, and Molly K. Richard (2012) "Juvenile Neurolaw: When it's Good it's Very Good Indeed, and When it's Bad it's Horrid" in *Journal of Health Law and Policy*, 15(1): 15–35.

Bayles, Michael (1982) "Character, Purpose, and Criminal Responsibility" in *Law and Philosophy* 1(1): 5–20.

Becker, Elizabeth (2001) "As Ex-Theorist on Young 'Superpredators,' Bush Aide Has Regrets" in *The New York Times*, Feb 9, p. A19.

Berman, Mitchell (2008) "Punishment and Justification" in *Ethics* 118(2): 258–90.

Bhabha, Jacqueline (ed.) (2011) *Children Without a State*, Cambridge: MIT Press.

Bonnie, Richard J. and Thomas Grisso (2000) "Adjudicative Competence and Youthful Offenders" in Thomas Grisso and Robert G. Schwartz (eds.), *Youth on Trial: A Developmental Perspective on Juvenile Justice*, Chicago: University of Chicago Press, pp. 73–103.

Brand, Myles (1977) "Identity Conditions for Events" in *American Philosophical Quarterly*, 14: 329–37.

Brink, David (2004) "Immaturity, Normative Competence, and Juvenile Transfer: How (Not) to Punish Minors for Major Crimes" in *Texas Law Review*, 82: 1555–85.

Bruck, Maggie and Stephen J. Ceci (1998) "The Suggestibility of Children's Memory" in *Annual Review of Psychology*, 50: 419–39.

Burgh, Richard (1982) "Do the Guilty Deserve Punishment?" in *Journal of Philosophy*, 79(4): 193–213.

Buss, Emily (2009a) "Rethinking the Connection Between Developmental Science and Juvenile Justice" in *The University of Chicago Law Review*, 76: 493–515.

Buss, Emily (2009b) "What the Law Should (And Should Not) Learn from Child Development Research" in *Hofstra Law Review*, 38: 13–65.

Carroll, Jenny E. (2015) "Brain Science and the Theory of Juvenile *Mens Rea*" in *North Carolina Law Review*, 94: 539–99.
Carter, Andrew M. (2006) "Age Matters: The Case for a Constitutionalized Infancy Defense" in *University of Kansas Law Review*, 54: 734–49.
Casey, B. J. and Kristina Caudle (2013) "The Teenage Brain: Self Control" in *Current Directions in Psychological Science*, 22(2): 82–7.
Chang, Ruth (ed.) (1998) *Incommensurability, Incomparability and Practical Reasoning*, Cambridge: Harvard University Press.
Christensen, David (1997) "What is Relative Confirmation?" in *Nous*, 31(3): 370–84.
Cleland, C. (1991) "On the Individuation of Events" in *Synthese*, 86: 229–54.
Coleman, Jules (1982) "Negative and Positive Positivism" in *Journal of Legal Studies*, v. 11: 139–64.
Cox, Steven M., Jennifer Allen, Robert Hanser, and John Conrad (2014) *Juvenile Justice: A Guide to Theory, Policy and Practice*, New York: Sage Publications.
Davidson, Donald (1969) "The Individuation of Events" in *Essays in Honor of Carl G. Hempel*, N. Rescher (ed.), Dordrecht: Reidel, pp. 216–34.
Davis, Michael (1986) "Harm and Retribution" in *Philosophy & Public Affairs*, 15(3): 236–66.
Delgado, Richard (1985) "Social Background: Should the Criminal Law Recognize a Defense of Severe Environmental Deprivation?" in *Law and Inequality*, 3: 9–45.
de Water, Erik, Antonius H. N. Cillessen, and Anouk Scheres (2014) "Distinct Age-Related Differences in Temporal Discounting and Risk Taking in Adolescents and Young Adults" in *Child Development*, 85(5): 1881–97.
DiIulio, John (1995) "The Coming of the Super-Predators" in *The Weekly Standard*, November 27.
Duff, Antony (2002) "Punishing the Young" in *Punishing Juveniles: Principle and Critique*, Ido Weijers and Antony Duff (eds.), Oxford: Hart Publishing, pp. 115–34.
Dworkin, Ronald (1986) *Law's Empire*, Cambridge: Harvard University Press.
Euling, Susan Y., Marcia E. Herman-Giddens, Peter A. Lee, Sherry G. Selevan, Anders Juul, Thorkild I. A. Sørensen, Leo Dunkel, John H. Himes, Grete Teilmann, and Shanna H. Swan (2008) "Examination of US Puberty-Timing Data from 1940 to 1994 for Secular Trends: Panel Findings" in *Pediatrics*, v. 121: S172–91.
Fagan, Jeffrey (2000) "Contexts of Choice by Adolescents in Criminal Events" in Thomas Grisso and Robert G. Schwartz (eds.), *Youth on Trial: A Developmental Perspective on Juvenile Justice*, Chicago: University of Chicago Press, pp. 371–401.
Feeley, Malcolm (1972) *The Process is the Punishment*, New York: Russell Sage Foundation.
Feld, Barry (1999) *Bad kids: Race and the Transformation of the Juvenile Court*, New York: Oxford University Press.
Feld, Barry (2000) "Juveniles' Waiver of Legal Rights: Confession, *Miranda*, and the Right to Counsel" in Thomas Grisso and Robert G. Schwartz (eds.), *Youth on Trial: A Developmental Perspective on Juvenile Justice*, Chicago: University of Chicago Press, pp. 105–38.
Feld, Barry and Donna Bishop (2012) *The Oxford Handbook of Juvenile Crime and Juvenile Justice*, Oxford: Oxford University Press.
Finkelstein, Claire (2003) "Is Risk Harm?" in *University of Pennsylvania Law Review*, 151: 963–1001.
Finnis, John (1980) *Natural Law and Natural Rights*, Oxford: Clarendon Press.
Fischer, John and Mark Ravizza (1998) *Responsibility and Control: A Theory of Moral Responsibility*, Cambridge: Cambridge University Press.

Gardinier, Bob (2013) "Homeless and Hungry Man Prefers a Jail Cell" in *Albany Times-Union*, January 23, 2013, http://www.timesunion.com/local/article/Homeless-and-hungry-man-prefers-a-jail-cell-4213734.php (accessed December 15, 2016).

Gardner M. and Laurence Steinberg (2005) "Peer Influence on Risk Taking, Risk Preference, and Risky Decision Making in Adolescence and Adulthood: An Experimental Study" in *Developmental Psychology*, 41(4): 625–35.

Goldberg, John C. P. and Benjamin Zipursky (2002) "Unrealized Torts" in *Virgina Law Review*, 88(8): 1625–719.

Greenberg, Mark (2011) "The Standard Picture and Its Discontents" in Leslie Green and Brian Leiter (eds.), *Oxford Studies in Philosophy of Law*, Oxford: Oxford University Press.

Greenberg, Mark (2014) "The Moral Impact Theory of Law" in *The Yale Law Journal*, 123: 1288–342.

Grisso, Thomas (1981) *Juveniles' Waiver of Rights: Legal and Psychological Competence*, New York: Plenum Press.

Grisso, Thomas and Robert G. Schwartz (eds.) (2000) *Youth on Trial: A Developmental Perspective on Juvenile Justice*, Chicago: University of Chicago Press.

Guggenheim, Martin and Randy Hertz (1998) "Juvenile Justice Reform: Reflections on Judges, Juries, and Justice: Ensuring the Fairness of Juvenile Delinquency Trials" in *Wake Forest Law Review*, 33: 553–93.

Hamilton, Vivian E. (2010) "Immature Citizens and the State" in *B.Y.U. Law Review*, 4(1): 1055–148.

Hart, H. L. A. (1961) *The Concept of Law*, Oxford: Clarendon Press.

Hart, H. L. A. (2008) "Prolegomena to the Principles of Punishment" in John Gardner (ed.), *Punishment and Responsibility: Essays in the Philosophy of Law*, Oxford: Oxford University Press.

Hartley, Catherine A. and Leah H. Somerville (2015) "The Neuroscience of Adolescent Decision-Making" in *Current Opinion in Behavioral Science*, 5: 108–15.

Hershovitz, Scott (2015) "The End of Jurisprudence" in *The Yale Law Journal*, 124(4): 1160–204.

Huigens, Kyron (1995) "Virtue and Inculpation" in *Harvard Law Review*, 108(7): 1423–80.

Huigens, Kyron (1998) "Virtue and Criminal Negligence" in *Buffalo Criminal Law Review*, 1(2): 431–58.

Husak, Douglas (1996) "The 'But-Everyone-Does-That!' Defense" in *Public Affairs Quarterly*, 10(4): 307–34.

Husak, Douglas (2016) *Ignorance of Law: A Philosophical Analysis*, Oxford: Oxford University Press.

Husak, Douglas (forthcoming) "What's Legal About Legal Moralism?" in *San Diego Law Review*.

Kagan, Shelly (2012) *The Geometry of Desert*, Oxford: Oxford University Press.

Kim, Jaegwon (1976) "Events as Property Exemplifications" in M. Brand and D. Walton (eds.), *Action Theory*, Dordrecht: Reidel, pp. 159–77.

Kohler-Hausmann, Issa (2014) "Managerial Justice and Mass Misdemeanors" in *Stanford Law Review*, 66: 611–94.

Kolber, Adam (2009) "The Subjective Experience of Punishment" in *The Columbia Law Review*, 109: 182–237.

Lederman, Cindy (2011) "From Lab Bench to Court Bench: Using Science to Inform Decisions in Juvenile Court" in *Cerebrum*, The Dana Foundation, http://dana.org/Cerebrum/Default.aspx?id=39466 (accessed April 16, 2016).
Lerner, Craig S. (2011) "Juvenile Criminal Responsibility: Can Malice Supply the Want of Years?" in *Tulane Law Review*, 86: 309–87.
Levy, Leonard W. (1968) *Origins of the Fifth Amendment: The Right Against Self-Incrimination*, New York: Oxford University Press.
Lewis, David (1997) "Finkish Dispositions" in *The Philosophical Quarterly*, 47(187): 143–58.
Leydet, Dominique (2014) "Citizenship" in *The Stanford Encyclopedia of Philosophy*, Edward N. Zalta (ed.), http://plato.stanford.edu/archives/spr2014/entries/citizenship (accessed February 25, 2016).
Mack, Julian W. (1909) "The Juvenile Court" in *Harvard Law Review*, 23: 104–22.
Manza, Jeff and Christopher Uggen (2008) *Locked Out: Felon Disenfranchisement and American Democracy*, New York: Oxford University Press.
Marmor, Andrei (2011) *Philosophy of Law*, Princeton: Princeton University Press.
Maroney, Terry (2009) "The False Promise of Adolescent Brain Science in Juvenile Justice" in *Notre Dame Law Review*, 85: 89–176.
Maroney, Terry (2011) "Adolescent Brain Science and Juvenile Justice" in Michael Freeman (ed.), *Law and Neuroscience*, Oxford: Oxford University Press.
Matthews, Gareth (1994) *The Philosophy of Childhood*, Cambridge: Harvard University Press.
McKenna, Michael (2012) *Conversation and Responsibility*, Oxford: Oxford University Press.
McLeod, Owen (2008) "Desert" in Edward N. Zalta (ed.), *The Stanford Encyclopedia of Philosophy*, http://plato.stanford.edu/entries/desert (accessed August 19, 2015).
Meares, Tracey (1998) "Place and Crime" in *Chicago-Kent Law Review*, 73: 669–705.
Moore, Michael (1993) *Act and Crime*, Oxford: Oxford University Press.
Mischel, Walter, Ebbe B. Ebbesen, and Antonette Raskoff Zeiss (1972) "Cognitive and Attentional Mechanisms in Delay of Gratification" in *Journal of Personality and Social Psychology*, 21(2): 204–18.
Mitchell, Ojmarrh, David B. Wilson, Amy Eggers, and Doris L. MacKenzie (2012) "Assessing the Effectiveness of Drug Courts on Recidivism: A Meta-Analytic Review of Traditional and Non-Traditional Drug Courts" in *Journal of Criminal Justice*, 40: 60–71.
Moore, Michael (2015) "The Quest for a Responsible Responsibility Test: Norwegian Insanity Law After Breivik" in *Criminal Law and Philosophy*, 9: 645–93.
Morris, Herbert (1968) "Persons and Punishment" in *The Monist*, 52(4): 475–501.
Morse, Stephen J. (1997) "Immaturity and Irresponsibility" in *Journal of Criminal Law and Criminology*, 88: 15–65.
Morse, Stephen J. (2011) "Severe Environmental Deprivation (AKA RSB): A Tragedy, Not a Defense" in *Alabama Civil Rights & Civil Liberties Law Review*, 2: 147–72.
Nelkin, Dana and Sam Rickless (2014) "Three Cheers for Double Effect" in *Philosophy and Phenomenological Research*, 89(1): 125–58.
Nozick, Robert (1981) *Philosophical Explanations*, New York: Belknap Press.
Owens, David (2012) *Shaping the Normative Landscape*, Oxford: Oxford University Press.
Pereboom, Derk (2001) *Living Without Free Will*, Cambridge: Cambridge University Press.
Raz, Joseph (1979) *The Authority of Law*, Oxford: Clarendon Press.
Raz, Joseph (1990) *Practical Reason and Norms*, Princeton: Princeton University Press.

Raz, Joseph (1994) "Authority, Law and Morality" in *Ethics in the Public Domain*, Oxford: Clarendon Press, pp. 210-37.

Reiner, Andrew (2013) "The Education Issue: Believing Self-Control Predicts Success, Schools Teach Coping" in *Washington Post Magazine*, April 11.

Rodham, Hillary (1973) "Children Under the Law" in *Harvard Educational Review*, 43(4): 487-514.

Rosenheim, Margaret K. and Franklin Zimring (2002) *A Century of Juvenile Justice*, Chicago: University of Chicago Press.

Scanlon, Thomas (2000) *What We Owe to Each Other*, Cambridge: Harvard University Press.

Scanlon, Thomas (2008) *Moral Dimensions: Permissibility, Meaning, Blame*, Cambridge: Harvard University Press.

Schapiro, Tamar (1999) "What is a Child?" in *Ethics*, 109(4): 715-38.

Schapiro, Tamar (2003) "Childhood and Personhood" in *Arizona Law Review*, 45: 575-94.

Scott, Elizabeth S. (2000) "Criminal Responsibility in Adolescence: Lessons from Developmental Psychology" in Thomas Grisso and Robert G. Schwartz (eds.), *Youth on Trial: A Developmental Perspective on Juvenile Justice*, Chicago: University of Chicago Press, pp. 291-324.

Scott, Elizabeth S. and Laurence Steinberg (2003) "Blaming Youth" in *Texas Law Review*, 81: 799-839.

Scott, Elizabeth S. and Laurence Steinberg (2008) *Rethinking Juvenile Justice*, Cambridge: Harvard University Press.

Shapiro, Scott (2011) *Legality*, Cambridge: Harvard University Press.

Shelby, Tommie (2016) *Dark Ghettos: Injustice, Dissent and Reform*, Cambridge: Harvard Press.

Sher, George (1987) *Desert*, Princeton: Princeton University Press.

Shoemaker, David (2012) "Blame and Punishment" in D. Justin Coates and Neal A. Tognazzini (eds.), *Blame: Its Nature and Norms*, New York: Oxford University Press, pp. 100-18.

Simons-Morton, B., N. Lerner, and J. Singer (2005) "The Observed Effects of Teenage Passengers on the Risky Driving Behavior of Teenage Drivers" in *Accident Analysis and Prevention*, 37(6): 973-82.

Steinberg, Laurence (2009) "Should the Science of Adolescent Brain Development Inform Public Policy?" in *American Psychologist*, 64(8): 739-50.

Steinberg, Laurence (2014) *Age of Opportunity: Lessons from the New Science of Adolescence*, New York: Houghton Mifflin.

Steinberg, Laurence and Robert G. Schwartz (2000) "Developmental Psychology Goes to Court" in Thomas Grisso and Robert G. Schwartz (eds.), *Youth on Trial: A Developmental Perspective on Juvenile Justice*, Chicago: University of Chicago Press, pp. 7-31.

Strawson, Galen (2010) *Freedom and Belief*, revised edition, Oxford: Oxford University Press.

Strawson, P. F. (1962) "Freedom and Resentment" in *Proceedings of the British Academy*, 48: 1-25.

Tadros, Victor (2007) *Criminal Responsibility*, Oxford: Oxford University Press.

Tanenhaus, David S. (2004) *Juvenile Justice in the Making*, New York: Oxford University Press.

Tanenhaus, David and Steven A. Drizin (2002) "'Owing to the Extreme Youth of the Accused': The Changing Legal Response to Juvenile Homicide" in *Journal of Criminal Law and Criminology*, 92: 641.

Taylor-Thompson, Kim (2003) "States of Mind/States of Development" in *Stanford Law and Policy Review*, 14: 143–73.

Thomas, Jacqueline Rabe and Mark Pazniokas (2015) "Malloy: Raise the Age for Juvenile Justice System to 20" in *The Connecticut Mirror*, November 6.

Tiboris, Michael (2014) "Blaming the Kids: Children's Agency and Diminished Responsibility" in *Journal of Applied Philosophy*, 31(1): 77–90.

United States Sentencing Commission (2016) "Recidivism Among Offenders: A Comprehensive Overview", http://www.ussc.gov/sites/default/files/pdf/research-and-publications/research-publications/2016/recidivism_overview.pdf (accessed March 10, 2016).

Van Duijvenvoorde, Anna C. K. and Eveline A. Crone (2013) "A Neuroeconomic Approach to Adolescent Decision Making" in *Current Directions in Psychological Science* 22(2): 108–13.

Von Hirsch, Andrew (2001) "Proportionate Sentencing for Juveniles: How Different than for Adults?" in *Punishment and Society*, 3(2): 221–36.

Ward, Cynthia (2006) "Punishing Children in the Criminal Law" in *Notre Dame Law Review*, 82(1): 429–79.

Watson, Gary (2004) "Responsibility and the Limits of Evil: Variations on a Strawsonian Theme" in *Agency and Answerablity: Selected Essays*, Oxford: Oxford University Press, pp. 219–59.

Weijers, Ido and Antony Duff (eds.) (2002) "Punishing the Young" in *Punishing Juveniles: Principle and Critique*, Oxford: Hart Publishing.

Westen, Peter (2008) "Individualizing the Reasonable Person in Criminal Law" in *Criminal Law and Philosophy*, 2: 137–62.

Williams, Allan F., David F. Preusser, and Katherine A. Ledingham (2009) *Feasibility Study on Evaluating Driver Education Curriculum*, Report of the National Highway Traffic and Safety Adminstration, DOT HS 811 108.

Williams, Bernard (1979) "Internal and External Reasons" in Ross Harrison (ed.), *Rational Action*, Cambridge: Cambridge University Press, pp. 101–13.

Yaffe, Gideon (2009) "Excusing Mistakes of Law" in *Philosopher's Imprint*, 9(2): 1–22.

Yaffe, Gideon (2010) *Attempts: In the Philosophy of Action and the Criminal Law*, Oxford: Oxford University Press.

Yaffe, Gideon (2012) "Intoxication, Recklessness and Negligence" in *Ohio State Journal of Criminal Law*, 9: 545–83.

Yaffe, Gideon (2014a) "Criminal Attempts" in *The Yale Law Journal*, 124: 92–156.

Yaffe, Gideon (2014b) "In Defense of Criminal Possession" in *Criminal Law and Philosophy*, 10(3): 441–71.

Yaffe, Gideon (2016a) "The Point of Mens Rea: The Case of Willful Ignorance" in *Criminal Law and Philosophy*, https://link.springer.com/article/10.1007%2Fs11572-016-9408-3 (accessed October 3, 2017).

Yaffe, Gideon (2016b) "Give Felons and Prisoners the Right to Vote" in *The Washington Post*, July 26.

Zhang, Wei (2010) *A Study on the Effectiveness of Iowa's Driver Improvement Program by Gender and Age*, Graduate Thesis, Iowa State University Digital Depository.

Zimring, Franklin (1998a) *American Youth Violence*, New York: Oxford University Press.